NINETEENTH-CENTURY SCOTTISH FICTION

NINETEENTH-CENTURY SCOTTISH FICTION

Critical Essays

edited by
Ian Campbell

BARNES & NOBLE
BOOKS
10 East 53d St., New York 10022
(a division of Harper & Row Publishers, Inc.)

Published in the U.S.A. 1979 by
HARPER & ROW PUBLISHERS, INC.
BARNES & NOBLE IMPORT DIVISION
ISBN 0-06-490953-0
Library of Congress catalog card number. LC 79-51072

Printed in Great Britain by
Billings, Guildford

CONTENTS

Preface

Each essay is prefaced by a brief biographical outline of its subject, and followed by the footnotes referring to that essay, and by a brief note on further reading which might supplement the main argument. In an effort to reduce to a minimum the distracting intrusion of notes into the text, quotations are identified where practicable by a key in parenthesis, which is explained on its first occurrence in each essay.

Introduction

TOWARDS the end of his engaging *Mansie Wauch,* David Macbeth Moir puts the following "conclusion and some philosophy" into the mouth of his hero-tailor from Dalkeith.

Perhaps I am going a little too far when I say, that the whole world cannot fail to be interested in the occurrences of my life; for since its creation, which was not yesterday, I do not believe . . . that there ever was a subject concerning which the bulk of mankind have not had two opinions . . . Englishmen, for instance, will say that I am a bad speller, and that my language is kittle; and such of the Irishers as can read, will be threaping that I have abused their precious country; but, my certie, instead of blaming me for letting out what I could not deny, they must just learn to behave themselves better when they come to see us, or bide at home.[1]

Blundering Mansie neatly phrases for us a common interest which is pursued almost unanimously in the following studies of nineteenth-century Scottish fiction. The interest lies in attitude: attitude on the part of author, of narrator, of reader. Not all our authors are speaking of homely Scottish scenes which they expect the reader to accept as norm — few could be less guilty of this than Stevenson in the novels of his which are here examined—yet none of them presents a picture of their imagined reality in any way simple-minded. Not even the kailyarder, frequently derided for sentimental nostalgia, depicts an uncritical rustic idyll; Thrums has its unpleasant side, Drumtochty its faint echoings of a changing Scotland.

What is interesting is the attitude which is conveyed to the characters and their environment. In Galt's hands, as in Moir's (indeed Moir may well have learned from Galt, whose *The Last of the Lairds* he severely edited for Blackwood in 1826, before the appearance of *Mansie Wauch* in book form in 1828[2]) the simple-minded narrator can be a subtle and frequently satirical commentator on the action, on his environment, on the reader's attitude. Like Hogg in the *Confessions,* Galt is careful to withhold from the reader the confidence of knowing just where he is with regard to the narrative voice: whether Balwhidder, or the "editorial" voice of Hogg, are authoritative or self-mocking is never completely clear, and the delicate tuning of these attitudes is frequently (as Professor Daiches argues with respect to Scott's own "voice" in *Waverley)* one of the most crucially difficult areas of a novel for the critic, and one of the most successful ways in which a book's value may be judged.

In this, of course, we always draw back to remember the exigencies of the conditions in which the authors wrote (Mrs Oliphant's biographers rightly stress how little opportunity she had to write what she wanted, and as she wanted), and the extent to which they may have mistaken their true intention. If Moir was not being disingenuous, he may have mistaken the extent to which his irony in the quotation from *Mansie Wauch* could operate to defuse criticism in advance.

> After all, how precarious a thing is literary fame! Things to which I have bent the whole force of my mind, and which are worth remembering ... have attracted but a very doubtful share of applause from critics; while things dashed off, like *Mansie Wauch*, as mere sportive freaks, and which for years and years I have hesitated to acknowledge, have been out of sight my most popular productions.[3]

In the hands of Galt, the characterisation of Balwhidder becomes much more than a sportive freak: the autobiographical Scot assumes a tone sufficiently consistent, sufficiently sharply characterised to defy easy typecasting. His *malentendus* function through irony, his provincialisms may mask satirical attack on the readers' preconceptions.

Yet *The House with the Green Shutters* reminds us, as immediately as does *Alec Forbes,* that the sharply-observed localisation of Scotland in a novel may be sharply-recollected, and that the vividness of the picture may be as much due to the unhappiness of the situation remembered, as to its picturesqueness. The satire of an author who presents the calculated ambiguity of his picture of Scotland may be self-directed, for not one of the authors studied in these pages treats Scotland as an earthly paradise. Mansie Wauch is surely jesting when he claims immunity from others' criticism of Scotland, while reserving the right to say what he wants about England and Ireland. Scott, Hogg, Lockhart, Galt, Macdonald, Mrs. Oliphant, Stevenson, Brown, even the kailyarders are all on record as showing that a Scotland evolving rapidly in its "united" political form was under continuous stress as existing institutions adapted themselves to new conditions, to influence from abroad and to "newfangledness", whether with sensational speed in *Adam Blair,* or with the unnoticed gradualness of *Annals of the Parish.* Improvements in transportation, changes in patterns of settlement and methods of agriculture, upheavals in worship, education and family life, an industrial and agrarian revolution and the Disruption could not avoid leaving permanent marks on a country which struggled throughout the nineteenth century to find a universal voice for its self-expression. Whether this leads to the "moralising scoundrel" so wittily, yet so unfairly, parodied by Crosland[4], or to the difficulty in finding a truly adult idea of Scotland pointed to by David Craig[5], it does go some way towards trying to close the gap between "the literary and the public experience"[6] — a gap which Edwin Morgan saw in 1962 as still conspicuous. No one novel, no one author could bridge and seal such a gap: the extent to which each writer tries to bridge some gap, both in his country and beyond, can be judged only by critical reading and re-reading of frequently — and often unjustly — neglected work, and it is to this end that the present volume of essays has been completed.

Ian Campbell
Edinburgh, 1977

NOTES:

1. *The Life of Mansie Wauch, Tailor in Dalkeith, Written by Himself* and edited by D. M. Moir (London and Edinburgh, 1911), 349-50.
2. I. A. Gordon, *John Galt, The Life of a Writer* (Toronto, 1972), 80-83.
3. D. M. Moir to Thomas Aird, 12 April 1845, quoted from Aird's memoir of Moir in *The Poetical Works of David Macbeth Moir* (second edition, Edinburgh and London 1860), I, 44.
4. T. W. H. Crosland, *The Unspeakable Scot* (London, 1902), 33.
5. D. Craig, *Scottish Literature and the Scottish People 1680-1830* (London, 1961), 163.
6. Edwin Morgan, "The Beatnik in the Kailyard", *New Saltire* 3 (Spring, 1962), quoted from Morgan's *Essays* (Manchester, 1974), 174.

SCOTT'S *WAVERLEY:* THE PRESENCE OF THE AUTHOR

by David Daiches

WALTER SCOTT (1771-1832) was already a well known narrative poet, editor and antiquary when *Waverley* was published anonymously in 1814. It was the first of a long series of historical novels that came to be known as the Waverley Novels, all published anonymously. *Waverley* had been begun as early as 1805 (hence its sub-title: "'Tis Sixty Years Since": the novel is set in 1745), but, becoming discouraged at a friend's adverse criticism of the first few chapters, he gave it up, to return to it in 1814 on accidentally finding the discarded chapters in a drawer.

The theme, tone and style of *Waverley,* together with its underlying philosophy, reflect with great accuracy Scott's concept of the historical novel (a literary form that he can be said to have invented). It is the story of a romantically minded Englishman on a visit to Scotland emotionally caught up in the Jacobite movement and so persuaded to join the Jacobite rising of 1745, and at the same time the story of his eventual realisation of the anachronistic and ultimately meaningless violence that the movement involved and his consequent withdrawal into the modern world of enlightened progress and humane feeling. It is also a story of *change;* a study of the last phase of the old heroic Highland way of life just before it gave way to influences from the south. "It was a very old attempt of mine to embody some traits of those characters and manners peculiar to Scotland the last remnants of which vanished during my own youth," he wrote of *Waverley* to his friend Morritt on 9 July 1814. And again, in the last chapter of the novel, he comments: "There is no European nation which, within the course of half a century, or little more, has undergone so complete a change as this kingdom of Scotland. The effects of the insurrection of 1745 — the destruction of the patriarchal power of the Highland chiefs — the abolition of the heritable jurisdictions of the Lowland nobility and barons — the total eradication of the Jacobite party, which, averse to intermingle with the English, or adopt their customs, long continued to pride themselves upon maintaining ancient Scottish manners and customs — commenced this innovation. The gradual influx of wealth, the extension of commerce, have since united to render the present people of Scotland a class of beings as different from their grandfathers as the existing English are from those of Queen Elizabeth's time". (492) The romantic fascination of the old heroic way of life and its inevitable replacement by a more enlightened and rational system is the theme of *Waverley* as it is the theme of so many of Scott's

novels. The present essay is offered as a footnote to the many critical discussions of the novel in recent years, pointing out the paradox of Scott's com-
bining a determined anonymity as author with a give-away personal style that
revealed him in almost every sentence.

I have used the Penguin English Library edition of *Waverley*
(Harmondsworth, 1972), edited by Andrew Hook, where the text is based on
the Centenary edition of 1870-71 with some readings restored from the manuscript. Page references refer to that edition.

ANYONE who has read through the twelve volumes of Scott's letters
edited by Grierson and others (London, 1932-7) must have been struck
by the fact that at almost every conceivable opportunity Scott quotes
"Patience, cousin, and shuffle the cards". Only once, so far as I can
recollect, does he reveal the source of the quotation — in a letter to Joanna
Baillie of 23 November 1810, when he prefixes it by saying "but, as
Durandarte says in the cavern of Montesinos . .". The quotation is in fact
from Part II, Book III, Section XXIII of *Don Quixote* (not, incidentally,
"chapter vi" as Andrew Hook says in his note in the Penguin edition:
Edgar Johnson in his edition does not identify it at all), but Scott's
imagination had dwelt so intimately with the book that the passage was
part of the familiar furniture of his mind that he revealed on the slightest
provocation without, except on the one occasion, considering it necessary
to identify it.

Anyone reading the anonymous *Waverley* when it first came out in 1814
must, if he knew Scott at all well, have sat up when he came to chapter 41
and found Fergus Mac-Ivor quoting to Waverley "But patience, cousin,
and shuffle the cards" (299). Scott put his favourite quotation into
Fergus's mouth not because Fergus was the kind of person who would
have been likely to know *Don Quixote* well enough to quote this otherwise
obscure sentence, but because he wanted Fergus to express that kind of
sentiment. It is in fact out of character for Fergus to use that sort of
quotation. As far as character and reading habits go, it was Waverley and
not Fergus who could have been expected to know and quote from *Don
Quixote,* as we know quite precisely from the account given of Waverley's
reading (which was Scott's own) in chapter 3. After reading chapter 41 of
Waverley no close friend of Scott and few who had any knowledge of his
daily conversation or regularly received letters from him could have been
in any doubt about the identity of the author.

Don Quixote is in fact an important key to *Waverley*. Northrop Frye, in
his book *The Secular Scripture*[1] (which he tells us grew in part out of an
abandoned essay on the Waverley novels), argues that the novel form
began — and indeed continued — as "a realistic displacement of
romance". *Don Quixote,* he points out, is "the supreme example of the
realistic parody of romance, . . which signalised the death of one kind of
fiction and the birth of another kind". And the Waverley novels "mark

the absorption of realistic displacement into romance itself. Scott begins his preface to *Waverley* by outlining a number of facile romance formulas that he is *not* going to follow, and then stresses the degree of reality that his story is to have. His hero Waverley is a romantic hero, proud of his good looks and education, but, like a small-scale *Don Quixote*, his romantic attitude is one that confirms the supremacy of real life".

This view agrees precisely with the position that I have taken in earlier essays on Scott.[2] But what I want to argue here is not so much that *Waverley* is "a realistic displacement of romance" as that in the tone in which Scott conducts his narrative and the ways in which he manages both to relish the set romantic scenes and convey a sense of a self-depre-cating author half apologising for them and half laughing at them he projects himself in a vivid personal way. If you have lived with Scott's letters for a period of time you recognise the voice at once — the com-bination of almost obsessive antiquarianism with sophisticated historical inquiry; of a passion for songs, ballads, anecdotes, anything traditional and *handed down* that reflects the past out of which it arose, with a highly sceptical view of romantic gestures and attitudes; of genial personal chat with an almost self-consciously formal expository prose.

> "In the succeeding spring, the perusal of old Isaac Walton's fascinating volume determined Edward to become 'a brother of the angle' ". (50)

This sentence, from Chapter 4, is a typical example of the occasions when Scott's voice comes through the fabric of the narrative. Walton was fascinating for him because he was "old"—i.e., he wrote in a previous age—and he loved fishing, as Scott did. (It will be remembered that *Waverley* was resumed after Scott had found the abandoned early chapters in a drawer while looking for fishing tackle.) Here the author's voice is not indicated directly, as it is, for example, in his ironical intro-ductory account of the kind of novel he is not going to write or in the opening of chapter 5:

> From the minuteness with which I have traced Waverley's pursuits, and the bias which these unavoidably communicated to his imagination, the reader may perhaps anticipate, in the following tale, an imitation of Cervantes. But he will do my prudence injustice in the supposition. My intention is not to follow the steps of that inimitable author, in describing such total perversion of intellect as misconstrues the objects actually presented to the senses, but that more common aberration from sound judgment, which apprehends occurrences indeed in their reality, but communicates to them a tincture of its own romantic tone and colouring. (55)

This is an important statement of the author's view of what he is doing in *Waverley*, but I am more concerned here with its tone than with its content. It is exactly the tone he uses in letters to friends — to Morritt, say — in talking about his work. Or consider Waverley's verses, "Mirkwood Mere":

> Late, when the Autumn evening fell
> On Mirkwood-Mere's romantic dell,
> The lake returned, in chastened gleam,
> The purple cloud, the golden beam . . . (60).

This is, in the most obvious and unquestionable way, the fluent throw-away poetic style of the man who wrote *The Lady of the Lake:*

> The stag at eve had drunk his fill,
> Where danced the moon on Monan's rill,
> And deep his midnight lair had made
> In lone Glenartney's hazel shade;
> But, when the sun his beacon red
> Had kindled on Benvoirlich's head,
> The deep-mouthed bloodhound's heavy bay
> Resounded up the rocky way,
> And faint, from farther distance borne,
> Were heard the clanging hoof and horn.

In writing *Waverley* Scott was using his own voice, not inventing a special authorial voice, as most novelists do. (Even novelists who introduce their own first-person comments into their narrative, like Fielding and Thackeray, or such a novelist as Sterne whose first-person voice takes control throughout, employ a deliberate *persona* rather than their genial and unguarded selves.) This may have something to do with the impression of carelessness Scott's novels often give and the charge of artistic laxity so often brought against him. Of course he often was careless and he could be lax. But he often seems to be more careless than he is precisely because of this unguarded quality of his narrative tone. This is true in spite of the passages of rather heavy descriptive prose and other stylistic artificialities that can be found in the novels. They represent Scott's voice too. E. M. W. Tillyard once attacked *Redgauntlet* because the two young men couch their correspondence in an intolerably artificial style. But that was an authentic style of educated young men in Enlightened Edinburgh, as it remained for a long time afterwards. Even in my own student days, members of the Diagnostic Society of Edinburgh University would rise and begin their observations with: "I rise to homologate the sentiments of the preceding speaker".

In later novels Scott did use other voices — that of Jedediah Cleishbotham in the *Tales of My Landlord,* for example — but even these reflected aspects of his own personality and interests. In *Waverley,* however, Scott's own voice is clear and undisguised. Consider this, for example:

> I know not whether, like the champion of an old ballad,

His heart was all on honour bent
He could not stoop to love;
No lady in the land had power
His frozen heart to move;
or whether the deep and flaming bars of embroidered gold which now
fenced his breast, defied the artillery of Cecilia's eyes; but every arrow
was launched at him in vain.
Yet did I mark where Cupid's shaft did light;
It lighted not on little western flower,
But on bold yeomen, flower of all the west,
Hight Jonas Culbertfield, the steward's son.
The introduction of four lines of a ballad followed by a facetious parody of
some well-known lines from *A Midsummer Night's Dream*, in a context of
genial chat and half-parody, represents an extraordinary way to carry on
the narrative. For the narrative is carried on; this passage is not an
excrescence, but tells us something quite specific about Waverley's lack
of interest in Cecilia Stubbs and Cecilia's consequent marriage to Jonas
Culbertfield. Scott goes on to crave pardon for his "heroics", just as
though he had been telling an anecdote at the breakfast table and had been
led (as he so often was) into quotation and parody in the telling. This is at
the end of chapter 5, which concludes with an even more direct authorial
intervention:

I beg pardon, once and for all, of those readers who take up novels
merely for amusement, for plaguing them so long with old-fashioned
politics, and Whig and Tory, and Hanoverians and Jacobites. The
truth is, I cannot promise them that this story shall be intelligible, not
to say probable, without it. My plan requires that I should explain the
motives on which its action proceeded; and these motives necessarily
arose from the feelings, prejudices, and parties of the times ... (63)

Scott is aware that he has been exhibiting his own historical and anti-
quarian interests — and when he could not get them directly into the
narrative he put them in notes — and indulging himself by introducing
into the narrative both his own poetry and quotations and parodies, and
without changing the tone of voice he explains that he does so to provide
proper motivation for the action of his novel. Northrop Frye argues in the
book from which I have already quoted that when great writers re-work
traditional material from narrative romance they usually try to change
merely episodic "and then" narrative into structured "hence" narrative
by supplying plausible motivation and other causal devices. This is
precisely what Scott tells us he is doing here. He tells us that he is using
history to explain the actions and inter-actions of certain kinds of
characters. The characters are explained both psychologically, culturally
and historically, but history is the most important causal factor. This, of
course, is the method of the historical novel as Scott invented it. But the

point I want to stress here is that he *talks about* his objective at the end of a chapter that moves easily between serious description and narrative, his own verse (attributed to his hero), quotation, parody and reflection. Superficially there would seem to be a range of styles employed here. In fact, everything emerges out of a single tone (if not a single style), a voice speaking (however formal the prose), Scott himself telling a story in the way demanded by his personality rather than by any aesthetic theory.

By making it clear that Waverley had in his youth indulged in exactly the same kind of reading that he himself had, Scott enables himself to use quotations from that reading in describing Waverley's reactions to particular events and situations. So in chapter 9, when Waverley is approaching the manor-house of Tully-Veolan, he thinks that he has reached "the castle of Orgoglio, as entered by the victorious Prince Arthur", and five lines of quotation from the eighth canto of Book I of *The Faerie Queene* follow. Shortly afterwards Scott is describing the scene in his own person, in terms of Ariosto's *Orlando Furioso:* "The scene, though pleasing, was not quite equal to the gardens of Alcina, yet wanted not the *'due donzelette garrule'* of that enchanted paradise, . . ." A reference to Tasso's Armida (in *Gerusalemme Liberata*) is then brought in. We are not told that these were comparisons that arose in Waverley's mind; it is the author speaking here; but in matters of this sort the author's mind and that of his hero are one.

Chapter 9 is indeed full of examples of Scott's telling his story in a way that indulges his own special interests and uses his own voice. The introduction of David Gellatley is made by having him sing a song, which Scott gives, adding in a footnote: "This is a genuine ancient fragment, with some alteration in the last two lines". He is quite right, of course. The lines he has David Gellatley sing are:

    False love, and hast thou played me thus
        In summer among the flowers?
    I will repay thee back again
        In winter among the showers.
    Unless again, again, my love,
        Unless you turn again;
    As you with other maidens rove,
        I'll smile on other men.   (82)

Scott probably found this in the two-volume 1776 edition of David Herd's *Ancient and Modern Scottish Songs*. On page 6 of volume two we find:

    False luve! and hae ze played me this,
        In the summer 'mid the flowers?
    I sall repay ze back again,
        In the winter 'mid the showers.

Bot again, dear luve, and again, dear luve,
   Will ze not turn again?
As ze look to ither women,
   Shall I to ither men.

When questioned by Waverley, Gellatley replies by singing another
song — "and, like the witch of Thalaba, 'still his speech was song' " —
which this time appears to be an original Scott version of one of the Lord
William and Burd Ellen ballads. The reference to the witch of Thalaba is
to the narrative poem *Thalaba the Destroyer* by Scott's friend Robert
Southey. He goes on to inform the reader that Gellatley appeared to
Waverley to be "not much unlike one of Shakespeare's roynish clowns",
which would indicate a pretty good knowledge of Shakespeare on
Waverley's part, for the word "roynish" (meaning "scurvy", "coarse") is
found only once in all the plays, and then in an unimportant scene (*As You
Like It*, 2:2: "My Lord, the roynish clown at whom so oft/Your grace was
wont to laugh . . ."). The paragraph concludes by describing Gellatley (is
it Scott's description, or Waverley's presented to us by Scott?) as "Old
Adam's likeness, set to dress this garden", which is a line from *Richard II*
(3:4) but clearly suggested to Scott by the Adam of *As You Like It*, since
that play was already in his mind. The whole paragraph is a characteristic
Scott *mélange*, and can be paralleled in many of his letters.

Chapter 10 opens with a description of Rose Bradwardine and an
account of her popularity as a local beauty and subject for generous toasts
by the hard drinkers of the Bautherwhillery Club. Then, as though this
had not all happened in 1745 but in his own day, or recently enough for
Scott to have been given oral information about what happened, he adds
in his own person: "Nay, I am well assured, that the sleeping partners of
the company snorted applause, and that although strong bumpers and
weak brains had consigned two or three to the floor, yet even these, fallen
as they were from their high estate, and weltering — I will carry the
parody no farther — uttered divers inarticulate sounds, intimating their
assent to the motion" (85). The parody that Scott says he will "carry no
further" is of part of the fourth section of Dryden's "Alexander's Feast":

He sang Darius Great and Good,
   By too severe a Fate,
Fallen, fallen, fallen, fallen,
   Fallen from his high Estate
     And weltring in his Blood.

Scott had already edited Dryden and, with his phenomenal memory,
knew much of his poetry by heart. As someone who had no real knowledge of or interest in music he nevertheless had a strong sense of rhythm
and tempo, and "Alexander's Feast" must have appealed to him
particularly as conveying a sense of music in rhymed and rhythmic
language, with varying tempi. "I do not know and cannot utter a note of

music," he wrote in his *Journal* in November 1825, "and complicated harmonies seem to me a babble of confused though pleasing sounds. Yet songs and simple melodies especially if connected with words and ideas have as much effect on me as on most people". And to his daughter-in-law Jane he wrote: "I who have no ear or almost none for *tune* have a perfect ear for *time* and never wrote a verse in my life for a measure with which I was familiar which was not quite adapted to it".

At one point or another almost everybody in *Waverley* sings. When Baron Bradwardine and his guests go to the local inn after the banquet, somewhat the worse for liquor, the Baron "imitating, as well as he could, the manner and tone of a French musquetaire" sings old French military songs and Balmawhapple, urged on by rivalry, sings snatches of ballads, including a "snatch of a ballad . . . composed by Andrew MacDonald, the ingenious and unfortunate author of Vimonda" (as Scott tells us in a footnote). On his way to visit Fergus Mac-Ivor "he heard the notes of a lively Gaelic song" (45), and when he is entertained by Mac-Ivor the family *bhairdh* chants "a profusion of Celtic verses" (165). In the extra-ordinary set piece in chapter 22, where Flora Mac-Ivor entertains Waverley in a deliberately contrived picturesque Highland setting, she explains to him that she had chosen that setting because "a Highland song would suffer still more from my imperfect translation were I to introduce it without its own wild and appropriate accompaniment" (177). She then entertains Waverley by singing her own English version of a Highland "Battle Song":

There is mist on the mountain, and night on the vale,
But more is the sleep of the sons of the Gael . . . (178).

This is in the same metre as "Young Lochinvar" (in *Marmion*) as well as of "MacGregor's Gathering", which has the same imagery and feeling:

The moon's on the lake, and the mist's on the brae,
And the clan has a name that is nameless by day; . . .

When Fergus comes to find his sister entertaining Waverley with her song, he addresses her ironically in verse:

O Lady of the desert, hail!
That lov'st the harping of the Gael,
Through fair and fertile regions borne,
Where never yet grew grass or corn   (181).

This is Scott parodying his own style in *The Lady of the Lake* and is quite inappropriate when put in the mouth of an ambitious and intriguing Jacobite clan chieftain. As though he realised this, Scott makes Fergus shift at once to a French pastoral song (Fergus's father had served in France after the failure of the 1715 rising and had married a French wife). Then he asks "little Cathleen" to sing, and she sings "with much liveliness a little Gaelic song, the burlesque elegy of a countryman on the loss of his cow, the comic tones of which, though he did not understand

the language, made Waverley laugh more than once" (182). Scott gives
the reader an explanatory footnote: "This ancient Gaelic ditty is still well
known, both in the Highlands and in Ireland. It was translated into
English, and published, if I mistake not, under the auspices of the
facetious Tom D'Urfey, by the title 'Colley, my Cow' ". Scott is here
building up a picture of a culture and at the same time showing the
psychological differences between different characters, all by means of
different styles of poetry and song. Again, we realise that Scott was always
doing this, in conversation, in his letters and later in his *Journal*. It is not
so much a literary technique he has invented as an easy deployment of his
own interests.

Both the heroines of the novel, Flora Mac-Ivor and Rose Bradwardine,
are given the opportunity to express themselves to Waverley in song.
Rose has already sung to him the ballad "St. Swithin's Chair" which he
gives the reader "although I conjecture the following copy to have been
somewhat corrected by Waverley, to suit the taste of those who might not
relish pure antiquity". What he is really saying here is that this is one of
Scott's own imitation ballads: it is *almost* a parody:

On Hallow-Mass Eve, ere ye boune to rest
Ever beware that your couch be blessed;
Sign it with cross, and sain it with bead,
Sing the Ave, and say the Creed. . . . (112).

Gellatley expresses himself in verse consistently, in the literary con-
vention of the clown or the mad rustic who communicates in this way.
Scott does the same thing with Madge Wildfire in *The Heart of Mid-
Lothian*. This gives him a marvellous opportunity to introduce at inter-
vals throughout the novel scraps of folk poetry, ballads, and imitation
folk-poetry of which his head was always full.

Sometimes Scott expresses dialogue through song to such an extent that
the novel almost turns temporarily into a ballad opera. The Jacobite wife
of the anti-Jacobite blacksmith of Cairnvreckan (in chapter 13) expresses
her defiance of the villagers by singing "Charlie is my darling" and then
telling them of the coming Jacobite rising in a modified fragment of
another traditional song:

Little wot ye wha's coming,
Little wot ye wha's coming,
A' the wild Macraws are coming   (236).

When her husband angrily bids her go home she replies contemptuously
with another snatch of folk-song:

O gin ye were dead, gudeman,
And a green turf on your head, gudeman!
Then I wad ware my widowhood
Upon a ranting Highlandman   (238).

There is another example of dialogue-through-quoted-poetry at the beginning of chapter 43 when the Baron quotes two lines of Virgil, followed by Robertson of Struan's translation, and Fergus replies "Or rather, hear my song" and proceeds to quote

She wadna hae a Lowland laird,
  Nor be an English lady;
But she's away with Duncan Graeme,
  And he's rowed her in his plaidy   (312).

There seems little point in arguing here against the psychological probability of Fergus's quoting, let alone knowing, this stanza. Scott is using what for him is a *natural* way of expressing himself. And in his creation of the character of Baron Bradwardine he is giving himself the apportunity to voice with splendid abandon all those antiquarian obsessions and relish for old feudal forms of speech and thought that had been with him most of his life. The Baron is a kind of walking Abbotsford. That this sort of thing is interfused in the novel with a formal neo-classic descriptive style as well as an occasional first-person sentimentality is bound up with the novel's theme, which is that in the end the heroic, however appealing, must give way to the reasonable and the kindly if civilisation is to progress. It is Scott's own voice that tells us, at the end of chapter 60, that now that Waverley has left the Jacobite army and seen the peaceful rhythms of agricultural life "the romance of his life was ended, and . . . its real history had now commenced" (416).

It is Scott's own voice, too, that we hear when Waverley is considering the case against joining the Jacobite army:

Whatever were the original rights of the Stuarts, calm reflection told him, that, omitting the question how far James the Second could forfeit those of his posterity, he had, according to the united voice of the whole nation, justly forfeited his own. Since that period, four monarchs had reigned in peace and glory over Britain, sustaining and exalting the character of the nation abroad, and its liberties at home. Reason asked, was it worth while to disturb a government so long settled and established, and to plunge a kingdom into all the miseries of civil war, for the purpose of replacing upon the throne the descendants of a monarch by whom it had been wilfully forfeited? (222)

This is the voice of the Scottish Enlightenment. Of course he was torn the other way too (as the novel makes clear). He discussed Jacobitism in a letter to Miss Clephane on 13 July 1813: "Seriously, I am very glad I did not live in 1745 for though as a lawyer I could not have pleaded Charles's right and as a clergyman I could not have prayed for him yet as a soldier I would I am sure against the convictions of my better reason have fought for him even to the bottom of the gallows". This shows to what a degree Scott was himself Waverley, which perhaps partly explains what a wooden figure he is, since Scott dreaded giving his inner self away directly in his novels. He would not give himself away in love scenes after his early and traumatic unhappy love affair with Williamina Belsches, and he would not directly reveal his kinship with Waverley. In writing to his friends he continually professed his inability to handle love scenes, while it was he himself who emphasised Waverley's woodenness, going so far as to call him "a sneaking piece of imbecility".

Scott's novels are a mixture of clear give-away and deliberate disguise. He includes, especially in the notes, a great deal of autobiographical chat but at the same time persisted in publishing the novels anonymously. His chosen motto *"clausus tutus ero"* ("closed up I shall be safe") reflected an important part of his character. But so did his whole style and manner of writing fiction — more so, I think, than he ever realised.

A final point, about the ending of *Waverley*. It can be said that the contrivance of having Colonel Talbot buy the forfeited estate of Baron Bradwardine and restore it to him, and indeed the whole ending of the novel, with Waverley's own complete escape from any consequences of his association with the Jacobite army, is improbable and sentimental. But it must be remembered that the Scottish Enlightenment preached humanity and compassion as well as reasonableness, and Scott wanted to show the movement of history as a progression from a cruel if in some respects splendid heroic way of life to a more compassionate as well as a more rational one. The ending, like the concluding dedication to Henry Mackenzie, at once the "Man of Feeling" and a stalwart of the Scottish Enlightenment, has this function. If this is sentimentality, it is balanced by the merciless fate of Fergus, who in death showed the heroism that had been beginning to seem a little tarnished in earlier scenes, and by the totally unsentimental matter-of-fact comment of Alick Polwarth after Fergus's severed head had been placed on the Scotch Gate at Carlisle: "It's a great pity of Evan Dhu, who was a very well-meaning, good-natured man, to be a Hielandman; and indeed so was the Laird o' Glennaquoich too, for that matter, when he wasna in ane o' his tirrivies" (477). To quote Northrop Frye again: "The happy endings of life, as of literature, exist only for survivors". For some of the most vividly drawn characters in *Waverley* there was no happy ending. Baron Bradwardine is perhaps the most unexpected survivor; but then his peculiar kind of anti-quarian pedantry was precisely how the older heroic way of life was to survive into the modern world, as an object of passionate inquiry by peace-loving antiquaries. It is perhaps true to say that Bradwardine is almost as much Scott as Waverley is, and a Scott whom he could reveal much more freely, for it was a side of him he had already opened to the public. For the rest, one can only say that in spite of his determined anonymity in publishing his novels, Scott in writing them found a style that really was *l'homme même* and must have given him away at every point to those who really knew him.

NOTES:

1. (Cambridge, Mass., 1976).
2. In *Literary Essays* (London, 1956), *Sir Walter Scott and his World* (London, 1971), "Sir Walter Scott and History", *Etudes Anglaises,* October-December 1971, and "Scott and Scotland", *Scott Bicentenary Essays* ed. A. Bell (Edinburgh and London, 1973).

FURTHER READING:

The selection is almost limitless. One can only provide outlines; the standard biography is the immense *Sir Walter Scott, The Great Unknown* (London, 1970) by E. Johnson, though Scott's own son-in-law Lockhart wrote a life that is still a classic (1837-8). W. E. K. Anderson edited Scott's noble and revealing *Journal* (Oxford, 1972). Tom Crawford's *Scott* (Edinburgh and London, 1965) remains an excellent brief introduction, and a sample of recent writing on Scott can be found in the stimulating *Scott Bicentenary Essays* ed. Alan Bell (Edinburgh and London, 1973). Of many other possible recommendations, Alexander Welsh, *The Hero of the Waverley Novels* (New Haven and London, 1963) especially deserves mention. The evaluation, and revaluation, of Scott continues.

GALT'S *ANNALS:* TREATISE AND FABLE

by David Buchan

JOHN GALT (1779-1839) was both businessman and author, and despite the demands of his first role achieved in his second a considerable output. He is best known for those works of fiction published within an astonishingly short period in the 1820s: *The Ayrshire Legatees* (1821), *Annals of the Parish* (1821), *Sir Andrew Wylie* (1822), *The Provost* (1822), *The Steamboat* (1822), *The Entail* (1822), *Ringan Gilhaize* (1823), *The Omen* (1826), and *The Last of the Lairds* (1826). His later writing, however, contains works of some merit unduly neglected through an accident of publishing history: *The Member* (1832), *The Radical* (1832), and a body of shorter fiction. Ian Gordon, whose *John Galt: The Life of a Writer* has cast much needed light on the editorial and publishing background of Galt's works, declares there that what Galt requires today is "a fresh judgment and available texts"; and a sign of a reawakening of interest in Galt is that in recent years available texts have appeared of five of his books: *Annals of the Parish, The Provost, The Entail, The Last of the Lairds,* and *The Member.* The variousness of Galt's appeal for readers can perhaps be appreciated from the way different critics have convincingly championed as his best book three quite different choices: *Annals of the Parish, The Provost,* and *The Entail.*

SOME years ago two major strains were detected in the development of the Scottish novel, the sentimental and the realistic.[1] It is a fact of some significance for this development that two of the early representatives of these strains quite specifically abjured what they took to be the novel form in their best known and most influential works of fiction. Henry Mackenzie in *The Man of Feeling* presents a series of vignettes of behaviour in a plotless book that nevertheless has its own structural principles of organisation; and John Galt explicitly disclaims for his *Annals of the Parish* the status of novel: "it is so void of any thing like a plot, that it lacks in the most material feature of the novel".[2] His opinion did not prevent its being received as a novel, however, a reaction Galt accepted with some equanimity, as can be discerned from the passage where he sets out what he conceived the book to be, if not a novel:

To myself it has ever been a kind of treatise on the history of society in the West of Scotland during the reign of King George the Third; and when it was written, I had no idea it would ever have been received as a novel. Fables are often a better way of illustrating philosophical truths than abstract reasoning; and in this class of compositions I would place the *Annals of the Parish;* but the public consider it as a novel, and it is of no use to think of altering the impression with which it has been received. . . .[3]

This non-novel, made up of a minister's year by year account (from 1760 to 1810) of an Ayrshire parish, is, then, both "a kind of treatise on the history of society" at a particular time and place, and a "fable".

Galt proffers further information about his fictional mode when he declares for both the *Annals of the Parish* and its companion piece *The Provost* that, however the public may have viewed them, "My own notion was to exhibit a kind of local theoretical history, by examples, the truth of which would at once be acknowledged".[4] The book is a history that is local, rooted in one parish over fifty years, and theoretical, designed to show the general from the particular; this "kind of treatise on the history" of a society is intended to illustrate "philosophical truths" about society and the relationship of man and society, in a "better way" than "abstract reasoning" can provide. As the derivation of the phrase "local theoretical history" from Dugald Stewart underlines, such an intention, expressing as it does one of the major preoccupations of the Scottish Enlightenment, places the book firmly in a Scottish intellectual tradition. If the sentence quoted in this paragraph is taken as a gloss on the earlier sentences, then one can see that by "fable" Galt means the depiction of truth by examples. These examples are designed to portray the events and processes of history and, concomitantly, man, both as social being and as individual. Indeed Galt felt — perhaps in response to the way the public received his works — that he achieved most success in the last regard: "if there is any merit in any of my sketches it is in the truth of the metaphysical anatomy of the characters".[5] There is a danger, however, especially clear in the light of his other statements, in assuming from this *post hoc* response that the picturing of characters as characters was his major aim; it was just one. The balance between his aims can be observed, partially at any rate, from the letter to Blackwood of 27 February 1821, in which he accepts a number of the publisher's suggested alterations but balks at others: "Some of them are characteristic of the garrulous humour of the old doited author, and the others are such events as are long remembered in country parishes besides they have all a vague reference to real events which happened about the time in Ayrshire — and are calculated, as I conceive, to give that degree of reality to the story that may induce *some* to think there has actually been an original chronicle".[6] Galt is concerned with the man his narrator and, at greater length, with the events of his history, in the composing of examples for his fable.

"Truth" is a term which Galt uses frequently in connection with his aims; we have already observed his references to the truth of the metaphysical anatomy of the characters and the fable's illustration of philosophical truths, and to these we can add his wish "to be estimated by the truth of whatever I try to represent",[7] but the most revealing use comes in his stated intention to create a "history, by examples, the truth of which would at once be acknowledged". From the last clause one can see, as one can in his description of the fable, the influence of Aristotle. What Galt is laying great stress on as an artistic value is the Aristotelian concept of recognition, whereby the reader, with profit and delight, readily perceives the truths of living in the imitation of reality. Galt's truths are of two kinds, what we may call, using his own terms, local and theoretical. Local or literal truth resides in that material which Galt incorporates into his work from his own memory of actual event and character and which he is pleased to see detected as such: "Some of the individuals who have been the models of the characters, were, on the publication, at once recognised, which tended to corroborate the favourable opinion I had myself formed of the work".[8] Galt, however, also aims at epitomising kinds of behaviour and event that catch the essence of the people and the processes of this time of social upheaval; he is after essential truths as well as literal. (There is a parallel to this in folk literature where certain historical ballads and legends recount not just literal facts but the traditionally perceived patterns of historical events.) Galt possessed a retentive memory, but the *Annals* is not a work of memorial recall, a charge he seems intent on implicitly rebutting by emphasising the role of artistic creation when he writes of seeing in the book "proofs of those kind of memorials to which I have been most addicted — things of which the originals are, or were, actually in nature, but brought together into composition by art".[9] The examples, then, of this history by examples are so chosen and created as to conform to the patterns of historical event, social process, and human behaviour, and thereby to present the essential truths of these patterns; and throughout, for the general context, Galt aims for what would nowadays be called verisimilitude but for which he had his own tentative term: "it has what my own taste values highly, considerable likeliness, if the expression may be used".[10] Galt's treatise-cum-fable, with its emphasis on truth, stands at some distance from the romances of contemporary fiction, and turns out on examination to be a quite individual species of historical realism. It is, after all, fairly radical for 1821 for a work to embody the premise that not just the essential truths of human nature but also the essence of social and historical event (for instance the industrial revolution in a "circumscribed locality") can be illustrated by fictional portrayal. The emphasis in Galt's comments on truth and its recognition, rather than any writer's gamesmanship, explains why he hoped "to induce *some* to think there has actually been an original chronicle" (a hope that was fulfilled): such recognition would supply objective proof of the efficacy of his method and the realisation of his aims.

So far we have been examining Galt's aims and intentions for the work, but we should also consider the aims and intentions Galt gives the narrator within the book. There are no fewer than five occasions on which Micah Balwhidder addresses himself to this topic:

> a faithful account of [my ministry], year by year, I now sit down, in the evening of my days, to make up, to the end that I may bear witness to the work of a beneficent Providence, even in the narrow sphere of my parish, and the concerns of that flock of which it was His most gracious pleasure to make me the unworthy shepherd. (*A*, 4)

> It is not, however, my design to speak much anent my own affairs, which would be a very improper and uncomely thing, but only of what happened in the parish, this book being for a witness and testimony of my ministry. (*A*, 46)

> But it is not for me to make reflections, my task and duty is to note the changes of time and habitudes. (*A*, 50)

> It belongs to the chroniclers of the realm to describe the [American War] . . . for my task is to describe what happened within the narrow bound of the pasturage of the Lord's flock, of which . . . he made me the . . . shepherd. (*A*, 80)

> [I am] not writing for a vain world, but only to testify to posterity anent the great changes that have happened in my day and generation — a period which all the best informed writers say, has not had its match in the history of the world, since the beginning of time. (*A*, 201)

This series of statements on the task illustrates two aspects of Galt's method, in its cumulative effect and in its arrangement: first, no one statement can be abstracted and labelled the minister's aim for the aim is the sum total of the statements with their varying emphases; and second, the series is so arranged as to give the final one a climactic force. In this group of excerpts one can see Galt balancing the demands of character and theme. In the first, second, and fourth he is establishing the minister's pastoral dutifulness and in the second and third the minister's comic blindness, for he is, of course, much given to speaking anent his own affairs and making reflections. In the preparatory third and the climactic fifth, on the other hand, the stress is laid on the great changes, the changes of time and habitudes, by which Galt is informing us that the burden of his treatise is the theme of social change.

Despite Galt's explicit declaration that the *Annals* was intended as a kind of treatise on the history of a society and not as a novel, there has been a tendency in Galt criticism for writers, after paying lip-service to the declaration, to proceed to discuss and judge it by the criteria of the novel. In doing this they have been anticipated by Galt's contemporary public, and perhaps been affected by Galt's reconciliation to the public's viewpoint, his straightforward assertion there was no plot, and in general the often deprecating attitudes adopted by this man of business to his writings. In any event, complaints have centred on the author's lack of artistic selectivity and the book's formlessness, which have, viewed reductively, sometimes verged on comments that this plotless non-novel lacks the plot of a novel. Considerable praise, on the other hand, has been accorded that standard element of the novel, the depiction of character. For the *Annals* to be seen in proper perspective what is required is a setting forth of the aims of this non-novel and an examination of the technique employed to realise these aims.

From the discussion of the aims, we have seen that the *Annals* as treatise is, above all else, concerned with history. Since the fifty years that it covers constitute the most explosively dynamic period in the history of Scotland, and the United Kingdom, Galt had rich veins of raw material to work. Just how rich can be gauged from the entertaining diversity of the old and the new *Statistical Accounts,* written in the 1790s and the 1840s by the parochial ministers, which provide interesting counterparts to the fictional chronicle.[11] Some of these ministers write with the same diverting idisyncrasy as Micah Balwhidder, and many also engage in the same itemised relation of the differences between past and present in their attempt to explain the nature of the social changes they had lived through. The depiction of social change, we have just noted, is a major aim of the book and not unexpectedly, for its half century saw the radical transformation of individual societies and the genesis of the modern world.[12] The *Annals* recreate this radical transformation. They reflect in their pages such international events as the American War, the French Revolutionary Wars and the Napoleonic Wars, and their progressive impinging on out-of-the-way places, and such national processes as the agrarian revolution, the industrial revolution, their concomitant social revolution, the commercial expansion of the West of Scotland, the improvement in land and sea communications, the growth of the ideas of the French Revolution, and the spread of education, literacy, and books. These affairs effected profound changes in social organisation and in the fabric of the life led by most people, and result in the supersession of one way of life with another. The treatise is not starved of raw data.

How, then, do the *Annals* as fable present the transformations of social change? The discussion of Galt's method will, in the minister's phrasing, come under four heads: the use of example, the use of detail, the structuring, and those elements of technique influenced by folk literature. "What happened in my parish" says Micah Balwhidder "was but a type and index to the rest of the world" (*A*, 186), and although his statement has a specific contextual reference it also has a larger reference in that it illustrates how examples can be made to fashion local theoretical history. Galt is intent on showing the national from the local, the general from the individual, and, above all, the abstract from the concrete, through examples that are types and indices. These examples take the form of characters and incidents. The agrarian revolution, for instance, is represented initially by the minister's father-in-law, Mr. Kibbock, "who was the first that made a speculation in the farming way in Ayrshire" (*A*, 32) and who specialised in dairy-farming, particularly the making of cheeses, and in the planting of trees; he, the first — speculative — kind of improver is followed in accordance with historical sequence by the thorough-going professional from the Lothians, Mr Coulter, "than whom there had been no such man in the agricultural line among us before" (*A*, 37). These are not just emblematic figures in a newly trig landscape, however, for their effects on others are made manifest. Mr Kibbock not only inspires neighbouring lairds to emulation (*A*, 102) but also raises a daughter, Miss Lizy, who "had been so ingrained with the profitable management of cows and grumphies in her father's house, that she could not desist" when she attained her redoubtable station as the second Mrs Balwhidder, and "was the mean of giving a life and energy to the housewifery of the parish". As with her father and Mr Coulter, her example animates others: "I began to discern that there was something as good in her example, as the giving of alms to the poor folk. For all the wives of the parish were stirred up by it into a wonderful thrift, and nothing was heard of in every house, but of quiltings and wabs to weave; insomuch, that before many years came round, there was not a better stocked parish, with blankets and napery, than mine was, within the bounds of Scotland" (*A*, 33). The activities of this "indefatigable engine of industry", paralleled by references in the *Old Statistical Account* to the passion for work that had people knitting as they walked along the road, furnish — as has been often noted — a steady source of humour, and pathos, in the way they reduce Mr Balwhidder to "a most solitary married man" (*A*, 138): at the human domestic level, the spirit of improvement could be hard to thole. And yet, it was her industriousness that enabled the Balwhidders after the first year of marriage to put his entire stipend into the bank, a detail which illustrates how one eighteenth century family engaged in the accumulation of capital. The second Mrs Balwhidder, sometimes regarded only as a source of comedy, Galt uses with her effects on the community, her husband's connubial comfort, and his bank account, to shed a number of different lights on the improving movement, at ground level.

The agrarian revolution and its ramifications which permeate the first part of the book profoundly altered the old patterns of social organisation, and it is no accident that persistent presences within this section are not improvers but the balancing figures of Lady Macadam, a "woman naturally of a fantastical" (*A*, 83), and the actively benevolent Lord Eglesham, contrasted representatives of the old stock of gentry. In like fashion the second half of the book, devoted in great part to the ramifications of the industrial revolution, contains as its pervasive character Mr Cayenne, the example of the entrepreneur in a world of new technological and commercial possibilities. He, the successful business man, has his antithetical shadow, the unsuccessful Mr Speckle, a balance that is repeated in the early flourishing and later failure of Provost Maitland in the commercial sphere. The disruption by the revolutions of the former patterns of class relation resulted in an intensified degree of social mobility, of which the main example is the Malcolm family. Ms Malcolm's three sons become a naval captain, a trading ship's captain, and a minister with a Doctorate of Divinity, and her two daughters marry into the gentry. Galt rather weights the scales in their favour, of course, with their genteel birth, innate grace, and decorous if impoverished upbringing, but the fact of their elevations remains, reinforced by such parenthetical details as: "... William Mutchkins, the father of Mr Mutchkins, the great spirit-dealer in Glasgow, set up a change-house" (*A*, 30), and "Robert Toddy ... set his own house to Thomas Treddles, the weaver, whose son, William, is now the great Glasgow manufacturer, that has cotton-mills and steam-engines; and took ..." (*A*, 123). The advances promoted by the revolutions in such areas as medicine and education have their exemplifying characters too. In medicine the Nanse Birrel who appears in the first half, "a distillator of herbs, and well skilled in the healing of sores" whom folk called a witchwife (*A*, 38-9) — a "skeely woman" — is succeeded in the second half by Doctors Marigold and Tansy. In education the dame-school of Nanse Banks who "learnt them reading and working stockings, and how to sew the semplar, for twalpennies a-week" (*A*, 13-14) is taken over by Miss Sabrina Hookie with her more advanced notions, and latterly she is replaced by Mrs M'Caffie and Mrs Pirn.

The spread of education brought mass literacy which in turn brought forth the phenomenon of the local poet, of whom Ayrshire had a plentiful number. The Dalmailing representative is Colin Mavis, who composes a patriotic song for the Volunteers, a poem on an infare, and a satire on Micah Balwhidder's efforts to reform burial customs, has some verses published in the *Scots Magazine,* and has either taken out a book or hopes to have one published by subscription (according to whichever annal, 1801 or 1807, one offers greater credence). "Thus", writes Micah Balwhidder, "has our parish walked sidy for sidy with all the national improvements, having an author of its own" (A, 174). To suggest, as has been done, that Galt's picture is incomplete because, for instance, it lacks any account of the stir created by Burns's poems in Ayrshire is to misinterpret his aims and method. Galt is not attempting a quirkily literal piece of retrospective reporting but trying to capture the essential truths of a society's history by examples, and the local example of the regional interest in poetry is Colin Mavis.

While the metaphysical anatomy of the characters does without doubt give pleasure, the importance of their function in relation to the book's main aim, the depiction of social change, should not be under-estimated. A point worth noting that will be returned to is that while some of these characters-as-examples stand on their own, others take part in an appositional pattern, and others make up a cumulative pattern.

Incidents as well as characters are used to typify the general from the particular and, especially, the national from the local. The disturbances that attend the placing of Mr Balwhidder in his charge (A, 5-6) reflect the troubles occasioned elsewhere by the exercise of patronage, just as the later alterations in church discipline and practice (A, 183-4) reflect changes widely accepted throughout the country. In these chapters the local event provides a type of happenings nationally, while in others it furnishes an index to what is going on in the world. The American War, for instance, is a national affair that has a steadily encroaching effect on the life of the parish. The first impingement comes when a soldier travelling with his troop to their transports at Greenock quarrels with and murders his camp-following woman within the parish bounds; later "the battle was brought, as it were, to our gates" (A, 80) when a recruiting party engages a married man with three or four of a family, and enlisting becomes "a catching distemper" so that "there was a wailing in the parish" (A, 81). For balance we are also given a picture of Charles Malcolm and Mr Howard "in their fine gold-laced garbs" which, "as we had tasted the sorrow, gave us some insight into the pomp of war" (A, 82). Chapter XXII for 1781 (A, 104-7) contains a different kind of exemplifying incident in the murder of Lord Eglesham by Mungo Argyle, which is based on the possibly accidental killing of a not altogether popular Earl of Eglinton in 1769 by an excise officer called Mungo Campbell.[13] Galt's exciseman, who in the chapter heading "grows a gentleman" and in the text takes to acting "as if he had been on an equality with gentlemen", shoots Lord Eglesham after he had been caught usurping a traditional privilege of the aristocracy, the hunting of game. Galt so reworks his material as to make it embody representatively attacks on the heritor class and their privileges and, in general, the strains besetting the old hierarchical social system. Lord Eglesham's death, however, does not stand alone, for it is one of a number of deaths in Chapters XXII to XXIV which cumulatively create an impression of the passing away of an old

order; here Galt uses in this series of incidents a simple version of the
reflector technique.

This local history is theoretical in that it reflects national doings and also
in that it investigates "philosophical truths" about man and society, most
notably the relationship of social change and human behaviour. Galt is
concerned not just with the typifying character and incident in themselves but with process, the interaction of people and event that makes up
social change, and here again he employs the exemplifying method. Early
in the book occur two occasions showing how a character can initiate
change; there is the accident of Lord Eglesham and the resultant trust-
road (A, 41-3), and there is the building of the steeple: "This was chiefly
owing to the instrumentality of Lady Moneyplack, who, in that winter,
was much subjected to the rheumatics, she having, one cold and raw
Sunday morning, there being no bell to announce the time, come half an
hour too soon to the kirk, [which] made her bestir herself to get an
interest awakened among the heritors in behalf of a steeple" (A, 38). They
exemplify, in small and comic compass, how little things lead to greater,
especially where the conveniences of the creature are involved. In a later
chapter Mr Balwhidder himself originates change from benevolent
motives when he reforms the old burial customs because they
"straightened many a poor family" (A, 188). The interaction is two-way,
however, for while the individual can effect change, change can also affect
the individual, who in turn influences others. The minister is profoundly
affected by the markings of change in the people of Glasgow: "I thought
the looks of the population were impaired, and that there was a greater
proportion of long white faces in the Trongate, than when I attended the
Divinity class" (A, 136). This leads him to the crucial realisation that
social progress, which had brought so many benefits to his parish, might
not be of unalloyed usefulness: "in that same spirit of improvement,
which was so busy everywhere, I could discern something like a shadow,
that shewed it was not altogether of that pure advantage, which avarice
led all so eagerly to believe". Consequently he delivers a series of sermons
on what was once called the vanity of riches but is now termed the evils of
capitalism, pointing out "that the rich man was liable to forget his
unmerited obligations to God, and to oppress the laborious and the
needful when he required their services" (A, 137); not unnaturally, such
statements result in complicated repercussions for the minister within the
parish. What Galt is presenting here, through the character of the
minister and the incident of his epiphany in the Trongate with its
parochial consequences, is one kind of exemplifying interaction between
the individual and the forces of social change where the interaction both
results from and contributes to the general processes.

In portraying the processes Galt deals not only with the effects on the
individual but also the effects on the social group of prosperities and, more

significantly, failures. Chapter XLIX (*A*, 197-200), for instance, begins with a statement on the former comparative remoteness of the parish from the ill effects of such national troubles as wars and, by contrast, the modern involvement in, and susceptibility to, the movements of national commercial affairs. The illustrative proof is supplied by the business of the cotton mill: "on the Monday, when the spinners went to the mill, they were told that the company had stopped payment. Never did a thunderclap daunt the heart like this news, for the bread in a moment was snatched from more than a thousand mouths". Stricken, the minister laments "what could our parish fund do in the way of helping a whole town, thus suddenly thrown out of bread", thereby underlining just how far commercial progress had outstripped the development of relevant social institutions: parish relief could not possibly cope with a town's unemployed. After the failure, an overseer at the mill who had himself once been a mill-owner commits suicide along with his wife. Here Galt first presents the "philosophical truth" in the abstract, then demonstrates it in human terms through the concrete example. The annal form, of course, lends itself to this organisation by generalisation and supporting evidence.

One advantage a writer of fiction has over the conventional historian in discussing the human effects of social change is that he can show more naturally differences in the ways of thinking and behaving, and in the ways individuals relate to one another; and Galt does not ignore the possibilities his medium allows. In Chapter XLIII (*A*, 175-8), for instance, the narrator makes the observation that a consequence of "the uncertain state of governments and national affairs" was "a great distrust between man and man, and an aching restlessness among those who had their bread to bake in the world". He goes on to furnish a manifestation of this, "Persons possessing the power to provide for their kindred, forcing them, as it were, down the throats of those who were dependent on them in business, a bitter morsel", and then the concrete example, the core of the chapter, in the treatment of Mr Cayenne by the London mercantile concern. At the end of the chapter, however, comes a balancing observation to the first: "mankind read more, and the spirit of reflection and reasoning was more awake than at any time within my remembrance". This too is followed by a manifestation, "Not only was there a handsome bookseller's shop in Cayenneville, with a London newspaper daily, but Magazines, and Reviews, and other new publications", and the example, comic this time, of Mr and Mrs Balwhidder jaunting through Ayrshire in the new Cross-keys chaise "by which our minds were greatly enlarged" for travelling is "one of the best means of opening the faculty of the mind". From the apposition, intrinsic and structural, of the ideas within the chapter, the implication is clear that a connection exists between the distrust and the new spirit of reasoning, that they are two aspects of one phenomenon. In this chapter Galt, particularly in the section on distrust, is portraying the kind of qualitative, non-material change in the texture of human relations that falls outside the scope of the standard history but which is grist for fiction's mill. Even the comic example of the modern opening of minds presents the generalisations of the history books with an immediately graspable actuality. This chapter, we can note on leaving it, illustrates certain aspects of Galt's structural method, a matter to which we shall return. In accordance with his dictum about fables, then, Galt illustrates through the examples of character and incident general truths about the features and processes of historical change.

Besides the typifying example Galt also employs the carefully selected detail, which is of course really the example writ small. The narrator's attitude to small incidents and their place in an overall design would seem to reflect the author's to his book: "a quiet succession of small incidents, none of which are worthy of notation, though they were all severally, no doubt, of aught somewhere, as they took up both time and place in the coming to pass, and nothing comes to pass without helping onwards some great end" (A, 100-1). Towards the great end of his treatise, Galt uses details in three main ways — singly, in apposition, and cumulatively organised. Some of the single details indicate how the threads that make up the fabric of living were being altered. Miss Sabrina Hookie, for instance, institutes a change in Christian names; she "began by calling our Jennies, Jessies, and our Nannies, Nancies; alas! I have lived to see even these likewise grow old-fashioned" (A, 49). In 1772, "there was a visible increase of worldly circumstances, and the hedges which had been planted along the toll-road, began to put forth their branches, and to give new notions of orderlyness and beauty to the farmers" (A, 65). Galt makes these hedges suggest visually the changes wrought in the everyday land-scape of the improvements, but he also in the one sentence shows how they are a side-effect of the new communications, and how they in turn create effects of the unquantifiable kind that maintain the momentum of change. On a number of occasions Galt follows a general statement of the minister, such as that a stage-coach was established between Glasgow and Ayr which passed through the town thrice a week, with a purely personal remembrance by the pastor: "it enabled Mrs Balwhidder to send a basket of her fresh butter into the Glasgow market, by which, in the spring and fall of the year, she got a great price, for the Glasgow merchants are fond of excellent eatables, and the payment was aye ready money — Tam Whirlit the driver paying for the one basket when he took up the other" (A, 131). Sometimes the variation in general and private perspectives results in a comic yoking, but almost invariably Galt uses the detailed garrulity of his narrator purposefully, to bring home the meaning of the generalisation concretely. Finally, two little linguistic touches would suggest that it would be unwise to underestimate Galt's use of the single detail. Cayenneville, we discover, is called by the country folk Canaille, a word found in both French and, derived therefrom, in Scots. In Scots it means gang, troop, as in "a canally o loons"; in French it means rabble, mob, which in the context is highly appropriate since the inhabitants are inspired by the "infidel and jacobin spirit of the French Revolution" (*A*, 193). Again, the name Balwhidder subsumes Galt's earlier choice of Bellwhidder,[14] appositely derived from "bellwether", the sheep that leads the flock, and contains too an echo of the related word "bellwaver" (to move here and there without a definite objective), with its verbal noun "balwavering", incoherence. Galt creates his, often apparently innocuous, details with no little care and a keen eye for their effect.

Language also enters into an example of Galt's appositional use of detail. When William Malcolm delivers his sermon, two reactions are juxtaposed: the minister and "the elderly people thought his language rather too Englified", but "the younger part of the congregation were loud in his praise, saying, there had not been heard before such a style of language in our side of the country" (*A*, 132). This mirrors the co-existence of Scots and English at the time and the differing feelings of the generations about the languages, and indicates, in the attitude of the younger generation, the future supersession of Scots by English.

Sometimes when treating a detail Galt will have the minister place it in the appositional context of then and now, as when Mrs Malcolm worries that Robert must sail to Norway via the Orkneys "for there was then no short cut by the canal, as now is, between the rivers of the Forth and Clyde" (*A*, 53), or when Gilbert Balwhidder is blinded by the smallpox for seventeen days "for the inoculation was not in practice yet among us" (*A*, 74). These look from the present moment to the benefits of the future, but the look can also be backward, to the comparative advantages of the past: "the people were grown so used to changes and extraordinary adventures, that the single enlistment of Thomas Wilson, at the beginning of the American War, occasioned a far greater grief and work among us, than all the swarms that went off week after week in the months of November and December of this year" (*A*, 148). On other occasions, the apposition is more implicit: Lady Macadam's jointure-house with the iron-gate that had "a pillar with a pineapple head on each side" is taken over by the rural businessman, Mr Robert Toddy, and transmogrified into The Cross Keys, the parish's first inn (*A*, 123); and this implicit apposition of the aristocratic and the commercial is followed by an explicit comparison of the new inn which brought "the evil practices of towns into the heart of the country" (*A*, 124) with the old change-house of Mr Mutchkins and his exemplary piety. These details all contribute to a sense, not of flux, but of a steady process of transformation. A different use of apposition occurs in the annal for 1763, in which year "The King granted peace to the French, and Charlie Malcolm, that went to sea in the

tobacco trader, came home to see his mother" (*A*,21), where Galt is
showing without comment that the two facts have equal importance for
the parish and that history for those who live through it is a compound of
both public and private detail.

Galt also employs details cumulatively to obtain his impressions and
effects. For instance, the running thread of the "firsts" provides a steady
reminder of the ongoing alterations in the fabric of parish life; there is the
first dancing school, man from the parish to go to sea, fair, Punch and
Judy show, troop of play-actors (*A*, 15,17,57,57,150), and such manifestations of the exotic outside world as the first parrot, ass, Muscovy duck
(*A*,22,39,65). Again, details can be so placed throughout the work as to
reveal the general pattern of developments, as in the matter of writing and
reading. In the first chapter Mrs Malcolm asks the minister to write a
letter for her to Provost Maitland (*A*, 9); in the last chapter the minister's
presentation server has a "well-penned inscription, written by a weaver
lad that works for his daily bread. Such a thing would have been a prodigy
at the beginning of my ministry, but the progress of book learning and
education has been wonderful since" (*A*,204). Towards the end of the first
half of the book a desire to know more of the American War's events
makes the minister, "no longer contented with the relation of the news of
the month in the Scots Magazine", join with his father-in-law "to get a
newspaper twice-a-week from Edinburgh", while Lady Macadam has
one sent three times a week from London (*A*,88); and towards the
beginning of the second half the Cayenneville bookseller "took in a daily
London newspaper for the spinners and weavers, who paid him a penny
a-week for the same" (*A*, 133). In this manner we can observe the spread
of literacy throughout the classes; and in like fashion we see the parish
people's exposure to new religious ideas as well as political. In the first
half, the minister meets an English Dean at Lord Eglesham's house, but
in the second the parish sees the arrival of a variety of denominations,
Roman Catholics, Quakers, Universal Redemptionists, and the establishment of the meeting house. Galt also concentrates little groups of
details in a kind of pointillism to bring home, almost subliminally, a social
fact. During three successive annals there occurs a series of references to
"a broken manufacturer's wife" (*A*, 170), "the widow of a custom house
officer" (*A*, 171), "a widow woman" (*A*, 173), and "a broken merchant"
(*A*,178), which together create the impression of widows and broken
merchants as common features of a troubled social landscape. Likewise,
that a newcomer into this rural Scottish parish is English is mentioned *en
passant* three times (*A*, 169,172,199) which provides indirect information, assimilated almost unconsciously by the reader, of the altering
patterns of geographical mobility in the new society. And there is the
series of details which shows not only the facts but also the changing
attitudes of a development — such as the introduction of tea. Initially

viewed (*A*, 12) as a luxury (just as ministers in the first *Statistical Account* denounce it as a species of inebriation) its status alters: "I lost some of my dislike to the tea, after Mrs Malcolm began to traffic in it, and we then had it for our breakfast in the morning at the Manse, as well as in the afternoon" (*A*, 19); and eventually it gains acceptance: "It was in this visit to Edinburgh that Mrs Balwhidder bought her silver tea-pot, and other ornamental articles; but this was not done, as she assured me, in a vain spirit of bravery, which I could not have abided, but because it was well known, that tea draws better in a silver pot, and drinks pleasanter in a china cup, than out of any other kind of cup or tea-pot" (*A*, 100). Here details are used cumulatively, in a comic sequence of character and manners, to indicate an actual process of adaptive reaction to innovation. Galt's details, apparently single and discrete at a casual reading, are often carefully selected to make up part of a larger design; what may appear intended only to represent the quirkiness of character of the minister may in fact belong to overall purposeful patterns built by Galt for his treatise.

If this non-novel possesses no plot, how, then, is it organised? Or is it formless, a haphazard concatenation of bits and pieces without any overall organisation? What we have seen of the typifying example and the carefully selected detail would suggest that possibility to be a *priori* unlikely. In fact this book has a unity of its own, a unity which, though without conventional plot, relies on other elements of the fiction-writer's technique. First of all the regular cast-list of characters helps to furnish narrative continuity, for they weave in and out through the book. Second, the work's major concern means that certain thematic strands will constantly recur since they are intrinsic to the general consideration of social change. Sometimes these themes can be keyed to specific characters, as in the central section of Chapter XXI where the two themes of improving and smuggling are treated through Mr Kibbock and Mungo Argyle; since both these themes and characters have been thoroughly established before, one way can be readily observed in which the chronicle builds up its own density of internal reference. Another, linked, way with which Galt achieves for the *Annals* its own network of inter-relations is the method whereby in a single chapter the past is put in perspective, the future is foreshadowed, and past, present, and future are linked by the narrator's looking backwards and forwards from the events of the current year. In Chapter XIX, for instance, which is centrally concerned with a resurgence of smuggling and Lord Eglesham's kindness to Willie Malcolm, the annal begins with a reference back to the past year and ends with a narratively whetting anticipation of the next year, while the body of the piece contains references to such previous affairs as the earlier smuggling, Mrs Malcolm's tea-selling, and Lord Eglesham's good offices, and foreshadows the death of Mungo Argyle (in a manner that Stevenson was later to employ). For the overall unity of the plotless chronicle, it is vitally important that the individual chapters do not become isolated parts, and this pitfall Galt avoids by his use of these interweavings, which also enable him to achieve effects comparable to some of those obtained by the novelist with his development of plot.

In both small compass and large, then, Galt gives his material significance and his book unity through the use of the singular and the cumulative. When dealing with example and detail he also, we have seen, employs apposition; and in fact the principle of apposition pervades the book as a whole. It is one of the major unifying forces in the work, operating both within individual chapters and within the total structure. James Kinsley has perceptively pointed out that the book has two halves and that "its centre is marked at chapter xxvi: '. . . here was an example plain to be seen of the truth of the old proverb, that as one door shuts another opens; for scarcely were we in quietness by the decease of that old light-headed woman, the Lady Macadam, till a full equivalent for her was given in this hot and fiery Mr Cayenne' ". He sees the essential concerns of the two sections as these: "The first half of the book is a picture of the old, settled world of the landed gentry (Lord Eglesham, Lady Macadam) and tenantry: an idyll marred only by common personal or parochial troubles, or by the familiar incursions of war. The second half introduces new themes (some typified by Mr Cayenne) of industry and urban settlement, religious anarchy, schism and decline, and the 'decay in the wonted simplicity of our country ways' " (A,x). This view, I would suggest, poses rather too sharp a contrast. It is not a matter of the first half dealing with a relatively static community and the second with its alteration, but rather of there being two eras of different kinds of change, proceeding at different paces, from slow to steadily accelerating. The first half deals with the agrarian revolution and the American War, the second with the industrial revolution and the French Wars. That general characteristics of the two halves are to a considerable extent typified by various character balances — Lady Macadam and Lord Eglesham, Mr Kibbock and Mr Coulter, Mr Cayenne and Mr Speckle — has already been noted. The symbolic replacement of Lady Macadam by Mr Cayenne at the beginning of the second period has in fact been foreshadowed at the beginning of the first when the widow of the minister's patron, "the Lady of Breadland, with her three daughters, removed to Edinburgh, where the young laird, that had been my pupil, was learning to be an advocate, and the Breadland house was let to Major Gilchrist, a nabob from India". He and his sister ("Lady Skim-milk") adopt a narrowly self-interested view of their responsibilities and not only neglect the policies but also, more important, ignore their social obligations to the old men and poor women previously helped by the heritors who now become dependent on the parish for relief, so that the minister "was necessitated to preach a discourse on almsgiving, specially for the benefit of our own poor, a thing never before known in the parish" (*A*, 18-19). Even at this stage the old network of social ties and responsibilities is being breached as a new class of money-making men take over from the heritors. Another kind of apposition that contributes to the book's overall unity is the balancing of theme and event at beginning and end that helps shape the chronicle: the overt linking of Micah Balwhidder and George III of *A*, 1 is paralleled on *A*, 204; the minister's induction in Chapter I is paralleled bs minister's retiral presentation in Chapter LI. In general terms, the structuring is — and there is an interesting comparison here to the fictions of folk narrative — not so much linear and sequential as spatial.

The appositional principle also operates within sections of the book. Throughout the second half, for instance, Galt balances against each other the two places, Cayenneville and the clachan — or "the town; for the term clachan was beginning by this time to wear out of fashion" (*A*, 149). The variations between their inhabitants illustrate not only the different kinds and rates of social change as they affected the manufacturing and agricultural communities but also how these differences in kind and rate led to the often entwined political and religious schisms that permeate so many of the later annals (e.g. *A*, 127-30, 152, 176, 179). The appositional principle also works to structure many individual chapters. Chapter XXIX (*A*, 127-30), for instance, begins with the building of Cayenneville which set "the whole countryside . . . stirring with a new life" but ends with a comment, growing out of an apparently irrelevant divagation on two bottles of wine, on the decline of the heritors that in the context of the chapter encapsulates an entire social movement: "our own heritors . . . were in general straitened in their circumstances, partly from upsetting, and partly by the eating rust of family pride, which hurt the edge of many a clever fellow among them, that would have done well in the way of trade, but sunk into divors for the sake of their genteelity". The Introduction illustrates how Galt uses themes to structure a chapter by apposition, for the central sermon is built on the balancing of old and young generations, past and present in the parish, particularly as seen in Micah Balwhidder's beginning and end as pastor, while the initial parallel between his pastoring and George III's links the local and the national. In Chapter IV it is the apposition of characters, and age and youth, that gives structural shape to the annal: Charlie Malcolm and the King, Kate Malcolm and first Miss Girzie Gilchrist then Lady Macadam, Patrick Dilworth and Mr Loremore, the first Mrs Balwhidder's death and her young brother's setting up in life. Chapter XXIII, which deals with Charles Malcolm's death, illustrates yet another aspect of the appositional method for here Galt by a careful balancing in incident and detail of the ordinary and the affecting, the satisfying and the sad, deftly works on the reader's emotions to create a moving chapter whose pathos, by the balances, is kept from the maudlin. There are more examples but enough evidence has been presented to demonstrate that the *Annals*, though without the conventional organisation of plot, possesses its own structuring, one directly suited to the book's aims, and that Galt works with a more conscious artistry than is sometimes realised.

Galt's use of the materials of folk tradition is a large and fascinating topic which here will be discussed only in relation to two elements of Galt's technique. First of all, point of view. Galt states quite specifically that for his narrator he wanted "a rural pastor" and that the clergymen of Irvine were "too urbane to furnish a model".[15] The reason for Galt's wanting such a minister becomes clear when one considers his method of presentation: the unsophisticated Micah Balwhidder represents an old-fashioned sensibility reacting to change's modifications. He has sympathy with what is but mostly adjusts to what comes, and Galt, by using the minister for his book's point of view, enables the reader to experience at first hand the process of adjustment and to gain an inside understanding of the transformations of social change. One of the main ways by which Galt establishes the old-fashionedness of the minister's sensibility is by his susceptibility to folk belief. Throughout, the pastor is shown to have a predilection for omens, portents, coincidences, and prophecies, which, besides underlining that the analogical and the conno-tative play a considerable part in his ways of thinking, demonstrates clearly that he is not a rational, urbane minister of the new school. The second area of technique involving folk tradition is where Galt's method goes beyond realism in its use of dream and symbol. In Chapter XXXIV Micah Balwhidder has a dream which not only foretells the French Revolution but also symbolically recounts the entire movement of society. This is a daring exercise in technique on Galt's part, but one which he has prepared us for through, generally, the predilection mentioned above and specifically the minister's earlier prophesying of the American War (*A*, 54). Here he achieves a sophisticated end through an interesting blend of means, in that the language is Biblical English but the form, as it were, — the dream — comes from folk literature. Galt also uses the minister's predilection for traditional modes of thinking to create a symbol of the glebe's special tree, which arrives on the scene in the settled days of 1762:

> There was no other thing of note in this year, saving only that I planted in the garden the big pear-tree, which had the two great branches that we call the Adam and Eve. I got the plant, then a sapling, from Mr Graft, that was Lord Eglesham's head-gardener; and he said it was, as indeed all the parish now knows well, a most juicy sweet pear, such as was not known in Scotland till my lord brought down the father plant from the King's garden in London, in the forty-five, when he went up to testify his loyalty to the House of Hanover. (*A*, 20)

In 1767, as changes begin to make their effects, its peculiar flourishing was thought "an ominous thing" (*A*, 45). In 1788, when a new spirit is abroad, the minister fears "that some change would ensue to my people, who had hitherto lived amongst the boughs and branches of the gospel" (*A*, 129). And in 1806, when the "infidel and jacobin spirit of the French Revolution" had so corrupted the Canaille folk that they set up another kirk "On Christmas day, the wind broke off the main arm of our Adam and Eve pear-tree, and I grieved for it more as a type and sign of the threatened partition, than on account of the damage" (*A*, 193-4). Initially the tree is associated with the slow-paced stability and leisurely growth that followed the Forty-five, but latterly it connotes social change in one of its crucial manifestations, the hostile divisions of the new society.[16] This literary symbol Galt creates through the old-fashioned minister's traditional sense of omens.

Annals of the Parish is not a novel *manqué*, but a highly individual work of historical realism, with a particular set of aims and a technique to suit. It contains without doubt an entertaining gallery of characters, an original approach to the use of Scots in fiction, and some skilfully realised scenes of comedy and pathos, all of which have been remarked on often enough by commentators, but these very virtues have served to obscure the importance of the book's social dimension. What, we should inquire for clear perspective on this subject, are the functions of these characters and comic and pathetic scenes in relation to the book's aims. This local theoretical history is both treatise and fable. As treatise it portrays, locally, the revolutions that transform a rural Ayrshire parish over fifty years, and, theoretically, some generalisations or philosophical truths about social change and human nature. As fable it employs typifying example and epitomising detail throughout and, more sparingly, dream and symbol, for the achievement of its ends. The fable's point of view has been objected to as restrictive, but John MacQueen has demonstrated tellingly in refutation that there is a conscious discrepancy between Micah Balwhidder's understanding and the understanding readers can have on the basis of information Galt, often indirectly, supplies.[17] In like fashion, complaints of the book's formlessness fail to take into account that behind Micah Balwhidder's apparently idiosyncratic narration of affairs is John Galt's structural ordering of event and detail and character. Galt, it would seem, has been all too successful at effacing himself as author. He is, the evidence of the *Annals* would suggest, a much more conscious artist than is often allowed and a writer whose works deserve a thorough critical revaluation.

NOTES:

1. J. B. Caird, "Lewis Grassic Gibbon and his Contribution to the Scottish Novel", *Essays in Literature*, ed. John Murray (Edinburgh, 1936), 143.

2. John Galt, *Literary Life, and Miscellanies* (1834), I, 155.

3. *Literary Life*, I, 155-6.

4. *Literary Life*, I, 226.

5. Letter of Galt to Blackwood, 12 April 1826, quoted in James Kinsley, ed., *Annals of the Parish* (Oxford, 1967), viii. All quotations from the book are from this edition which is hereafter referred to as *A*.

6. Letter of Galt to Blackwood, 27 February 1821, *A*, 206.

7. *Literary Life*, I, 231.

8. *Literary Life*, I, 154.

9. *Literary Life*, I, 157.

10. *Literary Life*, I, 155.

11. Sir John Sinclair, ed., *The Statistical Account of Scotland*, 21 vols. (Edinburgh, 1791-9): J. Gordon, ed., *New Statistical Account of Scotland*, 18 vols. (Edinburgh, 1843).

12. For an account of the sweeping alterations in another region of Scotland, the Northeast, see chapters 13 and 14, "The Revolutions" and "The New Society", in David Buchan, *The Ballad and the Folk* (London, 1972).

13. *Annals of the Parish*, ed. D. Storrar Meldrum (Edinburgh, 1895), II, 297; see also *A*, 231-2.

14. Jennie Aberdein, *John Galt* (London, 1936), 96, 101.

15. *Literary Life*, I, 152-3.

16. Galt reinforces the effect of this symbol with a skein of imagery which associates trees with settled prosperity and contentment (*A*, 3, 56, 114).

17. "John Galt and the Analysis of Social History", *Scott Bicentenary Essays*, ed. Alan Bell (Edinburgh, 1973), 334-8.

FURTHER READING:

Much that would be useful, like the *Autobiography* and *Literary Life*, are out of print and hard to find. Recent re-issues by the Oxford Press of the *Annals*, *The Provost* and *The Entail* have been supplemented by Ian Gordon's editions of *The Member* (Edinburgh and London, 1975) and *The Last of the Lairds* (Edinburgh and London, 1976). Elizabeth Waterston has edited the third volume of *Bogle Corbet* for a recent issue in Canada (Toronto, 1977). H. B. Timothy's edition of *The Collected Poems of John Galt, 1779-1839* (1969) further brings to public notice minor texts.

The standard book-length study is Ian Gordon's *John Galt* (Edinburgh and Toronto, 1972): important, too, Jennie Aberdein, *John Galt* (London, 1936) and E. Frykman, *John Galt's Scottish Stories, 1820-1823* (Uppsala, 1959).

"THE RAGE OF FANATICISM IN FORMER DAYS": JAMES HOGG'S *CONFESSION OF A JUSTIFIED SINNER* AND THE CONTROVERSY OVER *OLD MORTALITY*.

by Douglas S. Mack

WHEN JAMES HOGG (1770-1835) was six years old his father, a Border tenant-farmer, became bankrupt. As a result it was necessary for the young Hogg to leave school, which he had attended for only a few months in all, and the rest of his childhood was spent in service on various farms. By the time he reached his late teens Hogg was barely literate, but he had acquired an extensive knowledge of his native Ettrick's rich oral tradition of ballads, songs and tales. In 1801 Hogg began to send traditional ballads to Scott, for inclusion in *Minstrelsy of the Scottish Border*. The two men met in 1802, and five years later Scott persuaded Archibald Constable to publish Hogg's *Mountain Bard*, a collection of ballad-imitations. In 1813, when he was forty-two years old, Hogg's long poem *The Queen's Wake* was published. This work, which established his reputation as a poet, was followed by *The Pilgrims of the Sun* (1815) and *Mador of the Moor* (1816). Hogg then turned to prose, and in 1818 William Blackwood published his novel *The Brownie of Bodsbeck*, a tale of Ettrick life at the time of the Covenanters. This was followed by the publication of a number of Hogg's other prose works, including *Winter Evening Tales* (1820), *The Three Perils of Man* (1822), and *The Private Memoirs and Confessions of a Justified Sinner* (1824). During Hogg's final years many of his short stories, essays and poems appeared in periodicals. After Scott's death in the autumn of 1832, Hogg published his *Familiar Anecdotes of Sir Walter Scott* (New York, 1834). Hogg's own death followed in November 1835.

THE events of Hogg's *Confessions of a Justified Sinner* are narrated twice -
first by an "Editor" who tells the story from the evidence of "history,
justiciary records, and tradition",[1] and then again in the words of the
Private Memoirs of Robert Wringhim, the Justified Sinner. The
"Editor" begins his narrative by telling how, towards the end of the
seventeenth century, George Colwan, Laird of Dalcastle — "a droll,
careless chap" — married a young woman who was "the most severe and
gloomy of all bigots to the principles of the Reformation" (*JS*, 2). The
marriage proves to be a disastrous failure, and it is arranged that Lady
Dalcastle should live separately from her husband in the upper storey of
his house. In this situation, the Laird finds solace with a Miss Logan, who
later becomes his housekeeper, and who is described by Lady Dalcastle as
"that fat bouncing dame that visits the laird so often, and always by
herself" (*JS*, 11). Lady Dalcastle, meantime, seeks consolation in the
company of the Rev. Robert Wringhim, a clergyman whose teachings are
the source of her own theological views.

Two sons are born to Lady Dalcastle. The first is named George and is
brought up by his father and Miss Logan, but the Laird refuses to
recognise the second boy as his own and this child is brought up by his
mother and the Rev. Robert Wringhim. Indeed, he is eventually named
Robert Wringhim after the man who, it is strongly implied, is his real
father.

Hogg's Editor goes on to tell how Lady Dalcastle's two sons, by now
young men, accompany their respective fathers to a session of Parliament
in Edinburgh. The Laird attends Parliament as a supporter of the
Royalist, Tory cause, while the Rev. Robert Wringhim is a supporter of
the Whig party, the party which upheld the principles of the Reformation. While they are in Edinburgh, the two brothers meet for the first
time. Their meeting results in a public quarrel, and this sparks off a more
general conflict between the Whig and Tory factions. In due course
Robert murders George, and the Editor concludes his narrative by telling
how Miss Logan succeeds in establishing Robert's guilt. Officers are
dispatched "to apprehend the monster" (*JS*, 92), but Robert escapes and
is not heard of again.

In the second section of the novel, the Private Memoirs and
Confessions, Robert describes how he came to believe himself to be one of
the elect, a "justified person" (*JS*, 115) unalterably chosen by God for
salvation, and incapable of falling from his justified state through any
sinful act, no matter how heinous. Immediately after this, Robert is
befriended by a mysterious stranger, Gil-Martin, who encourages him to
set about purifying the world by murdering the enemies of true religion.
Gil-Martin (who is clearly the Devil in disguise) succeeds in persuading
Robert to murder Mr. Blanchard, a worthy old minister who opposes
Robert's theological views. This incident is followed by the murder of

George, and Robert also appears to be guilty of killing his mother, and a "beautiful young lady" whom he has seduced (*JS*, 191). The Private Memoirs end as Robert, in despair, prepares to commit suicide, finding "some miserable comfort" in the idea that his tormentor Gil-Martin will fall with him (*JS*, 239). There then follows a short final section, which tells of the discovery by the Editor of the manuscript of the Private Memoirs in Robert's grave on the summit of Faw-Law, in the Borders.

At the end of his main narrative, Hogg's Editor introduces Robert's Private Memoirs by writing: "We have heard much of the rage of fanaticism in former days, but nothing to this" (*JS*, 93). In the decade before the publication of the *Justified Sinner* in 1824 there had indeed been considerable controversy over the religious and political conflicts between the Whigs and Tories of seventeenth century Scotland, and it will be the purpose of the present essay to examine the influence of this controversy on Hogg's masterpiece. The controversy began in 1816, with the publication of Scott's *Old Mortality,* a novel which portrays the Whigs (or Covenanters) as a party strongly tainted by fanaticism. The Covenanters were revered by many of Scott's contemporaries as the founders of Scotland's civil and religious liberties, and the accuracy of the portrait of them in *Old Mortality* was vigorously attacked by such writers as Thomas McCrie, whose sympathetic biography of John Knox had been published a few years earlier. Scott replied to McCrie's criticisms in an anonymous review of *Old Mortality* which he wrote with William Erskine, and which was published in the *Quarterly Review* in January 1817. In the following year, 1818, Scott provided a more sympathetic portrait of the Covenanting party in his study of the Deans family in *Heart of Midlothian.* Hogg's strongly pro-Covenanter and anti-Royalist novel, *The Brownie of Bodsbeck,* was also published in 1818, although there is evidence that it had been planned and partly written some years earlier.[2] In his *Familiar Anecdotes of Sir Walter Scott,* Hogg tells us that, when *The Brownie* appeared, Scott told him: "As to its running counter to Old Mortality I have nothing to say. Nothing in the world. I only tell you that with the exception of Old Nanny the crop-eared Covenanter who is by far the best character you ever drew in your life I dislike the tale exceedingly and assure you it is a distorted a prejudiced and untrue picture of the Royal party". To this Hogg replied "it is a devilish deal truer than your's though; and on that ground I make my appeal to my country". Hogg tells us that he then "rose and was going off in a great huff", but Scott called him back, saying "You ought not to be offended at me for telling you my mind freely".[3]

Another novel which "runs counter" to *Old Mortality* is John Galt's *Ringan Gilhaize,* which was published in 1823, one year before the *Justified Sinner.* Galt writes in his *Literary Life:* "The book itself was certainly suggested by Sir Walter Scott's Old Mortality, in which I thought he treated the defenders of the Presbyterian Church with too much levity, and not according to my impressions derived from the history of that time. Indeed, to tell the truth, I was hugely provoked that he . . . should have been so forgetful of what was due to the spirit of that epoch, as to throw it into what I felt was ridicule".[4] Galt's novel traces the history of the Covenanting Gilhaize family for three generations, from the first stirrings of the Reformation to the triumph of their cause at the close of the seventeenth century. The book is totally in sympathy with the Covenanters, and its account of them is diametrically opposed to Scott's.

The *Confessions of a Justified Sinner* was published in 1824, one year after *Ringan Gilhaize*, and in it Hogg appears to make a number of references to Galt's novel. For example, the Wringhim group of characters (the father, the son, and Lady Dalcastle) support an extreme form of the theological and political views championed by Ringan Gilhaize — and it is worth noting that the Wringhims are called "the Ringans" on a number of occasions in Hogg's novel (see *JS*, 66 and 186). The most striking similarities between the two novels, however, can be seen if we compare the account of Wringhim's murder of Mr. Blanchard with the great closing scene of *Ringan Gilhaize*, in which Ringan kills Claverhouse at the Battle of Killiecrankie. This scene, which constitutes the concluding chapter of Galt's novel, is worth quoting extensively, as *Ringan Gilhaize* is a novel which is not as well known as it deserves to be:

> To whom the victory was to be given I could discern no sign; and I said to myself, the prize at hazard is the liberty of the land and the Lord; surely it shall not be permitted to the champion of bondage to prevail . . .
>
> . . . Presently I also saw Mackay with two regiments, all that kept the order of discipline, also in the plain. He had lost the battle. Claverhouse had won; and the scattered firing, which was continued by a few, was to my ears as the rivetting of the shackles on the arms of poor Scotland for ever. My grief was unspeakable.
>
> I ran to and fro on the brow of the hill — and I stampt with my feet — and I beat my breast — and I rubbed my hands with the frenzy of despair — and I threw myself on the ground — and all the sufferings of which I have written returned upon me — and I started up and I cried aloud the blasphemy of the fool, "There is no God."
>
> But scarcely had the dreadful words escaped my profane lips, when I heard, as it were, thunders in the heavens, and the voice of an oracle crying in the ears of my soul, "The victory of this day is given into thy hands!" and strange wonder and awe fell upon me, and a mighty spirit entered into mine, and I felt as if I was in that moment clothed with the armour of divine might.
>
> I took up my carabine, which in these transports had fallen from my hand, and I went round the gable of the house into the garden — and I

saw Claverhouse with several of his officers coming along the ground by which our hosts had marched to their position — and ever and anon turning round and exhorting his men to follow him. It was evident he was making for the Pass to intercept our scattered fugitives from escaping that way.

The garden in which I then stood was surrounded by a low wall. A small goose-pool lay on the outside, between which and the garden I perceived that Claverhouse would pass.

I prepared my flint and examined my firelock, and I walked towards the top of the garden with a firm step. The ground was buoyant to my tread, and the vigour of youth was renewed in my aged limbs: I thought that those for whom I had so mourned walked before me — that they smiled and beckoned me to come on, and that a glorious light shone around me.

Claverhouse was coming forward — several officers were near him, but his men were still a little behind, and seemed inclined to go down the hill, and he chided at their reluctance. I rested my carabine on the garden-wall. I bent my knee and knelt upon the ground. I aimed and fired, — but when the smoke cleared away I beheld the oppressor still proudly on his war-horse.

I loaded again, again I knelt, and again rested my carabine upon the wall, and fired a second time, and was again disappointed.

Then I remembered that I had not implored the help of Heaven, and I prepared for the third time, and when all was ready, and Claverhouse was coming forward, I took off my bonnet, and kneeling with the gun in my hand, cried, "Lord, remember David and all his afflictions;" and having so prayed, I took aim as I knelt, and Claverhouse raising his arm in command, I fired. In the same moment I looked up, and there was a vision in the air as if all the angels of brightness, and the martyrs in their vestments of glory, were assembled on the walls and battlements of heaven to witness the event, — and I started up and cried, "I have delivered my native land!" But in the same instant I remembered to whom the glory was due, and falling again on my knees, I raised my hands and bowed my head as I said, "Not mine, O Lord, but thine is the victory!"

When the smoke rolled away I beheld Claverhouse in the arms of his officers, sinking from his horse, and the blood flowing from a wound between the breast-plate and the arm-pit. The same night he was summoned to the audit of his crimes . . .

Thus was my avenging vow fulfilled, — and thus was my native land delivered from bondage. For a time yet there may be rumours and bloodshed, but they will prove as the wreck which the waves roll to the shore after a tempest. The fortunes of the papistical Stuarts are foundered forever. Never again in this land shall any king, of his own caprice and prerogative, dare to violate the conscience of the people.[5]

Various points in this passage immediately call to mind the killing of Mr. Blanchard in the *Justified Sinner*. For example, both Robert and Ringan lie concealed while the unsuspecting victim approaches, and both experience a supernatural vision as they fire their guns. The most striking point of similarity, however, is that both killers believe that they are serving the cause of Christ and his Church by cutting down an enemy of true religion. Thus Ringan ascribes the glory of his deed to God, while Wringhim tells us that he kills Mr. Blanchard in the belief "that the elect of God would be happier, and purer, were the wicked and unbelievers all cut off from troubling and misleading them" (*JS*, 137). However, although both killers have the same motivation and undertake the same action, the two scenes point as it were in opposite directions. It seems clear that Galt intends us to take Ringan's view of the killing of Claverhouse at face value: it does indeed represent the deliverance of Scotland and the Church from bondage. Hogg, however, clearly rejects the view that Salvation comes out of the barrel of a gun. When Wringhim pulls the trigger he believes that he is serving God in a great work of purification by Blood — but in fact he is acting at the Devil's instigation, with the Devil at his elbow. The deed which in Galt's novel marks the deliverance of church and nation from bondage, becomes in the *Justified Sinner* a decisive step in Wringhim's progress towards damnation.

It is clear, then, that the *Justified Sinner* contains some direct attacks on the views expressed by Galt in *Ringan Gilhaize*. Furthermore, it appears at first sight that Hogg's novel is in sympathy with the pro-Royalist views which Galt attacked. The Royalist or Tory point of view, the point of view with which Scott was identified in the controversy over *Old Mortality*, is represented in the *Justified Sinner* by three characters — the older and younger George Colwan, and Mrs. Logan (who was, we are told, "as much attached" to young George "as if he had been her own son") (*JS*, 19). These three characters — father, "mother" and son — are the Tory equivalents of the Wringhim group, and the Editor's narrative is essentially the story of the conflict between the Wringhims and the Colwans — a conflict which is reflected by the more general Whig and Tory conflict to be seen in the events which take place in Edinburgh, when the Wringhims and Colwans attend a session of Parliament at which party passions run high.

It quickly becomes clear that the sympathies of Hogg's editor lie entirely with the Tory Colwans. Thus he tells us that young George, during his boyhood, was a "generous and kind-hearted youth; always ready to oblige, and hardly ever dissatisfied with any body" (*JS*, 18). Robert, on the other hand, although he was "an acute boy, an excellent learner", nevertheless "had ardent and ungovernable passions, and withal, a sternness of demeanour from which other boys shrunk" (*JS*, 18-19). Similarly, the editor tells us that, when George was climbing Arthur's Seat one morning "he beheld, to his astonishment, a bright halo in the cloud of haze, that rose in a semi-circle over his head like a pale rainbow. He was struck motionless at the view of the lovely vision; for it so chanced that he had never seen the same appearance before, though common at early morn" (*JS*, 39-40). A little later, when George is sitting near the edge of a cliff, he sees another astonishing sight in the cloud of haze. This time the apparition takes the form of a "horrible monster", whose face is the face of George's brother, but "dilated to twenty times the natural size" (*JS*, 41). This fearsome monster proves to be a reflection of Robert, who has been creeping up behind George with the intention of throwing him over the cliff — an intention which is frustrated only because George involuntarily turns away from the horrible vision in the cloud. In spite of his narrow escape, George is still willing to seek a reconciliation, a course of action which, he suggests, would be "consistent with every precept of the Gospel". Robert rejects this idea with contempt, and replies that his reconciliation with George "is just as complete as the lark's is with the adder; no more so, nor ever can. Reconciled, forsooth! To what would I be reconciled?" (*JS*, 45).

According to Robert's theology, he is himself one of the elect and chosen of God, while his brother is a reprobate, doomed to eternal damnation before the beginning of time. For Robert, the elect and the reprobate, the lark and the adder can never be reconciled. For the Editor and his readers, however, the lark immediately suggests the happy and generous George, whose reflection in the cloud of haze appeared as "a bright halo". The adder suggests the would-be murderer, Robert, whose reflection appeared as a grotesque and evil monster. Similarly, George's offer of reconciliation is seen to be "consistent with every precept of the Gospel", while Robert's rejection of his brother's wish to exchange forgiveness is seen by the Editor, and his readers, as a direct rejection of the spirit of true Christianity.

At first we unquestioningly accept the Editor's Tory view that the Colwans represent sanity and happy normality, while the Wringhims represent an evil and disruptive fanaticism. The first hint that this view may be something less than the whole truth comes towards the end of the Editor's Narrative, when Miss Logan meets Bell Calvert, who forcefully expresses an opinion of George and his father the Laird which is much less favourable than the Editor's. At this meeting, Bell declares to Miss Logan: "you are callous, and have never known any feelings but those of subordination to your old unnatural master". Miss Logan then asks, in surprise, if Bell had known the Laird. She receives the reply: "Ay, that I did, and never for any good . . . I knew the old and the young spark both, and was by when the latter was slain" (*JS*, 60).

These words jar on the reader, who has been accustomed, up until this

point, to see "the old and the young spark both" in terms of the Editor's
warm approval of them. The reasons for Bell's low opinion of George
soon become clear, however, when she gives her own account of the
events of the night of his murder — an account which contrasts sharply
with the Editor's own version, which is given earlier in his Narrative.

The Editor tells us that George spent the early part of the evening before
his death in a tavern with some Tory friends. We hear that George, who
"was never seen so brilliant, or so full of spirits", exulted "to see so many
gallant young chiefs and gentlemen about him". Later in the evening the
gallant young chiefs "had pushed the bottle so long and so freely, that its
fumes had taken possession of every brain to such a degree, that they held
Dame Reason rather at the staff's end, overbearing all her counsels and
expostulations; and it was imprudently proposed by a wild inebriated
spark, and carried by a majority of voices, that the whole party should
adjourn to a bagnio for the remainder of the night" (*JS*, 50-51).

It is clear that, for the Editor, this madcap adventure of the gallant
young chiefs, although perhaps unwise, is not seriously culpable. When
Bell Calvert tells her story to Miss Logan, however, the reader comes to
see the events of that evening in a very different perspective. Bell explains
that, on the night in question, "I was . . . obliged, for the second time in
my life, to betake myself to the most degrading of all means to support two
wretched lives. I hired a dress, and betook me, shivering, to the High
Street, too well aware that my form and appearance would soon draw me
suitors enow at that throng and intemperate time of the parliament".
Soon after taking up her position in the High Street, Bell saw George and
his companions, and she resolved to keep near them, "in order, if
possible, to make some of them my prey. But just as one of them began to
eye me, I was rudely thrust into a narrow close by one of the guardsmen".
In spite of this, Bell continues, she went to the brothel to which George
and his friends were making their way, only to find that "they were all
housed and the door bolted". Bell then "resolved to wait, thinking they
could not all stay long; but I was perishing with famine, and was like to fall
down". For this reason, she goes on, she went to "a small tavern of a
certain description" which was nearby, and explained her plan to the
landlady. "She approved of it mainly, and offered me her best apartment,
provided I could get one of these noble mates to accompany me".

One of George's friends, the Honourable Thomas Drummond, soon
leaves the bagnio and is approached by Bell. She continues:

I beckoned him to follow me, which he did without farther ceremony,
and we soon found ourselves together in the best room of a house
where every thing was wretched. He still looked about him, and at me;
but all this while he had never spoken a word. At length, I asked if he
would take any refreshment? "If you please," said he. I asked what he
would have? but he only answered, "Whatever you choose, madam."

If he was taken with my address, I was much more taken with his; for he was a complete gentleman, and a gentleman will ever act as one . . . . I had great need of a friend then, and I thought now was the time to secure one. So I began and told him the moving tale I have told you. But I soon perceived that I had kept by the naked truth too unvarnishedly, and thereby quite overshot my mark. When he learned that he was sitting in a wretched corner of an irregular house, with a felon, who had so lately been scourged, and banished as a swindler and impostor, his modest nature took the alarm, and he was shocked, instead of being moved with pity. His eye fixed on some of the casual stripes on my arm, and from that moment he became restless and impatient to be gone. I tried some gentle arts to retain him, but in vain; so, after paying both the landlady and me for pleasures he had neither tasted nor asked, he took his leave. (*JS*, 70-72).

The Editor gives no hint of the considerations suggested by the picture of Bell "shivering" in her hired dress, "perishing with famine, and . . . like to fall down". George and his group of "gallant young chiefs", however, are reduced to very unheroic stature by Bell's repeated use of such phrases as "the best room of a house where every thing was wretched", "a wretched corner of an irregular house", and "the most degrading of all means to support two wretched lives". Drummond is made aware of these considerations by Bell's story, and he responds appropriately when he pays, with pity and disgust, "for pleasures he had neither tasted nor asked". He is however, the only member of the "group of noble mates" to emerge from Bell's account of the incident with anything like credit. The glamour of the Editor's picture of the "gallant young chiefs and gentlemen" has become somewhat tawdry.

The fact that the Editor, at best, sees only part of the truth is again underlined in the short concluding section of the novel. This section contains an account of how the Editor found the manuscript of the Private Memoirs, and it includes his comically obtuse attempts to interpret the document which he has printed in the previous section of the novel. Similarly, in the concluding section of the novel the Editor has to contend with the surly unhelpfulness of one James Hogg (an Ettrick shepherd), who carefully puts obstacles in the way of the Editor's attempt to find Wringhim's grave.

It appears from all this that the Editor's Narrative should not be regarded as the objective, unprejudiced account that it appears to be at first sight: the Editor sympathises entirely with the Tory Colwan group of characters, and he is blind to their faults. In view of this, it is not surprising that Hogg takes care to remind us again and again how prejudice can distort our interpretation of the world around us. For example, after the encounter of the brothers on Arthur's Seat, George is brought before the Sheriff to answer charges of assaulting Robert. The Sheriff is a Whig,

and the Editor comments: "It is well known how differently the people of
the present day, in Scotland, view the cases of their own party-men, and
those of opposite political principles. But this day is nothing to that in
such matters, although, God knows, they are still sometimes barefaced
enough" (*JS*, 48-49).

As the Whig Sheriff sifts the evidence, it becomes absolutely clear that
George is guilty, and he is sent to prison to be brought to trial in the High
Court. Here, however, the case is conducted by a different judge, and this
time the evidence is seen to prove that Robert, and not George, is the
guilty party. As a result George is released, and Robert in his turn is taken
into custody.

There are various trial scenes in the *Justified Sinner,* and in these
passages Hogg repeatedly stresses the difficulty of assessing the reliability
of witnesses. At the trial of Bell Calvert, for example, one witness is
"sifted most cunningly. His answers gave any thing but satisfaction to the
Sheriff, though Mrs. Logan believed them to be mainly truth" (*JS*, 63).
Bell's case is then remitted to the Court of Justiciary, where another
witness, Bessy Gillies, insists: "I am very scrupulous about an oath. *Like*
is an ill mark. Sae ill indeed, that I wad hardly swear to ony thing" (*JS*,
67). Bessy's scruples ensure that Bell Calvert is set free, although she is
guilty of the charges which have been brought against her. Conversely,
the young preacher who is accused of murdering Mr. Blanchard is found
guilty when he is brought to trial, although the reader knows that he is
entirely innocent. This causes Robert to remark, in words which form an
apt commentary on the trial scenes of the *Justified Sinner:* "from that time
forth I have had no faith in the justice of criminal trials. If once a man is
prejudiced on one side, he will swear any thing in support of such
prejudice" (*JS*, 142).

As we have seen, the Editor presents us with a Tory view of the events of
the novel, while of course Robert's Private Memoirs present us with a
very different Whig view of the same events. For Hogg both these views
are distorted by prejudice, and the effects of this distortion can be clearly
seen if we compare the two different accounts given in the novel of the
quarrel between the brothers, which takes place in Edinburgh while
George is engaged in a tennis match with some Tory friends (see *JS*, 22-
23 and 148-149). In both the Editor's account and in Robert's, the
essential incidents are the same. For example, the brothers collide, there
is a kick by Robert which does not properly connect, and there is a blow
by George which makes Robert bleed profusely. Nevertheless there are
differences which greatly influence the reader's reaction. In the Editor's
version, Robert stands close to George in order to spoil the game, while
Robert himself says that he does so simply because he wishes to observe
his brother closely. Similarly, Robert tells us that he goes boldly up and
kicks his brother — and this of course makes George look rather silly.

George is spared this indignity in the Editor's version, however, because here Robert's kick comes only *after* the brothers have collided and fallen.

Does Robert really have the courage to go boldly up to his brother and kick him, as he claims? Similarly, can we believe the Editor when he tells us that the puny Robert was able to summon up a kick so fearsome that it might easily have killed his athletic brother? Hogg does not allow us to answer such questions with certainty. All we can be sure of is that both the Whig and the Tory versions of the narrative give a prejudiced and distorted account of the events they record.

It is clear from all this that the *Justified Sinner* does not lend unqualified support to either the Whig or the Tory factions in the dispute over "the rage of fanaticism in former days". In the Private Memoirs section of the novel, however, Hogg indicates clearly where his own sympathies lie. It will be remembered that Robert, in his narrative, tells us of the series of murders he commits at the suggestion of his friend Gil-Martin, the Devil in disguise. At the end of his progress from murder to fratricide and matricide, Robert finally seals his damnation by committing suicide after praying, at Gil-Martin's suggestion, in words "susceptible of being rendered in a meaning perfectly dreadful" (*JS*, 238). That is to say, the Private Memoirs show us the process by which Robert loses his soul to the forces of Hell, and this section of the novel constitutes, as it were, a Pilgrim's Progress which ends with the damnation of the Pilgrim, instead of his salvation.

As he entices his victim to damn himself, Gil-Martin is not left entirely unopposed. In this way Robert tells us that, when he was climbing Arthur's Seat in order to attempt to murder George, he was "involved in a veil of white misty vapour, and looking up to heaven, I was just about to ask direction from above, when I heard as it were a still small voice close by me, which uttered some words of derision and chiding" (*JS*, 157-158). Robert then sees a vision of "a lady, robed in white", who warns him that his soul is in danger because of his murderous intentions. He resolves to heed this warning, but he is then again persuaded by Gil-Martin to proceed with his attempt to serve God by murdering his brother.

The lady robed in white first speaks in "a still small voice", and this is clearly a reference to the well-known passage in 1 Kings chapter 19, in which God speaks to the prophet Elijah in "a still small voice". Hogg's contemporaries would have immediately recognised the Biblical reference, and would have understood it as an indication that the vision of the lady robed in white is of Heavenly origin.

Robert also receives two distinct warning visions from Heaven before he murders Mr. Blanchard, and in addition he receives similar warnings from a number of human sources. One of the most impressive of these warnings is from Mr. Blanchard himself, and Robert tells us that this "eloquent and powerful-minded old man" "took both my principles and

me fearfully to task . . . and, before we parted, I believe I promised to
drop my new acquaintance [with Gil-Martin], and was *all but* resolved to
do it" (*JS*, 132). Later in his Memoirs Robert receives another warning
about his friendship with Gil-Martin, when his servant, the Cameronian
Samuel Scrape, tells him a story of how the devil deceived the pious
people of Auchtermuchty. In much the same way, during his childhood
Robert receives warnings about his conduct from John Barnet, the older
Robert Wringhim's shrewd beadle.

The warnings given to Robert by these men supplement the supernatural visions which are sent to him from Heaven, and the human
warners can themselves be regarded as the agents of Heaven, whose
words give Robert an opportunity to save himself from the Devil, before
his damnation is complete. The first of the warners, John Barnet, is
described more than once as a morally good man, and he behaves with
exemplary fairness and Christian charity, under extreme provocation,
when he discovers a boy named M'Gill attacking the young Robert.
Another warner, Samuel Scrape, is an essentially comic character who
quickly wins the reader's affection, even although he is a much less
impressive figure than Barnet. Scrape is a Cameronian — that is a
Presbyterian of the strictest kind — but he does not take his religion too
seriously, and when common sense suggests that he should adjust his
Cameronian principles, he is quite prepared to do so. Mr. Blanchard, like
John Barnet, is a man of blameless character, and he eloquently expresses
to Robert the theological views held by the Moderate Presbyterians of
Hogg's day. These three, together with the kindly farmer and the pious
hind who give Robert shelter towards the end of his life, can be regarded
as representing sanity, common-sense, and true religion.

The Wringhim group of characters, in contrast, represent deformed and
fanatical religion, while their Colwan opponents might be said to
represent non-religious, unredeemed natural man, amiable but flawed. It
is clear that Hogg's own sympathies lie entirely with the "true religion"
group, and that in the *Justified Sinner* he does not identify himself with
either the Whig or the Tory faction in the controversy over Scott's
portrait in *Old Mortality* of "the rage of fanaticism in former times".

This, of course, represents a change from Hogg's position when *The
Brownie of Bodsbeck* was being written some years before the publication
of *Old Mortality*. As we have seen, *The Brownie* is a novel which comes
down emphatically on the side of the Whig Covenanters, and it provoked
Scott because of its unfavourable picture of the Tory, Royalist party.
Hogg was by upbringing and instinct a supporter of the Covenanters, and
when he was writing the *Justified Sinner* he must have been tempted to
answer *Old Mortality* in the same way that Galt had done in *Ringan
Gilhaize* — by presenting the Covenanters as heroes and the Royalists as
villains. Instead, Hogg rejected this line of argument completely, by

writing a novel which — as the trial scenes for example show — is directed against *all* party prejudice, whether Whig or Tory. Indeed, Hogg answers Scott's criticism of Whig fanaticism by doing something which is at first sight rather strange — by presenting that fanaticism in an even more extreme form than Scott had done in *Old Mortality*. The Editor, it will be remembered, introduced Robert's Private Memoirs by saying "we have heard much of the rage of fanaticism in former days, but nothing to this" (*JS*, 93), and it is certainly true that nothing in *Old Mortality* can match Robert's horrific progress (in God's service) from murder to fratricide, matricide and suicide. Scott's attitude to the fanatics in *Old Mortality* — men like Habakkuk Mucklewrath — had appeared to such writers as Galt and McCrie to be one of cold distaste and rejection. Hogg answers *Old Mortality* by showing us that this attitude, while appropriate enough as far as it goes, is nevertheless shallow and inadequate. We are left in no doubt that Robert's damnation is fully deserved, but for all that he is by no means a mere caricature of evil: such things as his affectionate banter with Samuel Scrape establish him as a human being who deserves our understanding, and in spite of his crimes his fall arouses our compassion. That is to say, Hogg answers Scott, not in a partisan spirit as Galt had done, but demonstrating in a superbly imagined and magnificently realised novel that total rejection of Whig fanatics is not justified, and would not be justified even in the most extreme case of fanaticism which it is possible to imagine.

One of Scott's prized possessions at Abbotsford was a sword given by Charles I to the Marquis of Montrose, the great leader of the Royalist forces against the Covenanters. There was an occasion when Scott took great pleasure in showing this treasure to a visitor, John Morrison: "This is the very sword sent by King Charles to the gallant Montrose, the general of his armies in Scotland." Morrison replied: "It was drawn against the cause in which my fathers bled, and I should account it pollution to touch it". "Morrison, if you had lived in those times you would either have been killed or hanged". "And why not? . . . Might not this lucky hand have saved the hangman's trouble, as a predestined arm achieved in the case of his descendant and successor, bloody Clavers? But we will let the old fellows sleep". "So be it," Scott replied.[6]

We have reason to be grateful that the old fellows were *not* allowed to sleep. The contending feelings which they aroused produced, in the early decades of the nineteenth century, a series of excellent novels — a series which includes two of the supreme achievements of Scottish literature, Scott's *Old Mortality* and Hogg's *Private Memoirs and Confessions of a Justified Sinner*.

NOTES:

1. James Hogg, *The Private Memoirs and Confessions of a Justified Sinner,* edited by John Carey (Oxford, 1969), 92. All page references to the novel relate to this edition, and are identified by the abbreviation *JS.*
2. This evidence is discussed in my Scottish Academic Press edition of *The Brownie.*
3. James Hogg, *Memoir of the Author's Life* and *Familiar Anecdotes of Sir Walter Scott,* edited by Douglas S. Mack (Edinburgh & London, 1972), 106-7.
4. John Galt, *The Literary Life, and Miscellanies* (Edinburgh and London, 1834), I, 254.
5. John Galt, *Ringan Gilhaize* (Edinburgh, 1823), III, 304-310.
6. Quoted in Edgar Johnson, *Sir Walter Scott: the Great Unknown* (London, 1970), I, 382.

FURTHER READING:

There is no complete modern edition of Hogg: Rev. Thomas Thomson's two volume edition of 1866 is the most frequently seen in libraries, though especially in the prose works, the text is often unreliable. Douglas Mack has produced valuable modern editions of the *Memoirs of the Author's Life* and *Familiar Anecdotes of Sir Walter Scott* (Edinburgh and London, 1972), of the *Selected Poems* (London, 1970), and of *The Brownie of Bodsbeck* (Edinburgh and London, 1976). Douglas Gifford edited *The Three Perils of Man* (Edinburgh and London, 1972) and John Carey the *Confessions* (Oxford, 1969), superseding André Gide's issue of 1947. Superseding L. Simpson, *James Hogg: A Critical Study* (Edinburgh, 1962) and A. L. Strout, *The Life and Letters of James Hogg* (1946) is Douglas Gifford's wide-ranging *James Hogg* (Edinburgh, 1976), which incorporates a lot of the recent discussion of Hogg, most of which has centred on the enigmatic *Confessions.* The debate continues.

CHARACTER AND CRAFT IN LOCKHART'S *ADAM BLAIR*

by Thomas C. Richardson

JOHN GIBSON LOCKHART (1794-1854), the son of a Church of Scotland minister, was educated at the University of Glasgow and Balliol College, Oxford. In 1815 Lockhart went to Edinburgh to read law, and became an advocate in 1816. In 1820 he married Sophia, the daughter of Sir Walter Scott.

Lockhart began writing for *Blackwood's Magazine* in 1817 and in a short time had established his literary reputation (although somewhat infamous). His first major publication was *Peter's Letters to His Kinsfolk*, 3 vols., 1819, published as the "Second Edition." The second edition (published as "Third") also appeared in 1819. The most recent edition of *Peter's Letters* is a selected edition, edited by William Ruddick, Scottish Academic Press, 1977.

Lockhart published his four novels in as many years: *Valerius, A Roman Story*, 3 vols., 1821 (revised edition, 1842); *Some Passages in the Life of Mr Adam Blair, Minister of the Gospel at Cross-Meikle*, 1822 (second edition, revised, 1824); *Reginald Dalton*, 3 vols., 1823; *The History of Matthew Wald*, 1824. All of Lockhart's novels were reprinted in *Blackwood's Standard Novels*.

Other significant Lockhart publications include *Ancient Spanish Ballads: Historical and Romantic, Translated*, 1823; *Life of Robert Burns*, 1828; and the work for which he is perhaps most famous, *Memoirs of the Life of Sir Walter Scott, Bart.*, 7 vols., 1837-38 (second edition, 10 vols., 1839). A selection of Lockhart's critical studies has been edited by M. Clive Hildyard: *Lockhart's Literary Criticism* (Oxford, 1931). Gilbert Macbeth's study, *John Gibson Lockhart: A Critical Study* (Illinois Studies in Language and Literature, Vol. 17, 1935), contains a bibliography of Lockhart's numerous contributions to *Blackwood's Magazine* and the *Quarterly Review*.

Adam Blair, Lockhart's most successful work of Scottish fiction, was first published in 1822, although apparently as early as 1814 Lockhart was writing a novel or novels in which he wished to portray something of the Scottish character. As David Craig notes in his introduction to the Edinburgh University Press edition of the novel (1963), Lockhart in 1814 wrote to a friend that he was working on something "concerning the state of the Scotch, chiefly their clergy and elders. It is to me wonderful how the Scottish character has been neglected".[1] On 29 December 1814 Lockhart wrote to Archibald Constable regarding the publication of a novel about Scotland he was writing:

I am sensible that much has been done of late years in the description of our national manners, but there are still, I apprehend, many important classes of Scotch society quite untouched. The Hero is one John Todd a true-blue who undertakes a journey to London in a Berwick Smack, & is present in the metropolis at the same time w. the Emperor of Russia & other illustrious visitors in June last.[2]

But in February 1815 Lockhart wrote to Constable that he had decided not to send the manuscript for his consideration. When Lockhart's Scottish novel finally did appear it was certainly something new and bold, a tale of human nature told with a force rarely achieved in Scottish novel writing. In his novel of Scottish life, Lockhart attempts to capture the feelings of the nation, to join Sir Walter Scott's accomplishments in filling a gap in the portrayal of character left by the eighteenth-century intellectuals:

The most remarkable literary characters which Scotland produced last century, showed merely . . . the force of her intellect, as applied to matters of reasoning. The generation of Hume, Smith, &c, left matters of feeling very much unexplored. . . . Their disquisitions on morals were meant to be vehicles of ingenious theories — not of conventions of sentiment. They employed, therefore, even in them, only the national intellect, and not the national modes of feeling.[3]

Lockhart believed that for the modern age the novel was the best means of accomplishing the task of character portrayal. Lockhart regarded the novel as taking the place of drama in the modern society of educated, reading people, thus the novel provided for modern man what the drama had provided for previous ages, the "exhibition of human character under every light and shade which could result from the conflicting influence of principle and passion on every possible variety of temperament and constitution". Lockhart had a high regard for both the art and achievement of the novel form, a form that "has the appearance of being as natural . . . as any that exists", and the purpose of which is above all to excel in the "conception and delineation of *character*". "We read no fiction twice", Lockhart continues, "that merely heaps description upon description, and weaves incident with incident, however cleverly. The imitating romancer shrinks at once into his proper dimensions when we ask — what new character has he given us?"[4] Lockhart could answer his own question, of course, with Adam Blair. Adam Blair is a character who finds renewed life in generation after generation of us who are blind to our natures, to the varied and conflicting forces that shape our personalities. It is the purpose of this essay to examine both Lockhart's "exhibition of human character" and his efforts to develop the art of the novel in *Adam Blair*.

The idea for *Adam Blair* arose from a true story, which Lockhart heard from his minister father, involving a minister from the Presbytery of

Glasgow. In February 1822 Lockhart wrote to his brother, Lawrence: "I have since I was with you converted a story the doctor told us after dinner one day, into a very elegant little volume, under the name of 'Some Passages in the Life of Mr Adam Blair' ".[5] In a letter to his friend, Christie, Lockhart defended the novel for its truth and morality: "The story is a true, and, I think, a tragic and moral one, and old Henry Mackenzie, on one side, and Sir Harry Moncrief on the other, laud it highly. The former has sent Ebony a review of it, which I hope he will insert".[6] A review by Mackenzie did appear in the March 1822 issue of *Blackwood's Magazine,* and in it Mackenzie quotes from the General Assembly records of 1748 concerning the case which Lockhart apparently used as the germ of his novel. Mr George Adam, minister of Cathcart, confessed to the sin of fornication with his servant, Isobel Gemmel, and was duly deposed from his office. After a course of penance before his congregation which convinced the people of his sincere sorrow and repentance, "the patron, the whole heritors and elders and other parishioners" petitioned the Presbytery to have Adam restored to his charge. The Presbytery agreed and the restoration was approved by the General Assembly.

It is significant that such emphasis is placed on the truth of the story by Mackenzie, by Lockhart himself, and even by the narrator at the conclusion of the novel. Mackenzie, possibly with Lockhart's encouragement, felt the need to attest to the verisimilitude of the novel for both the English and Scottish readership: for the English this documentation was necessary to lend-credence to the severity of Blair's punishment, and for the Scots, to render credible the restoration of Blair to his parish ministry.

Secondly, Lockhart certainly anticipated the adverse criticism regarding the morality of the novel. A story of adultery and sexual passion, particularly in a minister, was a bold project for the puritan sensibilities of early nineteenth century Scotland. Lockhart probably hoped that the idea of telling a "true story" would ease the criticism. Again to his brother Lawrence, Lockhart wrote: "I am afraid the doctor may disapprove of some things: so take care you warn him to hold his tongue, i.e., in case he suspects me (which he will do)".[7] The novel did meet considerable criticism on moral grounds although it was generally well received in spite of (or perhaps because of) the boldness of the subject. *The London Magazine* published the only really scathing review: "We know not what real and pure interest can be excited, by this filthy betrayal of vice in characters and in situations to which we are accustomed to look for the decencies, the virtues, and the white enjoyments of life!"[8] In a letter to Lady Abercorn, Sir Walter Scott wrote concerning *Adam Blair:* "There is I think a want of taste in printing some part of the story something too broadly but perhaps that was unavoidable in telling such a tale".[9]

Finally the emphasis on the story as being true is important because the novel illustrates truths about the human condition. *Adam Blair* is a story of the conflict of the internal and external influences on the development of a man's character, a conflict of the natural needs and desires of man with learned attitudes and history, or in Lockhart's words, a conflict of "principle and passion". Blair's religion taught him that sexual intercourse outside the sanctity of marriage is a serious, damaging sin; however, it is the nature of man to desire sexual fulfilment and companionship. It is also the nature of man to ignore reality when such reality poses a threat to the complacency of his existence. Blair, a man of passion, ignored the reality of his physical desires rather than reconcile them to his principles as a Presbyterian minister.

Lockhart chose a Presbyterian minister as the subject of his study of human nature not only to follow the idea of the true story or, as Strahan says, because "We're all flesh and blood: a minister's but a man after all. . . ."[10] In the eighteenth century Scottish Presbyterian community the minister was not just a man — he was the defender of public morals, the archetypal good man, the figure for emulation. He personified the religious beliefs of the community, and for the people he was the living symbol of their salvation. In *Peter's Letters to His Kinsfolk* Lockhart provides some insight into the esteem of the people for their minister: "the Presbyterian Church possesses, in her formal and external constitution, very few of those elements which contribute most effectually to the welfare of the other churches in Christendom. But the most naked ritual cannot prevent the imaginations and the feelings of men from taking the chief part in their piety, and these, debarred from the species of nourishment elsewhere afforded, are here content to seek nourishment of another kind, in the contemplation not of Forms, but of Men. To the devout Presbyterian — the image of his minister, and the idea of his superior sanctity, come instead not only of the whole calendar of the Catholic Christian, but of all the splendid liturgies, and chauntings, and pealing organs of our English cathedrals".[11] The minister, then, was chosen for this role because the story of adultery in an ordinary citizen of the community would not have the impact on the reader as that of the keeper of the community's morals. Adam Blair, minister of Cross-Meikle, is an "everyman" figure, as his name implies.

It is for this impact on the reader, too, that Lockhart departed from the true story of George Adam and Isobel Gemmel. George Adam's sin was that of fornication, not adultery; he eventually married his companion in this affair. In the manuscript of *Adam Blair,* one can see that Lockhart was probably moving in the direction of such a fornication/marriage plot. Near the end of Chapter Five, following "a fair way to be so by her friends in Scotland", the manuscript continues:

Mr Campbell's death, however, occurred suddenly & unexpectedly one fine morning as he was in the act of dressing himself — and nobody could account for the apoplexy unless by coupling it with the extraordinary dinner (as Burgomaster in the chair) of the preceeding day.

Mrs Campbell not being so happy or so miserable as to have any children, had now no tie to detain her in Holland. After converting the continental property of her late husband into cash. . .[12]

It is easy to imagine the direction of this plot: Charlotte visits Cross-Meikle; Adam and Charlotte engage in immoral conduct; Adam, conscience-stricken, confesses and is deposed; Adam and Charlotte marry; after a period of penance, Adam is restored to his parish ministry. Apparently Lockhart believed that the sin of adultery and the resultant death of Adam's partner in this affair would present a greater challenge to Blair's existence, and thus add a greater depth to the story. This portion of the text, then, was crossed out in the manuscript and the story continued according to Craig's text.

The complete title of the novel, *Some Passages in the Life of Mr Adam Blair, Minister of the Gospel at Cross-Meikle,* is a significant indicator of the focus of the work, and substantially answers the critics who regard as shallow the characters of Sarah, Charlotte, Mrs Semple, Dr Muir, and John Maxwell. Lockhart's purpose in the novel is to reveal the character of Blair to the reader, to show through "some passages" in the life of the protagonist the universality of the conflict of natural passions and learned attitudes; all other characters exist in relation to Blair and for the purpose of developing this conflict. The structure of *Adam Blair* is more easily understood in the light of Lockhart's idea that the novel has replaced drama as a vehicle for character representation. Lockhart adopts the basic structure of the tragedy for *Adam Blair.* The rising action or conflict is set in motion by the death of Adam's wife, Isabel. The conflict builds through the relationship of Adam and Charlotte to the crisis, which occurs at the point of their adultery. The confession and resignation of Blair at the meeting of the Presbytery stimulate the catastasis. The catastrophe occurs, ironically, not with the death of the hero but with his restoration to his original position, minister of the parish of Cross-Meikle.

Adam Blair is a tragic tale of innocence and experience, the story of a man who moves from a comfortable state of "sinless" existence into the realm of experience and reality. It is tragic, however, not because Adam falls from his community pedestal as a result of a moral weakness in his character; it is tragic because Blair and the community fail to achieve a vision of reality from the experience. Blair, like Hawthorne's Young Goodman Brown, is compelled to have an experience that is a challenge to his established beliefs and representative of some confrontation with evil which emerges from within himself; however, he is complacent in his existence above sin, at least the public, black-and-white sins which can be witnessed by all members of the community, and thus he is blind to the necessity and the nature of the experience. Young Goodman Brown must leave the security of his home, his wife, Faith, and his community to meet with the devil in the forest. Here the self-righteous, *naïve* Brown "sees" that all those whom he previously thought righteous are indeed intimate with the devil and participate in his rituals of evil. As a result of this encounter Brown's vision of life is effectively destroyed so that his dying hour is gloom; it is gloom because Brown fails to achieve a vision of the nature of evil and of man from this experience. Brown is unable to rise above the convenient tradition of self-righteousness which has coloured his life to this point, which has been the basis of the faith of his family and his community. Adam Blair's life is characterised by a similar self-righteous complacency, a self-satisfied existence in innocence, sheltered from temptation and evil by a loving wife, a family history of public righteousness, and a supportive community of people whose vision of reality corresponds exactly and who allow their minister to bear the burden of righteousness which relieves them from the responsibility of attaining a knowledge of good and evil beyond superficial social indiscretions. Blair, like Brown, when confronted with a challenge to his moral existence, fails to meet the challenge; he is unable to see the short-comings in his own character.

Blair's self-righteousness and blindness to his nature derive from his recognition of his role as a minister in a Scottish community and an inherited family tradition. The graves of Blair's grandfather and father in the Cross-Meikle kirkyard serve as an ever-present reminder of the tradition which it is Blair's duty to promulgate; they also reinforce the memories of these two religious heroes in the minds of Blair's parishioners. Blair's grandfather was a simple peasant of the community who, like many of his generation, had become a folk hero for his role in the fight for Presbyterian freedom. Blair's father was minister of Cross-Meikle before Blair took the charge, and a tablet on the wall served "to record the pious labours of Mr Blair's father, who preceded him in the pastoral charge of that parish; and most of those who were present could still recall with distinctness the image of the good old man, and the grave tones of his voice in exhortation" (25). The elder, John Maxwell, is the living tie of Blair to his ancestors and the attitudes of the parish. Maxwell is a father-figure to Blair as well as his spiritual guide: "The priest felt in his soul the efficacious piety of the elder of Israel" (22). Maxwell dutifully comforts Blair after the death of Isabel, assuring Blair of the presence of his father's Lord: "I thought the Lord would never surely leave your father's son, and I see he has not left you" (19). Later it is Maxwell who responds to the despair of Blair and writes to Mrs Semple for help. When Blair leaves on his errand to Uigness it is Maxwell who follows, faithfully seeking after "my minister". At the end of the novel it is the feeble, dying

Maxwell who is instrumental in Blair's restoration to his father's place as minister of Cross-Meikle.

 Maxwell functions on a second important level in the novel: he symbolically links Blair to natural passions and thus serves as a touchstone for Balir's conflict between the natural and the learned. Maxwell, a farmer, is a simple man, a man of natural goodness, a figure on the level of Wordsworth's Simon Lee or leech-gatherer, but one whose ties to the natural world have been somewhat impaired by his religious training. Maxwell represents a blend of the learned Presbyterian attitudes and the natural passions although, as becomes clear at the end of the novel, he is by no means an ideal model for the reconciliation of Blair's conflict. Maxwell's wife died when he, like Blair, was a relatively young man. Maxwell coped with his natural passions, particularly grief and sexual desire, by suppressing them through labour. The farm kept Maxwell occupied to the point that he had no time for meditation (other than devotions and prayers), reading, or idle thoughts. His constant involvement with his work never permitted him to sink into the despair that Blair experienced: "Grieved and oppressed as I was, I could not be idle — I could not sit all day in the house with nothing but my book to take me up — I was obliged to rise with the cock and guide the plough — I behoved to mount my horse and ride to the town — I had bargains to make and fulfil — I was a busy man as I had been used to be — when the night came I was wearied, and I could not but sleep. . . . Take my word for it, if he had had two hundred acres on his hand instead of yon poor, starved, useless glebe, Mr Blair would have been a different sort of man ere now, than what he's like to be for many a day yet" (55-56). Adam has lost much of his effectiveness as a minister because of the despair and lack of physical fulfilment he experiences after the death of Isabel. Maxwell wants to divert Blair's energies into constructive channels. Maxwell is able to understand from his own experience the problems of passion that confront Blair, and he sees in the Protestant work ethic the relief that Blair is seeking; Maxwell believes that hard work provides adequate fulfilment of physical and emotional needs. Maxwell, after the death of his wife, not only occupied his mind with his work during the day, but at night he was too tired to think or read, or perhaps most importantly, to dwell on the unfulfilled passion which the death of his wife left him.

 The influence of Scott's *The Antiquary* (a work greatly admired by Lockhart) is evident in Maxwell's speech. After the funeral of his drowned son, Steenie, the poor fisherman Mucklebackit is mending his boat to return to sea. The Antiquary commends Mucklebackit for his ability to return so soon to work. "And what would ye have me to do," answered the fisher gruffly, "unless I wanted to see four children starve, because ane is drowned? It's well wi' you gentles, that can sit in the house wi' handkerchers at your een when ye lose a friend; but the like o' us maun to our warks again, if our hearts were beating as hard as my hammer".[13] The character of Mucklebackit, however, elicits a pathos which is not present in Maxwell. Mucklebackit continues living in the midst of death, and lives *with* his natural feelings; his unity with nature is favourably portrayed by Scott. Maxwell, on the other hand, uses his station in life as a means of suppressing his natural feelings, and thus his nature is clouded by his learned attitudes. Blair, who by the end of the novel is blind to the characteristics of natural passion, turns to the life of peasant labour as a self-inflicted punishment for his sin. Nature, often a source of comfort and strength to Blair before his adultery (*e.g.* after the death of his wife), becomes a vehicle for humiliation and degradation. Lockhart thus underscores the shortsightedness of Balir's vision, his inability to see and understand that "human nature will have its way, and the soul cannot long shut itself against the impressions of the bodily senses" (49).

Lockhart gradually and carefully develops the tragedy of Adam Blair through the relationship of Charlotte and Adam following the death of Isabel. The novel opens with Adam — a young, handsome, physical man — in a state of limited paradise, a post-lapsarian Eden where there is suffering and sorrow, but suffering that is endurable because it is temporary; there is always relief and happiness to follow; there is never a serious challenge to the moral consciousness of Blair. Blair is comfortable as keeper of the social mores of the parish, occasionally visiting Semplehaugh for the social and intellectual stimulus (albeit limited as Jamieson shows) not readily available to Blair in his contact with his "primitive" parishioners. But to Blair, happiness and comfort were ultimately inextricably bound with a healthy relationship with his wife, which meant, as the novel implies, sexual satisfaction. The satisfaction of Blair's passion was never a problem as long as his wife was healthy, but as Isabel's health declined, Blair experienced the mental, emotional and physical strain of the lack of female companionship. For a considerable time before the death of his wife Blair did not share the same bed with her. At the death of Isabel, Blair unleashed his frustrated passions: "He drew near to the couch — grasped the cold hand, and cried, 'Oh God! Oh God!' ... kissed the brow, the cheek, the lips, the bosom" (8). Blair, overcome by the intensity of the moment, rushed into the woods. Here, "Long-restrained, long-vanquished passions took their turn to storm within him. ... Again SHE returned, and she alone was present with him — not the pale expiring wife, but the young radiant woman — blushing, trembling, smiling, panting on his bosom, whispering to him all her hopes, and fears, and pride, and love, and tenderness, and meekness, like a bride" (9-10). The extreme energy of the emotions and the physical contact of these scenes illustrate the passionate feeling of Blair for his wife and the deep sense of loss he experienced from the moment of her death.

When Charlotte comes to visit Blair, then, Blair is emotionally keyed for the development of an intimate relationship. Blair is attracted to Charlotte not only because she is an old friend and a mother figure to his daughter; he is physically attracted to her as well. The relationship is made easier by the fact that Charlotte, too, is emotionally and sexually frustrated. Charlotte's present marriage to Captain Campbell, like her first marriage to young Arden, is a failure. She has never been loved and apparently the only true love she has to give is for Blair. In the striking scene in the graveyard of the Cross-Meikle kirk, Charlotte exclaims: "Oh, why was I not his wife! One year — not ten long blessed years — would have been enough for me, and I should have slept sweetly where I knew his eyes would every day rest upon my grave!" (103) Charlotte was stopped in the midst of her exclamations by the sensuous touch of Blair's hand upon her shoulder, which "she had, in her forgetfulness of all immediate things, permitted to become quite bare" (104). The arousing revelation of this scene could not have helped but make a powerful impression on the vulnerable Blair. Some weeks later at Semplehaugh, Blair displayed his sentiments publicly when Charlotte rescued Adam and Sarah from drowning. The scene is reminiscent of the affection displayed to Isabel at her death: Adam "fell upon his knees close beside Charlotte and his child, and throwing one arm round each, he drew them both towards his bosom, and began to kiss them alternately, cheek, and brow, and lip, and neck, hastily and passionately, as if ignorant or careless that he was within sight of any one" (155). The sexual attraction is reinforced by the narrator in the scene under the great phallic hawthorn tree after Charlotte and Adam had returned to Cross-Meikle from the near-disastrous day at Semplehaugh. Adam and Charlotte

> sat down together in a low garden chair, beneath the ancient and celebrated hawthorn tree, which stands (or stood) in the centre of the little green before the door of the Manse. This was by far the finest thorn in the whole vale, and its beauty had always been a matter of pride both with Mr Blair and his wife,—and indeed with everybody who had lived there. A few dozen yards off, one might easily have taken it for a small oak, it was so round in the head, so dark in the foliage, so straight and massive in the trunk, and so considerable in stature:—but at this time it was in full blossom, indeed so much so, that it had, at a little distance, the appearance of being quite covered with a feathering of snow-flakes (169-170).

While seated under the hawthorn tree, Adam and Charlotte are approached by a beggar who addresses the couple as man and wife. When corrected the beggar replied: "But though you're no man and wife now, ye'll maybe be sae ere yon braw thorn shakes down a' its white blossoms; and then ye'll no hae ony leisure to be angry at the auld man's mistake" (173). The beggar senses and acknowledges the glow and warmth of feelings that Adam and Charlotte display for each other, yet Adam himself remains blind to his own desires. Blair deludes himself with the thought that he is Charlotte's spiritual guide, a friend and comforter to her in her time of need. And when he frantically follows Charlotte to Uigness, he rationalises that it is after Strahan he is going to clear his and Charlotte's reputations; yet, Blair does not have the strength to stay out of Charlotte's bed. Blair is unable to understand himself, and thus he is compelled by his nature to commit adultery.

Blair is restored to his ministry after ten years of humble penitence. The irony of the restoration scene artfully disallows any apparent senti- mentality. Old Maxwell, bed-ridden for three years, is carried into Blair's cottage to make his last request: "let me not die until I have seen you once more in *your father's* place" 364, emphasis added). The story has returned to its beginning, with no one in the parish the worse for the experience, and tragically, no one the wiser. The people have triumphed; they have their minister again, purified, as clean as before; once again they are relieved of the burden of moral decision, the responsibility of knowing good and evil. With this in mind the reader is able to grasp the full significance of the ending of the novel:

> With [Sarah], the race of the Blairs in that parish ended—but not their memory.
>
> I have told a TRUE STORY. I hope the days are yet far distant when it shall be doubted in Scotland that such things might have been (367).

To remember the family of Blairs is to remind oneself of the nature of man. To doubt that such things might have been is to open the way for the return of the self-righteousness and blindness to self that characterised the generations of Blairs. *Adam Blair,* like the tragedy, exists to give the reader an experience from which he can emerge with a heightened vision of life.

That Lockhart was concerned with the art of the novel is evident in the considerable revisions from the first edition (1822) to the second edition (1824) of *Adam Blair.* The following account of the textual revisions of *Adam Blair* is by no means exhaustive; it is merely an attempt to demon- strate the process and direction of Lockhart's desire to find the most effective and artistic means of portraying *his* character.[14] In noting the revisions from the first to the second edition I shall refer to the edition most readily available to the reader, the Edinburgh University Press edition.

Henry Mackenzie was probably the greatest single influence on Lockhart as he revised *Adam Blair.* It is plausible to assume that Mackenzie exerted a great deal of unrecorded verbal influence on

Lockhart through their contact at Blackwood's. Written evidence of Mackenzie's influence is available in *Blackwood's Magazine* for April, 1822; in this issue appears an article by Mackenzie entitled "Hints for a Young Author, from a Very Old One," and directed toward the author of *Adam Blair*. In this essay Mackenzie referred to the novel as a "work of real genius," and he praised the author for "not dealing in high sentiment or romantic adventures, but in the walk of ordinary life, and among persons of middling rank." Mackenzie, however, went on to criticise the style of Lockhart's presentation; his criticisms are worth quoting at length:

> Redundant and diffuse in many parts where the narrative should be compressed and rapid. The descriptions of natural objects are well delineated, but are not always necessary to any purpose in the story, and but slight adjuncts to it. Moral reflections and abstract principles also seem too frequently introduced, and too much expanded;—they are anticipated by the reader, instead of being suggested to his mind, which takes away that interest which is always created by the discovery, or supposed discovery, of the reader himself. [15]

The obtrusiveness of the narrator in matters of description and moral commentary constitutes one of the major stylistic weaknesses of the first edition; Lockhart does much to rid the novel of its superfluities in the second edition, as the following revisions indicate.

> *Page 6/line 25* Doubt hung over him like some long-laid spectre risen again from a roaring sea, to freeze and to torture—Faith, like a stooping angel, blew the shadow aside, but the unsubstantial vapour grew together again into form, and stood within sight a phantom that would not be dismissed. *Deleted in the second edition.*

The deletion of this passage was probably considered by Lockhart to be in the interest of remaining close to reality, an effort to eliminate what might be construed as, in the words of Henry James, an "abuse of the fanciful element." In a comparison with *The Scarlet Letter* James praised Lockhart for the human, natural elements of his characters, for making his characters "more actual and personal" than those of Hawthorne's work.[16] It is important to realise that James's praise for the novel was likely based on a reading of the second edition, which would have been in print at the time of the writing of *Hawthorne*.

> *8/18* and exert all or many of its noblest powers. But these things are of the mysteries which human eyes cannot penetrate, and into which we should not be presumptuous enough to peer with all our blinding imbecility about us. *Deleted.*

This was one of several superfluous comments by the narrator which only detracted from the movement of the narrative and which Lockhart deleted to the improvement of the story.

> *17/28* when God's chosen race, and the true patriots of our country,

were hunted up and down like the beasts of the field—*Deleted*.

The role of the narrator is weak throughout the first edition of *Adam Blair*. The narrator fails to emerge as a character in the novel in the way, for example, Hogg's "editor" of *The Private Memoirs and Confessions of a Justified Sinner* becomes a character and establishes a point of view in contrast to that of the major character, Robert Wringhim. The narrator of the *Confessions,* as a man of reason and science, stands opposed to the religious fanaticism of Wringhim. He is a voice distinct from that of the author, and his point of view is as much in question as that of the devil. Through these contrasting points of view Hogg establishes the ambiguities which form the basis for the novel's impact upon the reader. Lockhart, however, fails to create such a complex and skilful device. Lockhart's narrator is a storyteller, indistinct from the author, whose comments are felt by the reader to be intrusions rather than effective manipulations of point of view. If Lockhart was unable to make his narrator an essential part of the story then he was undoubtedly wise to delete such passages as this and the following which are clearly distractive.

> 18/11 To their love he had 'titles manifold,' but not the least was his being the grandson and namesake of old Adam Blair, who had fought against bloody Clavers and the butcher Dalyell, at Bothwell-bridge, and endured torture, without shrinking, in the presence of *false Lauderdale. Deleted*.

Lockhart elsewhere makes the point that Blair's forefathers were an abiding influence both on the shaping of his character and the regard his parishioners had for him.

> 33/24 for the contemplation of dreary things was felt, in that diseased state of the mind, to constitute a sort of morbid luxury; and a sick fantasy was nothing loth to exert its feverish and fitful energies in brooding over and blending together the unseen troubles of a bleeding heart, and the too congenial images of external desolation. *Deleted*.

> 35/21 the elder, whose name we have already had occasion to mention more than once. *Deleted*.

This comment seems to imply that John Maxwell was such an unimportant person that he would easily be forgotten by the reader. There is a certain sense of snobbishness about several of the narrator's comments in the first edition which limits the effectiveness of such a character as John Maxwell.

> 60/6 There are some readers who may smile at such things; but I speak what I feel to be true, and wherever there is truth, there must also be wisdom. *Deleted*.

71/19 Although Mr Blair was by no means a profound Grecian . . . sun of genius. *Deleted.*

Another fault which Mackenzie finds in Lockhart's style is the apparent indiscriminate use of description, particularly of natural scenery. The descriptions, although good, are often merely tangential and detract from the verisimilitude of characterisation. Mackenzie writes:

> Let [the author], as the constructor of fable, look carefully on it as a whole, and not be satisfied if it give room for introducing brilliant or interesting parts, if they offend against the probability or interest of the work. In description, whether of natural scenery, or of other objects, let him be aware, that though *particularity* in detail is highly pleasing, yet *prolixity* fatigues the reader. . . . . Let the author of Adam Blair avoid this in the future, by making his pictures of still life, or his minute delineations of character, always such as belong to the story, not brought in from a distance.[17]

153/3 The scene surpassed all he had ever beheld, or conceived, of the still beauty of nature. Here, tall yellow crags. . . . *Revised to* The near surface of the sea was bright, and the tall, yellow crags . . . .

This is an important change for the sake of verisimilitude. As beautiful as the scenery might have been, it is difficult to imagine that Blair was admiring that beauty given the condition of his mind and the nature of the errand that took him to Uigness. This revision, with the three following similar revisions, provides for an effective alteration in the point of view in the second edition. The reader no longer witnesses the beauty of nature through the eyes of Blair; rather, he sees in nature a reflection of the solitude and despair which was the essence of the soul of Blair at this point. Thus, instead of repose there is gloom. The last two lines of this paragraph—"as the last crimson line of sunset kept sinking down lower and lower in the western horizon"—lose all implications for the beauty of a sunset and instead evoke a sense of the close of the day and the coming of night and darkness.

153/9 There, some fragrant . . . undermined it. *Deleted.*

153/18 The eye found repose on all sides amidst the purple hills. *Revised to* But Blair sought rather to gaze on the purple hills.

180/9 and groaning over the beautiful prospect which lay spread out below him. *Revised to* uttered one deep groan, and sunk backward.

158/19 drink, drink, dear Adam, and I will pledge you, I will pledge you gaily. *Revised to* drink, and I will pledge, I will pledge you once more.

The deletion of *gaily* is again an alteration for the sake of realism. There is no sense of gaiety about this couple, only desperation and the compulsion of the natural senses. There is a need for this relationship on the part of both parties; it is unavoidable. Adam and Charlotte are driven by forces stronger than their conscious wills, and indeed they act against the normal conscious desires of both.

187/7 and he drank abundantly, and felt refreshed to the core as he closed his eyes. *Revised to* he drank, and closed his eyes.

To this point Mackenzie's criticisms of Lockhart's style have certainly been justified and Lockhart's revisions followed the line of Mackenzie's suggestions to the unquestioned improvement of the novel. However, Mackenzie goes on to offer some inconsistent and unjustified criticism: criticisms:

> But the most striking fault, is the seeming unintentional indelicacy of some parts of the story; the loose dress, and the almost nudity of the heroine. Mrs Campbell, should not have been once mentioned in the strong colours which the author uses; but frequent repetition is offensive, and lowers the character of Blair, as if corporeal, not mental, or moral attractions, were congenial to his nature. Something of the same kind may be remarked in the catastrophe of Blair's seduction, which is brought about by the action of wine, and seems an imitation of the contrivance of *Lot's* daughters, but without the apology which the supposed failure of the human race made somewhat excusable in them.... The circumstances of Blair's horror on being laid, when thought to be dying, on Mrs Campbell's bed, is natural and striking; but it, too, may perhaps be censurable as indelicate.[18]

Mackenzie here demonstrates that he has missed the major thrust of the novel; Mackenzie reacts as a prudish Presbyterian concerned for propriety rather than as a seasoned novelist concerned for what makes the novel work. The portrayal of the sexuality of Mrs Campbell and the physical attraction which she had for Blair are essential to the purpose of the novel; physical desire was indeed congenial to the nature of Blair. Lockhart wisely made no changes that would seriously alter the impact of the sexuality, although, as the following revisions seem to indicate, he did make a token effort to eliminate some of the supposedly indelicate passages in the work.

56/14 virgin. *Deleted.*

Virgin is certainly not inappropriate in this instance. Is this Mackenzie's influence, on the grounds that the word itself is objectionable? There are two other similar revisions:

> *157/7* naked. *Revised to* undressed.

> *104/16* and, in short, she was now as thinly and as moistly clad as any goddess or nymph of the sea that ever Guido drew, or Flaxman modelled. *Deleted.*

Perhaps the suggestion for visual comparison was considered too bold.

> *74/24* The feelings of a brother and a friend were blended with those of a Christian and a priest, and being witness to misery, it was his business by all these titles to soothe it, even though it were by partaking it. *Deleted.*

Given the sexual implications of the context in which this passage occurred, the effect on Blair must certainly have elicited feelings beyond those suggested here. This comment would have been appropriate had it been presented as Blair's view of himself, adding strength to the view that Blair deluded himself concerning his feelings for Charlotte; as a comment by the narrator, it is out of place.

Another suggestion of Mackenzie's which Lockhart did not follow concerns the scene between Blair and Campbell in which Campbell forgives Blair for the wrong done to him and assures Blair that he will not expose his guilt. Mackenzie writes: "There should, we think, have been some action to shew [Blair's] sense of the depth of the injury, and the value of the forgiveness,—he should have thrown himself at Campbell's feet, and sobbed out his sense, though it did not rise into words, of the wrong he had done him". Mackenzie, perhaps, would have introduced such a scene but it certainly would not have been in keeping with Blair's character, nor would it have been appropriate for the state of mind which was Blair's at that time. Blair was convinced that Campbell could not be certain of his guilt. Also, Blair was still "quite incapable of summoning up the courage requisite for a solemn and deliberate confession of his guilt" to his friend, advisor, and father-figure, John Maxwell. It is not to be expected that Blair would be capable of such a public acknowledgement at this time, particularly to Campbell himself. In fact, it is implied that only in the night after this interview did Blair decide that he must confess.

In the second edition Lockhart does insert a paragraph concerning Campbell's attitude toward this adultery. Perhaps this was an attempt by Lockhart to lend credence to Campbell's act of forgiveness.

Following 204/24, the following paragraph is inserted:

I have spoken of Campbell as *certain* that he had been dishonoured; and he was not the less so because he had no positive legal proof in his possession. That deficiency he, under any circumstances, would have despised; now it scarcely ever occured to him.—Doubt he had none; he would have scorned himself had one shadow of it crossed his fancy. His mind was, as to this matter, as fixed and settled as it could have been, had he *really* seen all that had really happened.—Indeed, had this been otherwise, it is very possible he might have gazed with a harder eye on Charlotte's remains.

There are several other important revisions in the second edition worth noting here.

160/1 through 161/18, asterisks through "Suddenly," deleted.

Chapter Fourteen of the second edition begins: "It was morning. There came wafted from afar off the echo of a bell tolling slowly...." This is certainly one of the most effective changes in the second edition, doing much to relieve the novel of its melodramatic effect. The scene of the church bells awakening Blair to reality is superb, and the desperation that follows is skilfully depicted.

165/18 Mr Blair *Revised to* Adam Blair.

There are several instances in the second edition of changing "Blair" and "Adam Blair" to "Mr Blair", but this is the only instance of the change to "Adam". Presumably Lockhart wanted to emphasise the fallen man, the movement out of Eden and innocence into experience.

> *146/6* and the end of it was, that he got up and summoned. . . . *Revised to* the end of it was, that he persuaded himself everything else should be laid aside until he had seen Mr Strahan. Why not pursue him at once, and face him—Yes, face him, in the very presence of his victim?
> Mr Blair got up, and summoned. . . .

This is a very significant revision. Rather than going to Uigness after Charlotte, Blair is going in pursuit of Strahan to clear his name and to rectify the blow to his manhood. This presents a more consistent view of Blair as a man who has been deluding himself about both his feelings for Charlotte and the extent of his own passionate desires and needs.

247/3 The lines from Wordsworth's poem, "Lines. Left upon a Seat in a Yew-tree, near the lake of Esthwaite..." were deleted in the second edition. The quotation from St Paul, "Let him that thinketh he standeth take heed lest he fall", which appeared on the reverse of the half-title of the first edition, was also omitted in the second edition. Lockhart de-emphasises the role of pride in the second edition, making the conflict in Blair more directly one of natural desires and learned attitudes. Also, the omission of the lines from Wordsworth has the effect of accentuating the idea of the "true story," and rendering more effective the impact of the ambiguities in the last line: "I hope the days are yet far distant when it shall be doubted in Scotland that such things might have been."

The text of the second edition has been the text of all reprints until the Edinburgh University Press edition of 1963. Although the first edition of *Adam Blair* is valuable for scholarly purposes, the second edition is a far superior novel; for reading and study of the novel it is only fair to use Lockhart's revised edition in which considerable improvements were made for the sake of the art of the novel. The second edition of *Adam Blair* does much to discredit George Saintsbury's judgment that "Lockhart had every faculty for writing novels except the faculty of novel-writing".[19]

The publication of *Matthew Wald* in 1824, shortly after the publication of the second edition of *Adam Blair,* marked the end of Lockhart's career as a novelist. In 1825 Lockhart became editor of *The Quarterly Review* in London, a position he held until shortly before his death. As in the case of other promising novelists who, for one reason or another, ceased writing while in their prime, the question of what Lockhart might have written lingers unanswered. However, as an examination of *Adam Blair* makes evident to us as readers and critics, the subject of Lockhart's accomplishments deserves our immediate attention.

NOTES:

1. Quoted in David Craig's introduction to *Adam Blair* (Edinburgh, 1963), xi.
2. National Library of Scotland, MS. 331, ff. 220-221.
3. J. G. Lockhart, *Peter's Letters to His Kinsfolk*, 3rd ed. (Edinburgh, 1819), II, 360.
4. J. G. Lockhart, "Lives of the Novelists," *Quarterly Review*, 34 September, 1826), 349-378, *passim*.
5. Quoted in Andrew Lang, *The Life and Letters of John Gibson Lockhart*, 2 vols. (London, 1897), I, 295.
6. *op. cit.*, 302.
7. *op. cit.*, 295.
8. *The London Magazine*, V (May, 1822), 490.
9. *The Letters of Sir Walter Scott*, ed. H. J. C. Grierson, 12 vols. (London, 1932-37), VIII, 293.
10. J. G. Lockhart, *Adam Blair*, 2nd ed. (Edinburgh, 1824), 197. All references in the first part of this essay are to this edition.
11. *Peter's Letters*, III, 70-71.
12. National Library of Scotland, MS. 4818, f. 21.
13. Sir Walter Scott, *The Antiquary* (Edinburgh, 1816), III, 92.
14. An article listing in detail the revisions from the first to the second edition is forthcoming.
15. [Henry Mackenzie], "Hints for a Young Author, from a Very Old One," *Blackwood's Magazine*, XI (April, 1822), 466.
16 Henry James, *Hawthorne* (London, 1967), pp. 111,113. First pub. 1879.
17. Mackenzie, 467.
18. *op. cit.*, 466.
19. Quoted in Marion Lochhead, *John Gibson Lockhart* (London, 1954), 127.

FURTHER READING

There is no definitive biography of Lockhart nor is there an adequate critical study of Lockhart's works; his fiction has especially been neglected. Andrew Lang, *The Life and Letters of John Gibson Lockhart* (London, 1897) remains the most useful single study of Lockhart to date. Marion Lochhead's *John Gibson Lockhart*, 1954, adds little significant critical or biographical information. Gilbert Macbeth's critical study is largely about Lockhart and the *Quarterly Review*. Lockhart's biographies have been analysed in Francis R. Hart, *Lockhart as Romantic Biographer* (Edinburgh, 1971).

GEORGE MACDONALD'S EARLY SCOTTISH NOVELS

by Colin Manlove

GEORGE MACDONALD (1824-1905) is known today chiefly for fantasies and fairy tales such as *Phantastes* (1858), "The Golden Key" (1867), *At the Back of the North Wind* (1871), *The Princess and the Goblin* (1872), *The Princess and Curdie* (1883) and *Lilith* (1895). What is less known is that during his long and frequently unsuccessful literary career MacDonald wrote more than twenty-five three-decker novels of "real life", most of which sold well during his lifetime. They are little read now, like much of his work. Yet several of them concern accurately-portrayed scenes of Scotland, many relating to MacDonald's early life, and their sometimes equivocal descriptions of Scotland give a valuable insight into the workings of the author's mind.

MACDONALD began and ended his formal career with three years (1850-3) as minister of the Congregational church at Arundel, in Sussex. His heterodox views, particularly in his leaning to German theology and his belief that some provision was made for the heathen after death, caused increasing offence until he was forced to resign. As there was a campaign against heterodoxy throughout the country at the time, he found it impossible to secure another post. For the rest of his life he tried to support himself and a growing family in a freelance manner, writing, lecturing, taking occasional professorships, even going on tour with a family production of *Pilgrim's Progress* (1879-87); often only gifts from friends and relations saved him from penury. After a time the up-and-down life of an amateur in God's hand became more natural to him; it was this, together with a vein of fastidious unworldliness that could make him refuse such an offer as that made to him in 1873 during a lecturing tour of America of a stipend of $20,000 per annum should he take up the pastorate of a church on Fifth Avenue, New York.[1]

MacDonald began his literary career as a poet, but soon moved on to fantasy (which he considered a production of the poetic impulse) with *Phantastes,* which had considerable success. His publisher, George Murray Smith, of Smith, Elder & Co., told Macdonald that *Phantastes* held a unique place in literature and that he would be well advised to continue his gift for fiction in novels: " 'Mr. MacDonald . . . if you would but write novels, you would find all the publishers saving up to buy them of you' "[2] Nevertheless it would seem that MacDonald saved himself up: for it was not until 1863, five years later, that *David Elginbrod* appeared. Thereafter the novels appeared in a fairly steady stream.

It is clear from MacDonald's accounts of the creative imagination that he considered poetry, and that prose which aspired to the condition of poetry, to be the highest form of art.[3] (He once said that prose was only "broken-down poetry".[4]) Though he has left us his views on poetry, drama, fairy-tales and fantasy, there is little or nothing on the craft that preoccupied him for most of his literary life. Yet, if he could say, "I had no choice. I had to write for money, and prose pays best",[5] it would be mistaken to conclude that MacDonald regarded novel-writing as the mere bread-and-butter of his existence: it is quite clear that the novels were viewed by him as a substitute for the pulpit he had lost, a means of teaching by pleasing imitation. He told his son Ronald that

> having begun to do his work as a Congregational minister, and having been driven, by causes here inconvenient to be stated, into giving up that professional pulpit, he was no less impelled than compelled to use unceasingly the new platform whence he had found that his voice could carry so far.

> Through stories of everyday Scottish and English life, whose plot, consisting in the conflict of a stereotyped theology with the simple human aspiration toward the divine, illustrated the solvent power of orthodox Christianity, he found himself touching the hearts and stimulating the consciences of a congregation never to be herded in the largest and most comfortable of Bethels.[6]

Nevertheless, and despite their popularity, MacDonald would have regarded his novels as lower in status than fantasy or poetry.

The grounds on which he would have done so are those on which we would have initial qualms concerning works written with such a teaching intent—the distinction between "telling" and "showing". For him "The greatest forces lie in the region of the uncomprehended".[7] He wrote of the teaching artist,

> ever he must seek to *show* excellence rather than talk about it, giving the thing itself, that it may grow into the mind, and not a eulogy of his own upon the thing; isolating the point worthy of remark rather than making many remarks upon the point.[8]

MacDonald viewed the unconscious creative imagination as God at work in man. "For our consciousness is to the extent of our being but as the flame of the volcano to the world-gulf whence it issues: in the gulf of our unknown being God works behind our consciousness",[9] and since the things of God are incomprehensible to mere man, who can only glimpse sparks of the truth, that work which issues straight from the imagination untrammelled by the meddling and merely human intellect, and is left indefinite in character and meaning, will be most true to the nature of divine reality.[10] In such a view, didacticism, or "telling" rather than "showing", can only be abhorrent: it is man interposing his interpretations between God and mystic contact with His creation.

Yet MacDonald was not only an extreme Romantic of this sort: he was a Victorian; and preaching came naturally to Victorians—and especially to a Victorian clergyman without a pulpit. MacDonald occasionally felt impelled to justify his didactic intrusions: for example, after a spiritual aside on a sunset in *Malcolm,* he jerks round to:

> But, alas, it was not Lady Florimel who thought these things! Looking over her shoulder, and seeing both what she can and what she cannot see, I am having a think to myself.
>
> 'Which it is an offence to utter in the temple of Art!' cry the critics.
>
> Not against Art, I think: but if it be an offence to the worshipper of Art, let him keep silence before his goddess; for me, I am a sweeper of the floors in the temple of Life, and his goddess is my mare, and shall go in the dust-cart; if I find a jewel as I sweep, I will fasten it on the curtains of the doors, nor heed if it should break the fall of a fold of the drapery.[11]

First he says his work does not go against Art, but then says he will make it do so. And the plea of "life" as the criterion of such intrusions ignores the fact that they destroy the felt life of his work. There seems real uncertainty here—and a nervous irritability. Nevertheless, at whatever cost in tension, half of himself goes into the preaching that fills the novels. It may be that MacDonald resolved the conflict in his own mind at least by seeing himself as "telling" through his novels and "showing" through his fantasy and poetry. However he viewed himself, he would have been deluded if he had thus simplified the fantasy;[12] and likewise, as we shall see, with the novels.

The novels we shall be discussing here—*David Elginbrod* (1863), *Alec Forbes of Howglen* (1865), *Robert Falconer* (1868) and *Malcolm* (1875)[13]—are among not only the earliest, but the best that MacDonald wrote. They are largely about Scottish life, in the portrayal of which MacDonald has real claim to literary stature: his portraits of English society in other novels are far less sure. *Alec Forbes* and *Robert Falconer,* which will be our primary concern, are in part the working out of a theme which preoccupied MacDonald all his life—the Calvinist doctrine of the elect versus his own universalist position: and through this his whole attitude to the categories of good and evil, mercy and justice, freedom and constraint. Most of MacDonald's other novels are repetitious of motifs and themes which appear in these novels: in a sense he wrote himself out in them.

It may be helpful here to give brief accounts of the plots of these novels. *David Elginbrod* is the story of one Hugh Sutherland, descendant of an ancient Scottish family, who, during a university vacation, is made tutor in the laird's house on the estate of Turriepuffit (conceived as being in Aberdeenshire) and becomes very friendly with the laird's estate manager, the saintly David Elginbrod, and subsequently with his daughter, Margaret. Eventually the holiday ends and Hugh has to return to Aberdeen University, from where his contact with David by letter becomes increasingly perfunctory. When he comes down from university, Hugh is appointed tutor at the country house of a Mr. Arnold at Arnstead in Sussex. He soon finds his task of tutoring Mr. Arnold's son Harry interrupted by the attractions of Mr. Arnold's niece, Euphra, who is staying there. She flirts with Hugh and he becomes infatuated with her, but when he discovers that her frustration of his advances is owing to the fact that she is in a constant state of trance-like obedience to the mesmerist Funkelstein (who wishes to use her to steal from Arnstead for him), Hugh's love is wounded. He sets out to find Funkelstein in London, helped by one Robert Falconer whom he meets there. Funkelstein finally escapes, however, though Margaret Elginbrod, who now returns, helps Euphra to break free of his spell. Euphra dies, and Hugh and Margaret come together.

Alec Forbes of Howglen is in large part the story of a boy's life and development in a mid-century northern Scottish village, here named Glamerton (based on MacDonald's home-town of Huntly). But the novel is more than an account of "The Little Grey Town" (Mac-Donald's original title for the book): it follows Alec to university (in Aberdeen), to the development of an obsession for the beautiful flirt Kate whom he meets there; and, on his discovery that she loves his hated rival, Beauchamp, to a moral collapse into drinking and whoring. When Kate falls ill and dies, Alec too, falls ill, and returns to Glamerton. After he recovers, he takes a post as ship's doctor, and is the only survivor of a disaster on the Greenland coast. On his return, he is a changed man, and marries his childhood love, Annie Anderson.

Robert Falconer[14] again starts in the setting of a Scottish village, Rothieden, with the boyhood of the hero, and again the story proceeds to life as a student at Aberdeen University and Robert's enmity to a corrupt baronet, Lord Rothie. Central in Robert's boyhood is his conflict with his Calvinist grandmother: he develops an idea of a loving, merciful God, and, after an experience of mystical illumination while a student, resolves on a life of service to mankind. Driving him later too is the hope that he may one day find his long-lost and reprobate father. We follow him to London and pursue his numerous charities; and, when he finally discovers his father, we watch the charity with which he tries to remove his father's wickedness. Eventually his father becomes helplessly good, utterly dependent on

Robert, who now sets sail with him to India to work out his conversion to the full.

Malcolm is about a young fisher-boy of the village of Portlossie who falls in love with Florimel, daughter of the local laird, the Marquis of Lossie. Through her recommendation, Malcolm is made a sailor on the Marquis' yacht. He realises that Florimel is too far above him in station for his love to be successful, but defends her interests and those of the Marquis throughout. Eventually he finds that he is the legitimate son of the Marquis, and that Florimel is illegitimate (the Marquis married her mother without knowing that his first wife was still alive). Malcolm resolves to keep her secret, and, when the Marquis dies, allows Florimel to become Marchioness of Lossie. (In the sequel to this novel, *The Marquis of Lossie* (1877) Malcolm has changed his love for Florimel into brotherly affection, she being his half-sister. When Florimel insists on marrying the heartless Lord Liftore, Malcolm is forced to reveal the truth about herself to her, so that she will prefer the painter Lenorme, who really deserves her, and whom she secretly loves. After this, of course, Malcolm succeeds to the title.)

MacDonald has extraordinary ability in his portrayal of Scottish life and interrelationships in all these novels. He has perhaps not so much grasp of his villages as whole communities as of individuals who stand out even while they belong. David Elginbrod; Annie Anderson, the blind woman Tibbie Dyster, Murdoch Malison the schoolmaster, Cosmo Cupples the librarian in *Alec Forbes*; the vagabond Shargar and Robert's grandmother in *Robert Falconer*; the blind piper Duncan MacPhail (foster-father to Malcolm) and the mad outcast boy Stephen Stewart in *Malcolm:* all either live outside the village-society (*of*, but not *in* it) or else are extreme eccentrics. Perhaps the only exception to this is the unwelcome memorability of George Bruce, the tyrannical and mean shopkeeper with whom Annie is boarded in *Alec Forbes*. To bear out this point, it is worth contrasting MacDonald here with, say, Dickens, whose method of caricature is one which takes in all society: Micawber or Mrs. Gamp are locally vivid examples of a social matrix of caricatures in which they belong; Dickens' social worlds strike the reader with fairly even force, where MacDonald's is more Gothic, his characters lunging at the reader like gargoyles from a uniform pile behind.

MacDonald's physical descriptions are rarely memorable—which is strange in someone who was so moved by sights—but his descriptions of psychological landscape are often very fine and thoroughly felt. One thinks of the portrayal of the relation between the grasping Robert Bruce and his unwilling boarder Annie Anderson in *Alec Forbes*, or of Robert Falconer and his grandmother in *Robert Falconer* or of Duncan MacPhail and Malcolm in *Malcolm*; but the point can be illustrated from smaller contexts, like that of the relation between Mrs. Falconer, Robert's grandmother, and her wily maid Betty, which is a beautifully felt piece of Scottish feudalism: here, for instance, Mrs. Falconer is suspicious of what Robert keeps in the garret—

'What gangs he sae muckle up the stair for, Betty, do ye ken? It's something by ordinar' wi' 'm.

'Deed I dinna ken, mem. I never tuik it into my heid to gang considerin' aboot it. He'll hae some ploy o' 'is ain, nae doobt. Laddies will be laddies, ye ken, mem.'

'I doobt, Betty, ye'll be aidin' an' abettin'. An' it disna become yer years, Betty.'

'My years are no to fin' faut wi', mem. They're weel eneuch.'

'That's naething to the pint, Betty. What's the laddie aboot?'

'Do ye mean whan he gangs up the stair, mem?'

'Ay. Ye ken weel eneuch what I mean.'

'Weel, mem, I tell ye I dinna ken. An' ye never heard me tell ye a lee sin' ever I was i' yer service, mem.'

'No, nae doonricht. Ye gang aboot it and aboot it, an' at last ye come sae near leein' that gin ye spak anither word, ye wad be at it; and it jist fleys *(frights)* me frae speirin' ae ither queston at ye. An' that's hoo ye win oot o' 't.'*(RF, 53)*

The conversation is something like a dance of advance and retire. Part of our pleasure in the exchange is knowing that it is a time-worn one, even in a sense a constant game played out between two women. Doubtless Robert's grandmother is exasperated by Betty's prevarication, but there is also the sense that she needs such circumlocution and evasiveness on which to blunt her own purposes. Betty is not really interested in what Robert is doing with Shargar, while Mrs. Falconer implicates her in the boy's schemes much further that she has gone. At this Betty becomes evasive so far as the boy's secret concerns her, and finally is drawn to the point of being evasive for the sheer pleasure of baffling Mrs. Falconer. There is also pleasure for the reader in characters made so believable and real. Of course the language must help this, in the way that it insists on the local and individual nature of the scene simply by being Scots; and there is additional energy derived from the fact that both women are using the same dialect while apart in station (in the Lowlands the old lady would probably have talked King's English)—here that are no external signs of rank, only the regard and authority that are continually being earned. But MacDonald had the gift, shown by many Victorians, of being able to recreate his childhood with special vividness, as though he was present while he was describing the scene—and that without sentimentality or prosy awkwardness. One need not suppose that the characters of his novels are simply people he knew under different names: imagination has been at work, but that imagination could only thrive on a vivid experience and recall of the actual. For instance, the description of the drubbing given to Bruce's dog, or of the game of stopping cottage-chimneys with sods of turf, or of the "chain of beasts" in *Alec Forbes* (*AF*, 64-73, 81-6, 142-6) are all almost certainly reworkings of experiences MacDonald himself had once lived: they have a marvellous sense of detail, of going through the events described over again:

> 'Weel, it didna look a'thegither like respeck, I maun alloo.—I was stannin' at the coonter o' his shop waitin' for an unce o' sneeshin'; and Robert he was servin' a bit bairnie ower the coonter wi' a pennyworth o' triacle, when, in a jiffey, there cam' sic a blast, an' a reek fit to smore ye, oot o' the bit fire, an' the shop was fu' o' reek, afore ye could hae pitten the pint o' ae thoom upo' the pint o' the ither. "Preserve's a'!" cried Rob; but or he could say anither word, butt the house, scushlin in her bauchles, comes Nancy, rinnin', an' opens the door wi' a scraich: "Preserve's a'!" quo' she. "Robert, the lum's in a low!" ' (*AF*. 81)

Yet however delightfully vivid or human these and many other episodes may be, they are to be enjoyed only for themselves. The picture of "Murder" Malison the schoolmaster, whose tyranny is tamed when one day it goes too far; the rivetting but awful account of how when Malison is invited to preach for the first time in Glamerton church his mind goes blank during his sermon and he hides in his pulpit till the people have left; the portrait of blind Tibbie Dyster who defies but is killed in her house at the river by the flood raised by a great storm (" 'Lat it come . . . . The bit hoosie's fund't upon a rock, and the rains may fa', and the wins may blaw, and the floods may ca at the hoosie, but it winna fa', it canna fa', for it's fund't upo' a rock' " (*AF*, 281); the description of how the vagrant Shargar is found concealed in the garret of the house of Robert Falconer's grandmother; or the scene in which Robert and Shargar fly the kite they have built—all these are imaginatively realised, but the imagination that makes them is only locally operative: they are not symbolic of any larger theme implicit in the novels as wholes. The flood which ends Tibbie Dyster, for example, has none of the culminating symbolic force of that at the close of George Eliot's *The Mill on the Floss*. One can see something more of the precise problem in the description of the water in the bleach-fields outside Rothieden in *Robert Falconer*:

> The pleasure of the water itself was inexhaustible. Here sweeping in a mass along the race; there divided into branches and hurrying through the walls of the various houses; here sliding through a wooden channel across the floor to fall into the river in a half-concealed cataract, there bubbling up through the bottom of a huge wooden cave or vat, there resting placid in another; here gurgling along a spout; there flowing in a narrow canal through the green expanse of the well-mown bleach-field, or lifted from it in narrow curved wooden scoops, like fairy canoes with long handles, and flung in showers over the outspread

yarn—the water was an endless delight. (*RF,* 121)

No other reaction is offered but general delight, because no more subtle response is felt. Nor in the book as a whole is there any chain of related imagery that might turn this passage into a symbolic focus: MacDonald has seen this, has taken pleasure in the sight, and has tried to re-create it: that is all. He wrote of the creative imagination that "it takes forms already existing, and gathers them about a thought so much higher than they, that it can group and subordinate and harmonize them into a whole which shall represent, unveil that thought".[15] Such an imagination is not often evident in the novels. In relation to the passage on water quoted above one might mention another in his *Unspoken Sermons,* where he speaks of water as giving a mystical pleasure, an experience of divine immanence, or thought and form fused: "it comes bubbling fresh from the imagination of the living God . . . . The very thought of it makes one gasp with an elemental joy no metaphysician can analyse . . . . Water is its own self its own truth, and is therein a truth of God".[16] Such, however, is not our experience of the water in *Robert Falconer.* A little further on in the same account there is another and different kind of passage:

> On the grassy bank of the gently-flowing river, at the other edge of whose level the little canal squabbled along, and on the grassy brae which rose immediately from the canal, were stretched, close beside each other, with scarce a stripe of green betwixt, the long white webs of linen, fastened down to the soft mossy ground with wooden pegs, whose tops were twisted into their edges. Strangely would they billow in the wind sometimes, like sea-waves, frozen and enchanted flat, seeking to rise and wallow in the wind with conscious depth and whelming mass. But generally they lay supine, saturated with light and its cleansing power. (*RF,* 122)

Here the imagination has entered into the description: we are aware of the perceiving mind, remaking what it sees, in the "conscious depth, and whelming mass"; the mind is a part of the experience, rather than simply a delighted witness, as in the account of the water. In short, this passage has imaginative power. But it is a power which is only local: it does not draw into itself any of the larger issues of the novel, nor does it catch up any pattern of related images. It is also a power which, with an intrusive comment, MacDonald damps as soon as he has raised it:

> Falconer's jubilation in the white and green of a little boat, as we lay, one bright morning, on the banks of the Thames between Richmond and Twickenham, led to such a description of the bleachfield that I can write about it as if I had known it myself.

The absence of a continuous creative imagination at work throughout the novels has two broad effects: first, as we have seen, episodes become isolated from one another except as they advance the narrative or contribute to the general portrayals of youthful pleasures or Scots village life; and second, such themes as the novels have are put on them from outside, rather than felt from within. These effects are to be seen in many forms, which we can now consider.

One concomitant of the isolation of scenes and episodes is an uncertain attitude towards characters. When Robert Falconer has been trying to persuade his stern Calvinist grandmother to reverse her banishment of his friend Shargar from the house, by painting a picture of Shargar drowning himself, we are told that his grandmother "could be wrought upon", and that her severity of manner is a disguise for her warmth of human feeling: "I cannot help thinking that she not unfrequently took refuge in severity of tone and manner from the threatened ebullition of a feeling which she could not otherwise control, and which she was ashamed to manifest" (*RF*, 59, 60). But later, just before she finds and burns Robert's violin, we are told, "there was no smile in her religion, which, while it developed the power of a darkened conscience, overlaid and half-smothered all the lovelier impulses of her grand nature" (*RF*, 146). When in the same book comparison is made between the status of Mysie Lindsay and the saintly Mary St. John in the affections of the heroic Ericson, we are told that Mysie "was but a sickly plant grown in a hot-house" (*RF*, 294); but, when Mysie trusts herself to the villainous Lord Rothie, the word is "A world of innocence and beauty was about to be hurled from its orbit of light into the blackness of outer chaos" (*RF*, 306). In *Alec Forbes* the account of how the boys tie the village beasts nose-to-tail in descending order of size into a long serpentine monster which wanders through Glamerton is first of all comic, down to the picture of the cripple Andrew Truffey's white rabbit dead at the end of the procession

and so, by the accretion of living joints, the strange monster lengthened out into the dim fiery distance ....
Next came a diminishing string of disreputable dogs, to the tail of the last of which was fastened the only cat the inventors of this novel pastime had been able to catch. At her tail followed—alas!—Andrew Truffey's white rabbit, whose pink eyes, now fixed and glazed, would no more delight the imagination of the poor cripple; and whose long furry hind legs would never more bang the ground in sovereign contempt, as he dared pursuit; for the dull little beast, having, with the stiffneckedness of fear, persisted in pulling against the string that tied him to the tail of Widow Wattles's great tom-cat, was now trailed ignominiously upon his side, with soiled fur and outstretched neck—the last joint, and only dead one, of this bodiless tail. (*AF*, 142-3)

This is mainly amused, a mock-elegy; and the rabbit is almost blamed for its own fate. But on the next page the wrath of the stern and worthy Thomas Crann falls on Alec for causing the rabbit's death: " 'There's a heap o' fun ... that carries deith i' th' tail o' 't. Here's the puir cripple laddie's rabbit as deid's a herrin', and him at hame greetin' his een oot, I daursay' " (*AF,* 145). Now the comic element is small beside the moral one, and Alec, chastened, rushes off to try to repair the damage by giving Truffey a new rabbit; we are told, too, that "There had been a growing, though it was still a vague sense, in Alec's mind, that he was not doing well; and this rebuke of Thomas Crann brought it full into the light of his own consciousness. From that day he worked better" (*AF,* 146).

Some of the difficulties shown here can be attributed partly to the way MacDonald presents the same scene or event from different points of view which remain unreconciled, and partly to his continuous desire to moralise. As occasion demands he portrays the schoolmaster "Murder" Malison as a morally cretinous tyrant (*AF,* 61-2) and as a man whose fierceness is given awful sanction by prevailing theology (*AF,* 132-3); and the very fact that he has to enter with such explicit asides as "Let me once more assert that Mr. Malison was not a bad man" (*AF,* 132)—as if the name could convey otherwise—points to the fact that the moral analysis has not been present in the portrayal of the character. As he is presented, from the point of view of his charges, Malison is an inhuman sadist, who only reforms—and even *that* seems rather inconsistent—when he has so thrashed a boy as to render him a cripple for life. When last we see him, it is to feel pleasure at his discomfiture, when his mind goes blank before he is to deliver his sermon, and he becomes a "*stickit minister*" (*AF,* 253). Clearly the actual presentation simplifies: the moral asides attempt to impose a double view, but, not having grown out of the material as it is presented (and if they had, they would be unnecessary), lose grip and become contradictory. MacDonald did not as a novelist have the power to fuse two opposed apprehensions into a complex and felt whole. Consider, for example, his views on the loss to Scotland of the race of cottars (*RF,* 134): he begins with a heavy lament, "Alas for Scotland that such families are now to seek!"; but after eight doleful lines changes to "But well for the world that such life has been scattered over it, east and west, the seed of fresh growth in new lands"; finally trying to draw the two apprehensions into a theoretic unity, "The excellence must vanish from one portion, that it may be diffused through the whole"; there is more of the same until MacDonald tires, and becomes conscious that he has lost touch with his story: " 'Something too much of this' ".

That the themes of MacDonald's novels are most commonly grafted on to them from outside may be readily demonstrated by the way in which *Alec Forbes* and *Robert Falconer* fall in half. For the first third of *Alec Forbes* Alec is simply the ageless schoolboy, like Richmal Crompton's William: for the rest he is at Aberdeen University, developing—or devolving—morally and intellectually, learning from false loves, visiting his home from outside. One can put the gap in philosophical categories, as one between being and becoming: at first he is delighted in for what he is, but later he is reproved or commended for what he becomes; and in a real sense we feel there to be two Alecs in the book. The early earnestness of Robert Falconer—for example his opposition to his grandmother's harsh view of hell—does not produce this kind of disjunction when he becomes a great unofficial minister later on: but here there is a different kind of division, whereby a goodness thoroughly apprehended in the boy becomes lost in shrill idealising in the man. There are other discontinuities in *Robert Falconer*. From the point at which Robert leaves Rothieden for Aberdeen and subsequently London, no character is realised with force, though many are presented with spiritual fervour, even frenzy, on the part of the author. The movement from the childhood environment, as in *Alec Forbes*, marks a real break, but here there is a much more obvious change in language, from Scots to standard English: and this again with a loss of the variety of tones and the humour of the earlier section. Robert ceases to be looked at, and becomes looked with, in total complicity by the author, so that he becomes a mouthpiece of the sermonising which becomes marked as the novel proceeds. The plot—as in *Alec Forbes*—becomes melodramatic, riddled with sensational coincidences, lacking in all the random character of life. In short the author is making the experience, not life. That there should be a dichotomy at all between the two is the most revealing fact about MacDonald's novels: with his work we have an either–or situation where experience and reflection upon it cannot come together.

Let us look at some of these points in detail. Over halfway through *Robert Falconer* we are suddenly informed that the one purpose of Robert's life is to find his long-lost reprobate father: "For years he had regarded the finding of his father as the first duty of his manhood" (*RF*, 276). There has been small suggestion of this hitherto. The notion takes time to develop also, for later we are told, at the beginning of Part III of the novel, "His Manhood", that "Travel, motion, ever on, ever away, was the sole impulse in his heart. Nor had the thought of finding his father any share in his restlessness" (*RF*, 320). The tenuous nature of the theme's introduction could not be more clearly demonstrated. After this point the motif of search becomes more prominent, until with the eventual discovery of the father the last part of the novel is wholly devoted to the attempts made by Falconer to reform him. The book thus breaks in two.

There are parts of the earlier section of the novel in which the language grows stilted, particularly in the accounts of Robert's worshipping relation to the idealised Mary St. John, but there is nothing of the sentimentalism, melodrama and excessive intensity that creep in later. At Aberdeen University Robert meets the blond Eric Ericson, who has all the appearance of a Norse rover, and all the spiritual doubt and self-castigation of a nervous adolescent. Ericson, and his relation with Robert are treated without any irony.[17] Robert tells Ericson, " 'You remind me of Peter and John at the Beautiful Gate of the temple' " and the object of this adoration is similarly adored by the author:

> A smile broke up the cold, sad, gray light of the young eagle-face. Stern at once and gentle when in repose, its smile was as the summer of some lovely land where neither the heat nor the sun shall smite them. The youth laid his hand upon the boy's head, then withdrew it hastily, and the smile vanished like the sun behind a cloud. Robert saw it, and as if he had been David before Saul, rose instinctively . . . . (*RF*, 197)

Doubtless the best of MacDonald's feeling goes into this, but it is too simple and uncritical, and falls into sentimentality. The whole treatment of Ericson is an example of that Victorian habit of hero-worship which W.E. Houghton has so well documented:[18] what is strange is that Ericson lacks the spiritual certainty which usually aroused such hero-worship—he is in that state of despair from which those who looked to heroes were trying to escape. Much of Ericson's distress is a form of self-pity (see for example *RF*, 225, 257) which MacDonald prefers to portray as the wreck of a beautiful soul. Many of his febrile poems are quoted (*RF*, 198-319). It is a sign of MacDonald's loss of grip on this character that in the midst of his spiritual torments Ericson can be shown as falling in love with the trivial Mysie Lyndsay. When the saintly Mary St. John appears to nurse Ericson in his final illness, and supplants Mysie in his affections, the writing reaches an unbearable pitch of tropical sentimentality.

Similar are the later passages describing Robert's Christian life in London, and his relations with his father. We lose all sense of reality, of accuracy. This is a description of a London slum street in evening:

> Vague noises of strife and of drunken wrath flitted around me as I passed an alley, or an opening door let out its evil secret. Once I thought I heard the dull *thud* of a blow on the head. The noisome vapours were fit for any of Swedenborg's hells. There were few sounds, but the very quiet seemed infernal. The night was hot and sultry. A skinned cat, possibly still alive, fell on the street before me. Under one of the gas-lamps lay something long: it was a tress of dark hair, torn perhaps from some woman's head: she had beautiful hair at least. Once I heard the cry of *murder* . . . . (*RF*, 143)

If the tress of hair or the skinned cat suggest that this scene has been experienced by the author, the sense of experience has been lost in this shrill monochromatic portrayal. (It is interesting to note that MacDonald was probably reworking this passage—and to more integrated effect—in the visit of Vane to the city of Bulika in his fantasy *Lilith* (1895), ch.xxiv; there the fantastic medium guarantees an authorial distance which the novel does not.) This second half of the novel is packed with direct moral commentary by the author. One would not however argue that the material is unrealised because MacDonald is not involved with it: on the contrary, he is too involved—nearness as much as distance forfeits correct focal length. And, curiously, nearness can fall by its very violence into the inertia of distance: on one occasion, during a storm in London, Falconer has, at the moment of a flash of lightning, a vision of his father which in accuracy of detail exceeds any knowledge he has of his appearance; later this detail is drily explained:

"That I think was a quickening of the memory by the realism of the presentation. Excited by the vision, it caught at its own past, as it were, and suddenly recalled that which it had forgotten. In the rapidity of all pure mental action, this at once took its part in the apparent objectivity."

To return to the narrative.... (*RF*,376)

The descent from visionary rapture to psychological curiosity is startling.

This latter part of the novel has several moments of coincidence in the plot, which are of a piece with the melodramatic mode in which MacDonald is writing: it is odd to find the authorial persona of the book describing his early departure from a Strand theatre performance, "unable to endure any longer the dreary combination of false magnanimity and real meanness, imported from Paris in the shape of a melodrama, for the delectation of the London public" (*RF*, 372). Just before Falconer's lightning-flash vision, he has been saying of the crowded street where he experiences it, " 'Out of this mass may suddenly start something marvellous, or, it may be, something you have been looking for for years' " (*RF*, 376). While on a visit to Rothieden he walks to the bleachfield: there he eventually thinks of the vagrant mother, last seen in London, of his friend Shargar, and wonders, "Was it not possible, being a wanderer far and wide, that she might be now in Rothieden?" (*RF*, 360); he returns to the town at once and, no more to his amazement than to ours, finds her. Mysie Lyndsay tells Robert that when with her seducer Lord Rothie she happened to enter Antwerp Cathedral, someone was playing on the bells with such power that she was moved to make her escape from Rothie that moment; it was Robert, ignorant of her presence there, who had been playing (*RF*, 395-6). Such coincidences, false to the random character of reality, are symptomatic of an unbalanced authorial stance. One can see them, too, in *David Elginbrod,* where by sheer chance and circumstance the hero Hugh Sutherland fails to meet with his boyhood love Margaret Elginbrod when she is present as a servant-companion at the Sussex house where he is tutor; or in the way that his subsequent inamorata, the flirt Euphrasia, is made to die as a result of the effects of the prolonged mesmeric powers exercised on her by the villain Funkelstein, so that the road is clear for Hugh and Margaret to come together again.[19] Similar here is the death of the heartless Kate of *Alec Forbes,* whose removal makes it possible for Alec to return to his childhood sweetheart, Annie Anderson of Glamerton.

Two more general points concerning these novels are worth mention. First, we may note the occurrence in all four novels of a situation in which the hero falls in love with an unattainable woman: Hugh Sutherland with Euphra, Alec Forbes with Kate, Robert Falconer with Mary St. John, Malcolm with Florimel. With the exception of Mary St. John—"woman-angel" as she is once termed (*RF*, 368, cf. 268) — all are flirts. It has been said that MacDonald had an unpleasant experience with a flirtatious woman in his youth which obsessed him.[20] but in fairness it should be pointed out that he often contrasts these flirts with more humble women, in a theme of "getting" versus "giving" whereby the hero sloughs off the spiritual possessiveness of crude physical passion in his rejection by the flirt, and learns to love the humble and saintly other woman more purely, for herself, thereby (this theme is particularly dominant in the contrastive females of *Phantastes*). What is of concern to us here, however, is the class issue raised by this theme, and MacDonald's general attitude on the subject. His unattainable women are so not only in therir beauty and behaviour, but in their sophistication and their pedigree. It seems clear enough from the biographical facts we have that MacDonald suffered from his own uncouthness in society, and that he had an excessive veneration for titles. *Malcolm* is specifically about the discovery by the fisher-boy hero that he is in fact the successor to the Marquis of Lossie. All four novels are scattered with scenes in which the crude simplicity of the hero is put to shame or mocked by superior women. All these women speak well-turned English, and only in *Malcolm*—perhaps as defiance?— does the hero not purge himself of Scots dialect when in society. The issue is overt in *Robert Falconer*, where MacDonald has an ambivalent attitude towards dialect. He sees the King's English as a refinement and a civilising of Scots, and yet can maintain that their native coarseness of language comes the more naturally to his heroes in moments of great feeling. Thus, for example, when Robert is arguing with Ericson about faith, he falls back into broad Scots, and we are told of the English he had used up to that point,

> My reader may have observed a little change for the better in Robert's speech. Dr. Anderson had urged upon him the necessity of being able at least to speak English; and he had been trying to modify the antique Saxon dialect they used at Rothieden with the newer and more refined English. But even when I knew him, he would upon occasion, especially when the subject was religion or music, fall back into the broadest Scotch. It was as if his heart could not issue freely by any other gate than that of his grandmother tongue. (*RF*, 256)

Similar is the account of Dr. Anderson's reversion to dialect on his death-bed (*RF*, 347). In a context like that when Robert is overcome by the beauty of Mary St. John, MacDonald is more one-sided: "Robert was thrown back into the abyss of his mother-tongue, and out of this abyss talked like a Behemoth" (*RF*, 284). The trouble is that the protagonists often switch between Scots and English not on the basis of feeling, but simply on that of their interlocutors: Alec Forbes speaks English to Kate and Scots to the people of Glamerton or Cosmo Cupples, and Robert Falconer grows to reserve his Scots for Rothieden, his grandmother and Shargar (though when Shargar rises socially and drops his accent, there is uncertainty: see for example *RF*, 391). We begin to feel, in short, that the hero becomes an indeterminate hybrid, neither here nor there—even, at times, a hypocrite. In a chapter of *Robert Falconer* entitled "Shargar Aspires", there is a passage where this and Robert's uncondemned patronage of the vagabond Shargar come together. Shargar has come to Robert with information concerning the wicked Lord Rothie. First Robert berates him for his habit of eavesdropping: " 'gin ye want to be a gentleman, ye maunna gang keekin' that gate intil ither fowk's affairs' "; and Shargar submits, " 'Weel, I maun gie 't up. I winna say a word o' what Jock Mitchell tellt me aboot Lord Sandy' ". Upon which Robert shifts at once, " 'Ow, say awa' ' "; but now the boot is on the other leg, " 'Na, na; ye wadna like to hear aboot ither fowk's affairs' ". Robert now reverts to imperialist's English: " 'What is Lord Sandy after? What did the rascal tell you? Why do you make such a mystery of it?' said Robert, authoritatively, and in his best English"; and when Shargar has told him what he knows, climbs back on his moral pedestal, " 'Well, take care what you're about, Shargar. I don't think Dr. Anderson would like you to be in such company' " (RF, 297). It is a significant comment on MacDonald that the potential ironies of this scene escape him. Similar too is the afterword to *Alec Forbes*, in which Annie Anderson, whom Alec marries, is promoted from her previous low station: "The first time Curly [the boy she refused] saw Annie after the wedding, he was amazed at his own presumption in ever thinking of marrying such a lady" (*AF*, 440).

The second general point concerning the novels is their nature as *Bildungsromanen*. MacDonald is quite good at portraying moral decline, as in the cases of Hugh Sutherland or Alec Forbes, but his conversions tend to be rather sudden. Hugh Sutherland, having lost Euphra, swings round to Margaret Elginbrod and returns to Turriepuffit to repent in the last pages of the novel: up to then his soul has been more or less a wilderness. The conversion of Alec Forbes, and the revelation that he loves Annie Anderson occur offstage, while he is a ship's doctor stranded in the Arctic, and are reported by him on his return.[21] Robert Falconer, who has watched his adored Mary St. John give her love to his friend Ericson, and Ericson die, and who has seen Lord Rothie seduce Mysie Lyndsay, leaves the country for four years, during which time he commits himself to the service of God. The account of his conversion is relatively brief, and in summary form, so that we are not in touch with the psychological and spiritual alteration in Robert, but are presented with his change as little other than a *fait accompli*:

> By the end of the month it had dawned upon him, he hardly knew how, that the peace of Jesus (although, of course, he could not know what it was like till he had it) must have been a peace that came from the doing of the will of his Father. From the account he gave of the discoveries he then made, I venture to represent them in the driest and most exact form that I can find they will admit of. (*RF*, 329)[22]

There follows a list of Falconer's spiritual discoveries, under the heads of First, Second, Third and Fourth. As for his subsequent career, we hear and see nothing of spiritual doubts or tests of faith: he is the fully resolved Christian hero. MacDonald is conscious of this, sometimes irritably so, as in this on Falconer in *David Elginbrod*:

> Those who are in the habit of regarding the real and the ideal as essentially and therefore irreconcileably opposed, will remark that I cannot have drawn the representation of Falconer faithfully. Perhaps the difficulty they will experience in recognizing its truthfulness, may spring from the fact that they themselves are un-ideal enough to belong to the not small class of strong-minded friends whose chief care, in performing the part of the rock in the weary land, is—not to shelter you imprudently.[23]

This, however, is to forget the fact that though the Christian is meant to be an image of Christ, that image must by the nature of sin and mortality be a broken one. Generally with these novels we may note therefore a thinness in MacDonald's portrayals of the process and maintenance of conversion in his heroes. We may attribute this partly to the "Victorian" need for a grand human example to follow, but also to a curious detachment from the world which the author's own conversion involved, and his own refusal to admit subsequent doubts.[24] It is interesting to note that with *Malcolm* MacDonald drops the idea of a developing hero: Malcolm is perfect from the outset, and all that is at issue is the manifestation and proper recognition of that perfection; significantly the novel never moves away from the northern Scottish fishing village in which it is set.

Perhaps the basic problem that MacDonald had in expressing his Christian themes in his novels was that he could only "tell" them, not "show" them. He tells us of conversions, but we do not really see them happening—or, if we do, what we witness is a process of spiritual bludgeoning which we cannot accept as true to life (the alterations wrought in Euphra Cameron or Falconer's father). He tells us that God is present in the commonest and ugliest sights, and yet it is their ugliness or commonness which preoccupies him: the MacDonald who in the context of nature can speak of God being on top of, in the show or manifestation of a flower,[25] here speaks of him as buried beneath the other side of life—its

vileness: " 'Could you,' " Falconer asks the fictionalised MacDonald of
the latter part of *Robert Falconer*, " 'Could you believe in the immortal
essence hidden under all this garbage—God at the root of it all?' " (*RF*,
405). A hard question indeed. But the issue is not merely one of the
pleasant versus the less pleasant. It is not even that MacDonald can only
find God immanent in certain phenomena—jewels, stairways, steeples,
mountains, flowers and the wind,[26] though this explains why much of the
assertion that God is present in the everyday sounds a trifle *voulu*. It is
that for the recreation of religious experience MacDonald needed a less
articulate and articulated medium than the novel form as he saw it and
made it:

> But think what language must become before it will tell
> dreams!—before it will convey the delicate shades of fancy that come
> and go in the brain of a child!—before it will let a man know wherein
> one face differeth from another face in glory! I suspect, however, that
> for such purposes it is rather music than articulation that is need-
> ful—that, with a hope of these finer results, the language must rather
> be turned into music than logically extended. (*RF*, 186)

It was towards such a condition of music that he worked in his fantasies.
There the appeal is directly to the imagination and the divine spark
MacDonald believed inhabited it; there a form and purpose no longer
need be intelligible, since God is the maker and the object of imitation.
That at least was the aim: how far MacDonald succeeded is another
matter. But in the novels we can go no further than:

> A gentle wind, laden with pine odours from the sun-heated trees
> behind him, flapped its light wing in his face: the humanity of the world
> smote his heart; the great sky towered up over him, and its divinity
> entered his soul; a strange longing after something 'he knew not nor
> could name' awoke within him, followed by the pang of a sudden fear
> that there was no such thing as that which he sought, that it was all a
> fancy of his own spirit; and then the voice of Shargar broke the spell,
> calling to him from afar to come and see a great salmon that lay by a
> stone in the water. But once aroused, the feeling was never stilled; the
> desire never left him; sometimes growing even to a passion that was
> relieved only by a flood of tears.
>   Strange as it may sound to those who have never thought of such
> things save in connection with Sundays and Bibles and churches and
> sermons, that which was now working in Falconer's mind was the first
> dull and faint movement of the greatest need that the human heart pos-
> sesses—the need of the God-Man. There must be a truth in the scent
> of that pine-wood: some one must mean it. There must be a glory in
> those heavens that depends not upon our imagination: some power
> greater than they must dwell in them. Some spirit must move in that
> wind that haunts us with a kind of human sorrow; some soul must look

up to us from the eye of that starry flower. It must be something human, else not to us divine. (*RF*, 123)

It is interesting that Shargar and the salmon, who equally belong in God (compare the later " 'There is not a gin-palace, or yet lower hell in London, in which a man or woman can be out of God' ", (*RF*, 386)), are considered a worldly interruption. In this passage MacDonald is describing the experience, telling his readers how to recognise it and what to recognise in it: he is not trying to do all these things by making them experience the desire for themselves. In fact it is not far removed from an inductive argument based on human experience—though Paley's *Natural Theology*, a storehouse of such arguments, is later attacked (*RF*, 366).

MacDonald's novels thus exhibit a range of self-divisions. One side of him is content to portray life and society simply for themselves; the other wants to make it intelligible. On the one hand the world appears too much with the author; on the other, too little, where all existence is marshalled under mind and moral purpose. Turriepuffit, Glamerton and Rothieden allow only "being": London and the Arctic are the scenes of "becoming". Such, with occasional lurches from one side to the other, continued to be the character of the novels after *Robert Falconer*. In *Malcolm* MacDonald tells a plain romantic story of love and class with only scattered moral commentary: though the characterisation is fine, the book, lacking even imposed significance, is limited in power. Similar in the opposite direction is *The Seaboard Parish* (1868), which is given over almost entirely to preaching.

There is as much of a division between the novels and the fantasies, as indeed between the literary principles in both. The novels deal largely with consciousness: they treat of the world as it appears to the waking and the human eye, and at the same time have intelligible purpose. But the fantasy is largely concerned with the world as it appears in dreams or to the imagination, and the purpose, inseparable from this portrayal, is precisely to go beyond human standards of intelligibility: "The greatest forces", MacDonald wrote in this connection, "lie in the region of the uncomprehended".[27] (Even the fantasy itself shows self-division in MacDonald's creative purpose when he sometimes imposes intelligible meaning on that which he set out to leave obscure.[28] To write fantasy MacDonald deliberately attempted to jettison his conscious mind—will, intelligence, overt moral intent; to write novels he was forced to do without his unconscious imagination. The polarities we have seen within the novels are the product of a sensibility at once possessed of a strong sense of life and burdened by an intense desire to make that life morally and spiritually instructive; those between the novels and the fantasy stem from what makes MacDonald far more unusual in his time, the fact that he was both a Victorian and an extreme Romantic.

MacDonald's novels do not, on the whole, have claim to major literary status, and the teaching for which in part they were so popular in their day no longer speaks to most of us. Yet the evocation of Aberdeenshire characters that they contain shows a power of vivid portrayal the equal of which is only to be found in the finest of Scottish novels. Even their failures testify to the powers of the thought and feeling which were at variance in them. MacDonald himself would not have considered the worth of his novels as literature finally so important as their efficacy: as he saw it, the best of himself went into his poetry and fantasy. For us they will be perennially alive for their variety of human characters, and constantly fascinating, perhaps moving, as a picture of the diverse currents of a passionate spirit.

NOTES

1. The full, if biased biography of MacDonald is his son's *George MacDonald and his Wife* (1924 hereafter *GMDW*).

2. Quoted, *GMDW*, 318.

3. E.g. "The Imagination: Its Functions and its Culture" (1867) and "The Fantastic Imagination" (1893) in MacDonald, *A Dish of Orts, Chiefly Papers on the Imagination and on Shakspere* (1893). See also J. Oswald Cochran, "George MacDonald", *Methodist Magazine* (April, 1951), which quotes MacDonald as saying: " 'My business is poetry; I write novels because I have to' " (p.156).

4. *GMDW*, 44.

5. Quoted in Paladin [pseud.], *Glances at Great and Little Men* (Lauder 1890), 189.

6. Ronald MacDonald, 'George MacDonald: A Personal Note', in *From a Northern Window: Papers, Critical, Historical and Imaginative*, ed. Frederick Watson (London 1911), 67.

7. *A Dish of Orts*, 319.

8. Op. cit., 38.

9. MacDonald, Éptea Áptera, *Unspoken Sermons, Second Series* (1885), 113. See also MacDonald, *The Hope of the Gospel* (1892), 37; *A Dish of Orts*, 24-5.

10. See my *Modern Fantasy: Five Studies* (Cambridge, 1975), 62-6.

11. MacDonald, *Malcolm* (Cassell, 1927), 232.

12. See *Modern Fantasy*, 66-91.

13. All first published in three-volume form, the first three novels by Hurst and Blackett, *Malcolm* by Henry S. King. References to *Alec Forbes* and *Robert Falconer* are to the one-volume, undated editions also published by Hurst and Blackett; hereafter abbreviated as *AF* and *RF*.

14. When asked which of his novels he thought the best, MacDonald replied, " 'I had most models before me in *Robert Falconer*' " (W. Garrett Horder, "George MacDonald: A Nineteenth Century Seer", *Review of Reviews*, 32 (Oct., 1905), 362.

15. *A Dish of Orts*, 20.

16. MacDonald, Éptea Áptera, *Unspoken Sermons, Third Series* (1889), 67-8.

17. Apparently Ericson was a portrait of MacDonald's brother John Hill MacDonald, who was in fact the author of those poems of Ericson's scattered throughout *Robert Falconer* (*GMDW*, 164).

18. Houghton, *The Victorian Frame of Mind, 1830-1870* (New Haven and London, 1957), 281-7, 305-40. The *British Quarterly Review*, 47 (Jan., 1868), finds Ericson's "perhaps the most finished and masterly portrait in the whole range of George MacDonald's works", praising Ericson's heroic character (p.12).

19. Most tenuous of all, perhaps, is the way in which the plot is so manipulated that Margaret, equipped with a veil which chance or the wind keep continually falling, can also do duty as a ghost, the veiled lady of Arnstead: see *David Elginbrod* (Hurst and Blackett, n.d.), 202-3, 221, 223, 363. It is worth remarking, however, that this novel comes at times near to a symbolic mode, by which it might be possible to argue that Hugh cannot see Margaret because he is not yet 'ready' to, and that she must play the ghost because for him she has temporarily lost reality; and similarly, that Euphra's death could be seen as the outward symbol of the inner death of that in Hugh which responds to Euphra (though see p.257). There are several passages describing the external world as the extension of the spirit: see pp.169, 272, 312, 376. Euphra, as somnambulist, is described as " 'a creature of [Funkelstein's] imagination for the time, as much as any character invented' " (p.338). As the first of MacDonald's 'real-life' novels, coming shortly after *Phantastes* and during the composition of his shorter fairy-tales and his story of Celtic 'second sight', *The Portent* (1864), *David Elginbrod* could be expected to show some of the symbolic idiom so characteristic of the fantasy.

20. Robert Lee Wolff, *The Golden Key: A Study of the Fiction of George MacDonald* (New Haven, 1961), 16-17, 36-7, 59-60, 115-6, 195-8, 222-6, 283, 297-8, 304, 316-9, 361, 381.

21. Similarly reported and therefore rather unreal is the conversion of Euphra in *David Elginbrod*, 313, 347.

22. See also the spiritual transformation, on hearing just one sermon, of Thomas Wingfold's rector in MacDonald, *Paul Faber, Surgeon* (1879), I, 69-100, 140-58. 140-58.

23. *David Elginbrod*, 396. MacDonald also told Lewis Carroll that Falconer was an "ideal character" (R. L. Green, ed., *The Diaries of Lewis Carroll* (London, 1953), I, 192 (10 Feb., 1863).

24. By going into "The Wilderness" (the title of the chapter in Greville's biography which follows the account of his father's departure from his short professional life), MacDonald could remain proudly and safely isolated from the intellectual controversies of his day. For an account of this, see *Modern Fantasy*, 58-60.

25. See e.g. *Unspoken Sermons, Second Series*, 235-7; *Unspoken Sermons, Third Series*, 48, 62-9; *A Dish of Orts*, 257-8.

26. See e.g. MacDonald, *Adela Cathcart* (1864), II, 231-2 (passage used again in *A Dish of Orts*, 234); *RF*, 325-7; MacDonald, *Castle Warlock* (1882), III, 274-5; *GMDW*, 348-51, 485, 530, 543. Stairs are used symbolically in "The Golden Key" (1867), *The Princess and the Goblin* (1872), *Donal Grant* (1883) and *Lilith* (1895).

27. *A Dish of Orts*, 319.

28. See *Modern Fantasy*, 60-71, 75-83, 90-1.

FURTHER READING:

MacDonald's novels are frequently difficult to find, and have rarely been reprinted in modern editions, except for some of the more popular fantasy works. C. S. Lewis edited an anthology of George MacDonald in 1946. The main biographical and critical studies have until lately been those of Greville MacDonald, *George MacDonald and his Wife* (London, 1924), and Robert Lee Wolff, *The Golden Key: A Study of the Fiction of George MacDonald* (New Haven, 1961): Colin Manlove's own important essay on MacDonald is in *Modern Fantasy: Five Studies* (Cambridge, 1975).

MRS. OLIPHANT'S SCOTLAND: THE ROMANCE OF REALITY

by Robert and Vineta Colby

Early widowed, MARGARET OLIPHANT (1828-1897) found herself writing not just for pleasure, but to support herself, her children and other members of her family. She wrote hastily and often the haste shows through her professional and sometimes excellent prose. Sometimes, too, her writing reflects a Victorian taste which is far removed from what is popular, or even acceptable today. Some of her work, like her history of the Blackwood's publishing house, is excellent. But the shadow of poverty hung over her incessantly: "For the next three years", she wrote to a friend, ".. I can look forward to nothing but a fight *a outrance* for money: however, it is to be honestly come by. I don't care how much or how hard I work...". Her short stories are often excellent, and constitute an enjoyable introduction to her work.

The wandering Scot, patriotic and energetic, pushing his fortunes at the ends of the earth, canny and practical, yet moved always by the memory of his old home, is a familiar figure in the real life of experience and in the imaginary life of literature.

Lionel Johnson, "R. L. Stevenson",
The Academy, 3 June 1893

IN a literal sense Margaret Oliphant (1828-1897) was a "wandering Scot". She left the land of her birth at about the age of ten, returned in 1860 as a struggling young widow to live in Edinburgh for less than a year, and thereafter knew Scotland only as a visitor on business and summer holidays. No doubt a good measure of her devotion to Scotland was as practical as it was sentimental. Working throughout her life under almost incredible financial pressures and family responsibilities, she exploited her native land as marketable literary material. It was by natural right her heritage; and the post-Sir Walter Scott revival of interest in Scottish history and culture that came with Queen Victoria's choice of Balmoral for her summer retreats made it a likely source for Mrs. Oliphant to tap, turning her knowledge and experience (much of them acquired not at

first-hand but from her Scottish mother to whom she was devoted) into
articles and books.

More important—Scotland fired her imagination. Though remote, it
was alive with subjects that appealed to her. Family-minded, a dedicated
mother with a fierce loyalty to all her kin, she found in the close ties and
strong matriarchal figures of the Scottish family a source of personal as
well as artistic inspiration. Scotland stimulated her highly developed
sense of history, and most of her Scottish novels, from the early *Katie
Stewart* to the late *Kirsteen*, are set in the past. It offered colourful personalities—the strongly individualistic, ruggedly independent characters,
eccentric, sometimes comic, almost always sympathetic, that she found in
Walter Scott and John Galt. Although Mrs. Oliphant's public image was
strictly proper and conventional, we know from her letters and autobiography that she was an independent thinker who always had a lurking
admiration for non-conformists and rebels. And finally, Scotland offered
a spiritual appeal. Not herself drawn to superstition or spiritualism, she
nevertheless was fascinated by Scottish folklore and legends.

The portrait medallion of Mrs. Oliphant in St. Giles' Cathedral in
Edinburgh is inscribed: "That we may remember her genius and power
as a novelist, biographer, essayist and historian"—a tribute to her literary
fertility and versatility. In all these *genres* Scotland figures prominently
from the beginning of her career to the end. She made her debut as a
novelist at the age of twenty-one with a feigned memoir of a pious spinster
"of discreet years and small riches", *Passages in the Life of Mrs. Margaret
Maitland of Sunnyside* (1849). Her first contribution to *Blackwood's
Magazine* was *Katie Stewart* (1852), a short fictional reminiscence of the
days of Bonnie Prince Charlie. John Knox is depicted in her early
historical novel *Magdalen Hepburn: A Story of the Scottish Reformation*
(1854). From a long list spread out over four more decades such titles as
The Laird of Norlaw (1858), *A Son of the Soil* (1866), *The Minister's Wife*
(1869), *The Primrose Path: A Chapter in the Annals of the Kingdom of Fife*
(1878), *It Was a Lover and His Lass* (1883), *The Wizard's Son* (1884), *Effie
Ogilvie* (1886), *Kirsteen* (1890), and *That Little Cutty* (1898), reflect a
continuing and complex relationship to the home of her ancestors.

Furthermore, as a biographer Mrs. Oliphant produced studies of
important Scottish theologians and religious leaders—Edward Irving,
Thomas Chalmers, Principal John Tulloch. Among her historico-travel
books is *Royal Edinburgh: Her Saints, Kings, Prophets, and Poets* (1890);
and one of her last books was *A Child's History of Scotland* (1895). As a
reviewer for numerous magazines she grappled with important historical,
religious, and polemical works by Scottish writers of the order of John
Hill Burton, Dean Ramsay, John Stuart Blackie, the Rev. Robert Story,
and Lord Archibald Campbell. The most tangible evidence of her attachment to her native land was her life-long relationship with the firm of

William Blackwood and Sons, the most enduring of a career which brought her into business association (not always on the best of terms) with many other publishers, British and American. She worked for several generations of Blackwoods—as writer, reviewer, editor, manuscript reader, adviser (sometimes her advice was unsolicited but she gave it), and finally as their historian, reading proof for her *Annals of a Publishing House* (1897) on her deathbed. Her career indeed encompassed nineteenth-century literary Scotland. She was nurtured on Scott and Galt. As a girl she was tended by the physician-writer David Macbeth Moir ("Delta"). In her youth she met Christopher North. As an established writer she helped George MacDonald to get his first novel published. She interviewed Carlyle while she was at work on her biography of Edward Irving ("I bearded the lion in his den," as she phrased it). In 1849 that formidable critic Francis Jeffrey had hailed the author of *Margaret Maitland* as a fresh new voice; in her last years she in turn saluted two promising young Scottish writers—Robert Louis Stevenson and James M. Barrie.

It is, unfortunately, for quantity rather than quality that Mrs. Oliphant is remembered. Her ironic gift of facility in words, "that strange faculty of expression—which is as independent of education, knowledge, or culture as any wandering angel"[1]—which produced 125 books and innumerable periodical articles and enough income to support a dying husband, two improvident brothers, two brilliant but unlucky young sons, a nephew, a houseful of nieces and cousins, and a fairly high personal standard of living—also produced a cynical and embittered woman who was forced to acknowledge early in her life that whatever talents she had would be compromised and traded off in an unfair deal with life: "It has been my fate in a long life of production", she wrote in 1892, "to be credited chiefly with the equivocal virtue of industry, a quality so excellent in morals, so little satisfactory in art" (Preface to *The Heir Presumptive and the Heir Apparent*).

Whether we read Mrs. Oliphant as a Scottish writer or an English writer we must recognise in her work the dominating presence of what, in quite another context, Matthew Arnold called "the personal estimate." Out of her massive bibliography the work that remains the most beautiful and moving is her posthumously published *Autobiography and Letters* (1898), written and carefully filed away to pay off her debts and provide for her dependents. It is her best work because it is an expression of the heart, full of flashes of wit, shrewd intelligence, the ability to catch the essence of a personality or a scene, and her endless grace and facility of language. To read Mrs. Oliphant *into* her novels is not the futile and *naïve* exercise it would be with the major Victorian novelists who could transcend themselves in their art. Her life itself was dramatic, even tragic, offering better material than any plot she ever devised. And her imagination, if not of the highest order of creativity, was lively. She was in fact a novelist by default. She never wanted to be one; she admitted that she preferred writing biography and criticism. But she was obliged by circumstances and by the nature of the nineteenth-century novel itself (its popularity, the steady demand for it) to be a novelist, just as she was obliged to capitalise on Scotland, to squeeze every memory and impression until bone dry for whatever charm, interest and information it would offer.

Scotland gave Mrs. Oliphant a pride and distinction that otherwise, being of undistinguished family background with no education or social position, she would not have possessed. As Henry James discerningly observed in an obituary on her in his *London Notes* (August 1897): "She showed in no literary relation more acuteness than in the relation—so profitable a one as it has always been—to the inexhaustible little country which has given so much, yet has ever so much more to give, and all the romance and reality of which she had at the end of her pen. Her Scotch folk have a wealth of life, and I think no Scotch talk in fiction less of a strain to the patience of the profane".

The bulk of her fiction was not regional. The most popular of her works was a semi-sensation novel *Salem Chapel* (1863), one of a series of novels about an imaginary community, Carlingford. The several novels that constitute her obviously Trollope-inspired "Chronicles of Carlingford" are set in a provincial English town. Some of them are delightful social satire (*Phoebe Jr.*, *The Perpetual Curate*, *Miss Marjoribanks*), but they were ephemeral, quickly overshadowed by the competition of Collins, Dickens, Mrs. Henry Wood (from whose *East Lynne* she borrowed several details for *Salem Chapel*). Oddly enough, some of her Scottish novels, though written more from memory than observation and carefully tailored to the demands of the marketplace, survive the erosion of time better—perhaps because their regional details give them freshness and colour. Apart from Susan Ferrier, who until recently has been even more neglected than Mrs. Oliphant, she is the only woman novelist whose pictures of Scottish life are today remembered. Although she refreshed her memory by trips to Scotland, she was not writing out of the immediate experience that shapes the genuine regional novelist. Hers is a mixture of purely cerebral knowledge and sentiment—family pride based on a dim connection with the ancient Oliphants of Kellie in Fife,[2] who traced their lineage back to The Bruce, and a kind of misty-eyed tribute to her warm-hearted, sharp-tongued Scottish mother.

Mrs. Oliphant's Scottish novels, no less than much other Victorian fiction, could be characterised as "novels with a purpose"—a purpose never very adroitly concealed and occasionally bobbing to the surface. In one of the last, *Kirsteen*, which looks back like *Vanity Fair* to the "teens" of the century—the turbulent times between Elba and Waterloo—she refers to another altercation, "the standing feud between Scotch and

English, and the anger and jealousy with which the richer regarded the invasions of the poorer..." (Ch. XXIII). Among the ordeals endured by the courageous young heroine of this novel (who has left her native Argyllshire to seek her livelihood in London) are the taunts of her new compatriots: "Fierce jests about the Scotch who came to make their fortune off their richer neighbours, about their clannishness and their canniness, and their poverty and their pride, and still lower and coarser jibes about their supposed peculiarities ..." Whether or not Mrs. Oliphant was recalling her own experience as expatriate, she exerts one of her self-imposed functions as novelist—to set the Sassenachs straight about their kin north of the Tweed.

Actually the novels transfer to the realm of fiction a campaign she conducted intermittently through the pages of *Maga* to break down what she regarded as *naïve* stereotypes retained by English readers about Scotland and the Scottish people based on prejudice or on accounts by unreliable witnesses. "There are few subjects of study so interesting and picturesque as that of national character ... There is so much attraction in this kind of study, that everybody dabbles in it more or less", she wrote in an article in 1860, "and even harmless tourists who have had a summer's holiday in Switzerland feel themselves warranted henceforward to deliver verdicts upon the 'character of the people' ".[3] The book she was reviewing, *Reminiscences of Scottish Life and Character*, by E. B. Ramsay, Dean of Edinburgh, established her point that only one born and bred in Scotland can really speak for its "natural character", that there can be no substitute for "intercourse of people who have the gift of eyesight, without having added thereto the dangerous advantage of that traveller's pen, of which haste and exaggeration are the attendant sprites". Hard as she could be on the Cook's Tour pundit hot for "beauties" and quaintness, she was no less scornful of a scholar like the historian Buckle who, "instead of seeking his evidence in the golden Lothians, headquarters and stronghold of superstition as they are ... has found a safer and less troublesome field of observation in the British Museum", from which he documents his characterisation of the Scottish people as self-mortifying ascetics.[4] She was equally unhappy with the caricature perpetuated by hack English journalists of "a nation of adventurers, bound upon getting all the good things that come within their reach, and not at all over-scrupulous as to the means by which they obtain them ... high cheek-boned, red-haired—covetous, but enterprising ..."[5]

It may be true, as Stevenson observed, that being born in Scotland does not guarantee one's looking good in a kilt, but Mrs. Oliphant seems to have assumed that being born in Musselburgh gave her a special *cachet* as cultural ambassador from Midlothian. Populariser of learning and mediator of issues of the day to readers of *Maga* for nearly half a century (1852-1897), the role of preceptress came as easily to Mrs. Oliphant as it

had to her Mistress Margaret Maitland. Along with such recondite
interests as Italian poetry and the French monastic revival, she early
turned her attention to what she called "the national heart" of her own
people.[6]

In one of her reviews Mrs. Oliphant commended the historian John Hill
Burton for his factual approach to Scotland's past, his scrupulousness
with evidence, rejecting legend and antiquarian lore.[7] With her own
passion for fact, her sense of her audience nevertheless did not allow her
to let slip the opportunity offered by her native land as "a field of amusing
and picturesque observation first opened by Sir Walter".[8] As early as
Adam Graeme of Mossgray (1852) she was recognised for her "admirable
pictures of Scottish life and scenery".[9]

In an early historical novel, *Magdelen Hepburn*, she strains after the
picturesque in this so-called "grand scene" that begins a chapter:

> Grey and muffled in the morning mist, like some ancient mariner
> watching by the sea, North Berwick Law lowered dimly into the white
> haze which overspread the Firth. Still and dreaming by its foot, the
> fisher cottages sent up no household smoke, gave forth no household
> sounds upon the unawakened morn (Ch. VII).

Not so self-consciously grandiose and more akin to genre painting is this
setting for Kellie Mill in *Katie Stewart*:

> The mill lay at the opening of a little uncultivated, primitive-looking
> valley, through which the burn wound in many a silvery link between
> banks of bare grass, browned here and there with full sunshine which
> fell over it all the summer through, unshaded by a single tree (Ch. I).

She had an eye for landscape but was convinced that "readers prefer
people to trees", as she remarked in one of her omnibus reviews of fiction
for *Maga*. Accordingly she laid stress on the figures in the landscape.
"Few countries, perhaps, have been placed in a position so well adapted
for the development of *character*, as distinguished from merely intellectual gifts or outside customs, as this our kingdom of Scotland, ancient,
hardy, pugnacious, and poor ..." she declared in her review of Dean
Ramsay's domestic history.[10] Her Scottish novels, in line with this conviction, might well have been subtitled in a way familiar to Victorian
readers, "Illustrations of Scottish Character".

Author of a book called *Dress* (in MacMillan's *Art at Home* Series, 1876),
Mrs. Oliphant never neglected to clothe her figures carefully. We learn
what Mistress Margaret Maitland wore at her nieces' wedding: "I was
laying by my gown (it was silk, of a silvery gray colour, like the bark of a
beech tree, and was the same as Mary, my sister's—we had both got them
from Edinburgh for the occasion ...)" (Ch. XXII). Katie Stewart and her
sisters "are all dressed in a very primitive style, in home-made linen, with
broad blue and white stripes; and their frocks are made in much the same
form as the modern pinafore" (Ch. I). In her late novel *Kirsteen*, where

the heroine becomes a professional mantua maker, she early practises her skill by indulging her father's aristocratic taste for fine linen: "Kirsteen's hemming was almost invisible, so small were the stitches and the thread so delicate. She was accomplished with her needle according to the formula of that day" (Ch. VII).

Intent on her mission of educating readers to the ways of Scottish life, Mrs. Oliphant furnishes houses, calls attention to matters of etiquette, sometimes to quaint customs. Her best gifts, however, were displayed more in her appeals to the ear than to the eye. Her attempts to recover archaic speech in her historical novels could be as stilted as those of G. P. R. James whom she was undoubtedly emulating (" 'You maun e'en do your war yourself, boy, if words are the weapons ... My day of sword and buckler is well nigh ended, but none shall say of Roger of Lammerstane that he left a knight's arms for a priest's ...' ") (*Magdalen Hepburn*, Ch. I). But she could also render colloquial Scots speech with a ring authentic-sounding at least to outsiders:

> But matrimony is an honourable estate, Miss Margret ... in especial with a licentiate—I am meaning with a placed minister of the Kirk. The leddy of a minister may haud up her head with any leddy of the land, and you ken it is far otherwise with a single woman, living her lee-lane in the world ... (*Margaret Maitland*, Ch. XXII).

> He's maybe no' a' that folk could desire, this king, but he's a decent man, sae far as I can hear; and anyway, he's better than a Papish. Ony-thing's better than a Papish. (*Katie Stewart*, Ch. XXII)

> No that I mean to say I believe in fate ... though there is little doubt in my mind that what happens is ordained. I couldna tell why, for my part, though I believe in the fact—for most things in life come to nothing, and the grandest train of causes produce nae effect whatso-ever; that's my experience. (*A Son of the Soil*, Ch. VI)

Such externals help to vivify Mrs. Oliphant's people and scenes, but her main interest was in personifying "Scottish National Character". She manages to do this at times even in her polemical journalism, especially when she domesticates Anglo-Scottish relations—poor Scotland "always dwelling next door to the rich brother, who vexed her soul with osten-tatious display of his greater wealth", until she is compelled to fall back on "the pride and brag of a poor gentlewoman wrapping herself in her pinched cloak in self-defending bitterness, while her plump neighbour laughs beside her, full and lavish, mocking the pomp of poverty".[11] Else-where she likens the uneasy union of the two countries to a marriage in which the husband, while loving his wife, enjoys casting aspersions on her ancestors and relatives.[12]

Largely defences of Scotland's people and traditions, Mrs. Oliphant's

Scottish novels are not belligerent in tone but tend to make virtue out of necessity, stressing the strength of character that has grown out of the poverty and inferior position to which, she believed, the Scottish nation had been traditionally reduced. What survived and endured was Scottish piety, pride, and resourcefulness, centered most strikingly in the institutions of the Family and the Church, representing a kind of collective Scottish consciousness exemplified. "How real, how living, are our old fathers and mothers in their old Scotland yonder, so much poorer a Scotland than it was in our days!" she wrote in *Maga*. "We cannot imitate them; but the only way to preserve the distinct character of our country, as of every other, lies in the truth, reality, and spontaneous nature of individual life".[13]

One of the "distinct character" types she brings to life is the Scottish spinster, to whom she pays special tribute in her essay on "Scottish National Character":

> In no other region has the genus 'old-maid' developed itself so notably ... These were not the gentle souls of modern romance, benign sufferers from some youthful disappointment, spending their placid lives in recollection of a lost love ... So far from conceiving themselves set apart into such a mild twilight of retirement by their unwedded condition, this class of celibates behaved themselves with great energy and emphasis in the world, and have worked their reminiscences into the history of their time with a force and clearness not to be surpassed.[14]

In a humbler sphere are Marg'ret Brown, the stoical, resourceful servant who comforts Kirsteen Douglas in her family distress and stands by her during her "exile" in London, and Marg'ret's sister Jean, who employs Kirsteen in her London shop. But the prototype of the spinster-matron in Mrs. Oliphant's fiction is Mistress Margaret Maitland, an old maid by choice, content with her "lone tabernacle at Sunnyside".[15] She has refused one suitor because his principles were not of the strictest. (Mistress Maitland comes from a clerical family, her father, brother, and nephew all ministers.) A far remove from "the gentle souls of modern romance, benign sufferers from some youthful disappointment, spending their placid lives in recollection of a lost love", this spinster heroine is distinguished for her mental energy, spark and independence. She has had some formal education, befitting her social rank, "with a Miss Scrymgeour, a discreet gentlewoman, who kept a genteel school for young ladies, to learn divers things that were thought needful in those days, and also how to behave myself in polite society", but adds candidly that "I aye found the breeding of the Manse of Pasturelands to serve me better than what I got in the school at Edinburgh" (Ch. I). She seems to lean heavily on native wisdom in her capacity as mentor to the young (in the tradition of the didactic novels of the time), and she guides her two young nieces into suitable marriages.

The wise Scottish spinster had her fictional uses and her charms, but essentially Mrs. Oliphant's sympathies were with the matron-mother: "Capable women, unswayable by circumstances, queens of their position—imperative Spartan mothers, sparing of indulgence, willing their own will and having it ... knowing neither age nor weakness when succour was needed, brave to do all and bear all".[16] In her *Autobiography* she was to memorialise her own mother, who had kept the household together, as "all in all". Significantly Mistress Maitland recalls of her mother: "Truly she was of a most uncommon spirit, being more like a lanthorn holding a great light than any other thing; for she was gifted with a mind that drew others to it, as the loadstone that bairns play with draws the needle ..." (Ch. I).

The mother keeps the fires burning in Mrs. Oliphant's Scottish households where fathers tend to be either absent or silent. Katie Stewart's mother,

> a little fair-haired woman, rather stout nowadays, but a beauty once, and with the pretty short-gown, held in round her neat waist by a clean linen apron, and her animated face, looked yet exceedingly well, and vindicated completely her claim to be the fountain-head and original of the beauty of her children (*Katie Stewart*, Ch. I).

She is "absolute sovereign of Kellie Mill". (There is a father named John, but "muckle he kens about the role o' a household", Mrs. Stewart says [Ch. VIII].) As quintessential mother, she upholds the traditional rural virtues. She is torn between family pride and ambition for her daughter as she confronts Lady Betty Erskine who has invited Katie to be part of the retinue at Kellie Castle:

> "You see, my lady, we have nae occasion to be indebted to onybody for the upbringing of our bairns. My man, I am thankful to say, is a decent man, and a well-doing, and if we're spared, we'll have something to leave to them that come after us; but I dinna dispute the advantage of being brocht up at the Castle. The Castle's ae thing, the mill's anither ...".

However, she lays down her conditions firmly:

> "She mustna be learned to lightly her ain friends—they're a creditable kind no better than ... her ain sisters. She's to come to the mill aye when she can win, to keep her frae pride she has nae right to ... And she's to get to the kirk ... She's at no hand to gang down to Pittenweem, to the English chapel; I couldna suffer that ... And she's to get nae questions but the right question book. It's easy bending the minds of bairns, and I canna have her turned to the English way, my lady" (Ch. II).

An especially memorable figure is Jeannie Campbell, a farmer's wife, mother of the idealistic young minister Colin of *A Son of the Soil*. Unlike some of the Spartan matriarchs who dominate Mrs. Oliphant's hearths, she is outwardly delicate, "gentle-voiced", with "soft, dark, beaming eyes ... the softest pink flush coming and going over her face ...", but she is buttressed from within by her strong will and her faith. This,"mistress of Ramore Farm" encourages her son's intellectual aspirations: "I hear there's some grand schools in England ... no that they're to compare wi' Edinburgh", she inquires at the beginning of the novel of a wealthy young friend of Colin's who has been to Eton; "You'll be at ane o' the great schools, I suppose? I aye like to learn what I can when there's ony opportunity. I would like my Colin to get a' the advantages, for he's well worthy o' a good education, though we're rather out of the way of it here" (Ch. I). Colin goes on to university (first to Glasgow, later to Oxford), with the predictable result that he becomes filled with immortal longings somehow not satisfied in Ramore. Most touching is Mrs. Campbell's perplexity, "pondering with a troubled countenance upon this new aspect of her boy's life. Amid the darkness of the world outside, this tender woman sat in the sober radiance of her domestic hearth, surrounded and enshrined by light; but she was not like Hero on the tower" (Ch. XII). The greatest upset to her is Colin's momentary doubt as to his vocation for the ministry; and she tries to call him back to a fundamental faith: "Eh, Colin, sometime ye'll think better ... after a' our pride in you and our hopes! ... It's mair honour to serve God than to get on in this world ... It's maybe nothing but a passing fancy—but it's no what I expected to hear from any bairn of mine ...". (Ch. XII).

"What life, what force, what a flood of vital power!" proclaimed Mrs. Oliphant of the daughters of Scotland, a country noteworthy, she contended, for women "not of genius but of character".[17] Women tend to dominate her novels, but to at least one class of men—the clergy, and especially the Scottish clergy—she allotted a share of sensitivity and wisdom. In one of her essay-reviews she observes that whereas the French curé and the Italian monk figure frequently in fiction and travel diaries, "the Scotch minister has, almost up to the present time, been a personage almost as unknown in England as is the un-polemical priest of a Catholic country, unfretted by heresy, and calm in his own established rights and duties".[18] Here she identifies another "distinct character" who emerges in her fiction.

The minister as a presence in Scottish society is related to larger religious controversies in which Mrs. Oliphant became engaged through her journalism. "There is a great deal of bad taste, to use the lightest expression, in the attitude assumed by English Churchmen generally towards the Church of Scotland", she complained in one of her reviews in *Maga*.[19] On religious as well as secular questions Mrs. Oliphant acted as something of a national apologist. The Church of Scotland, in particular, was a subject of lively interest during the 1850s and '60s when the best of her Scottish novels were written, the Free Kirk movement of 1843 having taken place within the recent memory of many of her readers. In *The Minister's Wife*, published in 1869 but looking back to the time when Edward Irving's influence had been strong, she takes her readers inside a Kirk Session, which she reminds them was "the vestry, the guardians, the churchwardens of a Scotch parish all in one . . . And at the period of which we write, before any great rent had been made in the Church of Scotland, its authority was real and considerable" (I, Ch. XI). Earlier on, Mistress Maitland had made veiled reference to this "rent", her own family having been involved:

> . . . it is not my purpose to speak of the solemn and great things of the Kirk in a simple history like this . . . But my brother, the Minister, and Claud, my nephew, and many of their brethren . . . left their temporal providing at the appointed time, and came out with the pure and free Kirk into the wilderness; for who would heed to green pastures and still waters, if the light of the Lord's countenance was lifted away? (Ch. XXII).

Her nephew Claud adopts an ecumenical attitude towards this disruption (echoing, one suspects, Mrs. Oliphant's own): "Certainly I hold leaving the church, and leaving the establishment, to be two very different things; but the servants of the church are not confined to one locality. I may serve my Master as well in another place" (Ch. XXII).

With *A Son of the Soil* a new generation has superseded the old:

> When Sunday morning dawned upon the Holy Loch, it did not shine upon that pretty unanimous church-going so well known to the history of the past. The groups from the cottages took different ways . . . The reign of opinion and liking was established in the once primitive community. Half of the people ascended the hillside to the Free Church, while the others wound down the side of the Loch to the Kirk, which had once accommodated the whole parish (Ch. III).

Through the hero Colin Campbell, who comes of age in this period of transition, a part of "the advanced party, the Young Scotland of his time", we get one of Mrs. Oliphant's most searching fictional inquiries into the nature of the minister's vocation—its conflicts, frustrations, and rewards.

Son of a farming family, poor but proud, Colin is the archetypal minister of the Church of Scotland as Mrs. Oliphant represents it—humble in origin and of the people.[20] With his sensitivity and idealism, his ambition to "be a prince in his own country without, at the same time, following anything for his own glory or advantage", he answers to her characterisation of its ministry as "pervasive and profound . . . [in] its influence—working, as every good agency works, not always to the glory of the instrument, but through many disappointments and trials, to the benefit and improvement of the country".[21] Young Colin has his share of "dis-

appointments and trials", including a romantic infatuation for an aristocrat who spurns him for one of her own class, and a certain disenchant-
ment with his home parish after travel to Italy and a taste of the intellectual atmosphere of Balliol College. Mainly, like a number of Mrs.
Oliphant's young clergymen, he is beset with doubts as to his calling. "If I
cannot bear the yoke conscientiously I cannot bear it at all", he protests in
a moment of pique to his sceptical friend Lauderdale; "... and as for
ambition ... what does it mean?—a country church, and two or three
hundred ploughmen to criticise me, and the old wives to keep in good
humour, and the young ones to drink tea with—is that work for a man?"
(Ch. XLVI). His greatest trial derives from the very democratic nature of
the Church of Scotland—his being subjected to "the bar of the
presbytery". He makes his initial appearance in the pulpit in the parish of
Afton "not to instruct the congregation, but to be inspected, watched,
judged, and finally objected to" (Ch. XLV). At a crucial moment he is
struck with a "sudden sense of incapacity", preaching his sermon "with
pale lips and a heart out of which all the courage seemed to have died for
the moment" (Ch. XLVI).

Eventually Colin weathers this crisis. At first distrusted by his congregation for his lofty ideas and his English university background, he is
finally accepted, and settles into the quiet round of a rural ministry. It is
possible to read Colin's history as a tale of disillusionment—his
discovery, as the narrator puts it, of "the impossibility of the fundamental
romance which at the bottom of their hearts most people like to believe
in". But at the same time we are left to infer also that Colin's self-doubts,
questionings, and spiritual pains (and a less than happy marriage) may
have made him all the more fit for his calling in a religious society grown
unsure of itself but still in need of guidance. "You'll no make Scotland of
your way of thinking, Colin", his friend and tutor consoles him, "but
you'll make it worth her while to have brought ye forth for a' that" (Ch.
XLV). After his ordeal Colin discovers that "he had begun to stretch out
hands for his tools almost without knowing it, and to find that, after all, a
man in a pulpit, although he has two flights to ascend to it, has a certain
power in his hand" (Ch. XLVI). Mrs. Oliphant herself concluded her
article "Clerical Life in Scotland": "The pastor of the poor, himself not
rich, may link the peasants in the highest bonds of Christian friendship
and kindness with the great and gifted".

With fictional heroes like Colin Campbell and Arthur Vincent of *Salem
Chapel*, Mrs. Oliphant came as close as ever she could to portraying a
complex, conflicted character caught in the struggle between intellect and
emotion. As a novelist she almost but never quite succeeded in creating a
tragic hero. But in a single work of biography, her *Life of Edward Irving,
Minister of the National Scotch Church, London. Illustrated by his Journals
and Correspondence* (2 vols., 1862), she achieved what so much of her

fiction aspired to—a portrait of a noble Scot self-betrayed by his idealism. Her heart, she once confessed to her publisher William Blackwood, had "sickened" at the traffic of novel writing, the formulas and conventions that the literary marketplace and the endless urgent needs of her family demanded.[22] Criticism, literary history, and biography especially engaged and stimulated her mind as fiction never could, and *The Life of Edward Irving* is by far the best of her books.[23] No small measure of its success is its Scottish-ness. Here truly Mrs. Oliphant went back to her national roots, not in an artificial reconstruction of the historical past, but in a labour of conscientious research, interviewing witnesses who had known Irving, including Henry Drummond, a founder of the Irvingite Church who had commissioned the book in 1858, and Jane and Thomas Carlyle, friends of his youth. In search of letters, journals, documents, she travelled to Rosneath where Irving's friend Dr. Robert Story had lived, and she visited every Scottish and English scene with which he had been connected.

Out of all this effort came not only a colourful portrait of her subject but a vivid, sensitive picture of the remote provincial Scotland from which Irving had emerged. With more life than her fictional Carlingford or Afton, she created the real rural Annan of 1792—"this little neutral-coloured community, living in a little round of social gaieties" (Ch. I); and the Kirkcaldy where, brilliant and ardent, young Irving preached his first sermons to simple, puzzled parishioners: "The people listened doubtfully to those thunder-strains which echoed over their heads . . . 'He had ower mickle gran'ner,' the good people said, with disturbed looks" (Ch. IV). As Irving moves on to Glasgow and then to London, winning more converts, stirring up controversy and notoriety, Scotland looms as his nemesis:

> Wherever he went, crowds waylaid his steps, turning noble country houses into impromptu temples and seizing the stray moments of his leisure with jealous eagerness. His own Church was crowded to overflowing at those services which were least exclusively congregational. Amid all this his own eyes, burning with life and ardour, turned not to fashion or the great world, not to society or the givers of fame, but were bent with anxious gaze upon the "grey city of the North," where the Scotch Assembly gathered. ... (Ch. XVI).

When finally in 1833 Irving's preaching the identity of Christ's nature with all human nature and the practice of glossolalia in his congregation were declared heresy—on charges, among others, that he had allowed his services to be interrupted "by persons not being either ministers or licentiates of the Church of Scotland"—it was by the Presbyters of his own church in Annan. Mrs. Oliphant rises to dramatic heights she never achieved in her fiction as she describes him walking out of this church in which he had been baptized and ordained—

through crowds of confused and wondering spectators ... contemporaries of his own, who had watched his wonderful progress with a thrill of pride and amaze ... to this bleak afternoon of March, slowly shadowing, minute by minute, upon those clouds of eager faces growing pale in the darkness, what a brilliant interval, what a wonderful difference! (Ch. XVIII)

A broken man, Irving did not long survive his downfall. Mrs. Oliphant measured him sympathetically but realistically as a man who "looked for suffering on an heroic scale, not the harassing repetitions of Presbyterial prosecution" (Ch. XII), a tragic figure reduced to failure by his self-delusion: "Unconsciously his thoughts elevated themselves, and grew into fuller development; unconsciously he assumed in his own person the priestly attitude, and felt himself standing between God and the people" (Ch. XII). The delusion was perhaps more romantic than theological or philosophical, a blindness that Mrs. Oliphant significantly links with a word of Scottish origin, *glamour*, the magic that transforms those over whom it is cast:

Irving had so much of the "celestial light" in his eyes, that he unconsciously assigned to everybody he addressed a standing-ground in some degree equal to his own. The "vision splendid" attended him not only through his morning course, but throughout all his career. The light around him never faded into the light of common day. ...
This *glamour* in his eyes had other effects, melancholy enough to contemplate; but even though it procured him trouble and suffering, I cannot find it in my heart to grudge Irving a gift so noble (Ch. XII).

Realistic and clear-eyed as she could be, Mrs. Oliphant herself retained a lingering love for the romance of Scotland. The terrible blows of her own life, the deaths of her husband and her children, the grinding schedule of hard work that never produced as much money as she needed, the grim realisation that with all her talents and efforts she would never rank as a first-rate writer—these were endurable only because she was sustained with a belief in what she called "the Unseen". She was not, however, a mystic, nor did she seek comfort in any of the flourishing spiritual movements of her day. Her stories of the supernatural range from bland dream visions like *The Little Pilgrim in the Unseen* to the sublimity of "A Beleaguered City". In between are ghost stories like "The Secret Chamber" and "The Open Door", and novels like *The Wizard's Son* which draw on Scottish folk traditions.

In one of her best ghost stories, "The Library Window", she conjures up a fable of the life of the imagination out of an atmosphere of Scottish glamour. A late story (first published in *Maga* in 1896), it is told in retrospect by an elderly widow returning to her homeland after years abroad and recalling a strange episode from her youth. Delicate in health, bookish and shy, the girl is visiting with an aunt in St. Rule's, surrounded by a circle of genteel elderly Scots folk. She spends hours staring out of the window at the College Library across the road and gradually becomes fascinated by a strangely illuminated window there through which she sees a man writing busily. The vision is neither morbid nor frightening. Rather it possesses a curious kind of fascination that she associates with the hazy lights of the long Scottish midsummer evenings—"daylight, yet it is not day, and there is a quality in it which I cannot describe, it is so clear, as if every object was a reflection of itself"—and the peculiar glinting lights of an old diamond ring worn by one of her aunt's guests, a sybilline figure, Lady Carnbee. Of course there is no window and there is no writing man. And the girl's aunt, alarmed by her fantasies, sends her back home. But for years the vision haunts her, the man appears to her in crowds "as a face I knew", but then vanishes.

There is no resolution, no dramatic climax, in "The Library Window". The writing man remains anonymous, and we never even learn what he was writing—certainly not poems, the narrator concludes, "because no one could possibly write poems like that, straight off, without pausing for a word or a rhyme". Such a writer could only have been one gifted (or perhaps cursed) with the facility of words, "the equivocal virtue of industry", that marked the writer Margaret Oliphant herself. But she was also the ageing widow telling the story, recalling her early life in Scotland, the enchantment of which haunted her through all her years as "a wandering Scot".

NOTES:

1. From her novel *The Athelings, or the Three Gifts* (1857)—relating to Agnes, the literary daughter of the family, presumably modelled on herself.
2. See her story "The Heirs of Kellie: an Episode of Family History", *Blackwood's Magazine* 159 (March, 1896), 325-62.
3. "Scottish National Character", *Blackwood's Magazine* 87 (June, 1860), 715.
4. "Scotland and Her Accusers", *Blackwood's Magazine* 90 (Sept., 1861), 274.
5. *op. cit.*, 267.
6. *op. cit.*, 244.
7. "The History of Scotland", *Blackwood's Magazine* 101 (March, 1867), 317; rev. of Burton's *The History of Scotland from Agricola's Invasion to the Revolution of 1688.*
8. "Scottish National Character", 722.
9. *Morning Post* (as quoted in advertisement at end of Vol. I of *The Minister's Wife* [1869]).
10. "Scottish National Character", 717.
11. *Ibid.*
12. "Scotland and Her Accusers", 267.
13. *op. cit.*, 731.
14. *op. cit.*, 721.

15. The full title of this novel suggests a female counterpart of Lockhart's *Some Passages in the Life of Mr Adam Blair* (1822), but its technique of impersonation and its autobiographical mode hearken back to the fictitious "annals" of John Galt and to David Macbeth Moir's *The Life of Mansie Wauch*.

16. "Scottish National Character", 722.

17. *Ibid.*

18. "Clerical Life in Scotland", *Macmillan's Magazine* 8 (July, 1863), 208; rev. of *Memoir of the Life of the Reverend Robert Story*, by his son, Robert H. Story; and *Life of the Reverend James Robertson*, by the Reverend A. H. Charteris.

19. "New Books", *Blackwood's Magazine* 112 (Aug., 1872), 203-8, referring to *Lectures on the History of the Church of Scotland*, delivered in Edinburgh by Dean Stanley. Here Mrs. Oliphant commends Dean Stanley for one of the very few tolerant and sympathetic views of this church expressed by an Anglican.

20. "Clerical Life in Scotland", 208. Some details of Colin's characterisation seem to be derived from the biography of the Reverend James Robertson, one of those reviewed in this article. Robertson was the son of a farmer, and was educated at the University of Glasgow.

21. *Ibid.*

22. Blackwood MSS 4650, May 4 [1896].

23. One redoubtable witness is Thomas Carlyle who, according to Jane Carlyle's report, said that the book "was worth whole cartloads of Mulocks, and Brontёs, and Things of that sort ... Nothing has so taken him by the heart for years as this biography" (*Autobiography and Letters*, 186).

BIBLIOGRAPHICAL NOTE:

Because there is no standard uniform edition of Mrs. Oliphant's works, some of which in fact are not available to us in the United States except in periodicals, we have confined our citations from the novels and *The Life of Edward Irving* to chapter rather than page references. One exception is the posthumous *Autobiography and Letters of Mrs. M. O. W. Oliphant*, Arranged and Edited by Mrs. Harry Coghill. Edinburgh: Blackwood, 1898; reprinted (facsimile), with an Introduction by Q. D. Leavis. Leicester: University of Leicester Press, 1974, to which we have given page references. Additional material on Mrs. Oliphant's life and career is drawn from her letters to her publisher Blackwood in the National Library of Scotland in Edinburgh (here cited as Blackwood MSS) and from our *The Equivocal Virtue: Mrs. Oliphant and the Victorian Literary Marketplace*. Hamden, Conn.: Archon Books, 1966.

PARABLES OF ADVENTURE: THE DEBATABLE NOVELS OF ROBERT LOUIS STEVENSON[1]

by Alistair Fowler

ROBERT LOUIS STEVENSON (1850-94) is arguably the finest prose stylist in either English or Scottish literature. He began as an essayist and travel writer, with *An Inland Voyage* (1878); *Edinburgh: Picturesque Notes* and *Travels with a Donkey* (1879); *Virginibus puerisque* (1881); *Familiar Studies* (1882); and *The Silverado Squatters* (1883). But his first really popular book was an adventure story, *Treasure Island* (1883). Subsequently he wrote in a great variety of kinds, some of which he invented or mixed creatively. His *oeuvre* can only crudely be classified as: historical "romances" or novels: *Kidnapped* (1886), *The Black Arrow* (1888), *The Master of Ballantrae* (1889), *Catriona* (1893), and the unfinished *St. Ives* (1897); symbolic light romances or tales: *New Arabian Nights* (1882), *More New Arabian Nights* and *Prince Otto* (1885), and *The Wrong Box* (1889); a picaresque romance, *The Wrecker* (1892); psychological tales such as *Dr. Jekyll and Mr. Hyde* (1886); and numerous other novellas and short stories, some unfinished. In 1887 he left Europe for the U.S.A., and then for the South Seas, where he eventually settled, in Samoa (1890). There he enjoyed a period of mature production, interrupted by journalism and political activity on behalf of the Samoans. *The Ebb-Tide* (1894) belongs to a group of late fictions that includes *The Beach of Falesá* (1893); *St Ives*; many of the Fables; and *Weir of Hermiston*, an unfinished novel published posthumously and sometimes called his best work. Stevenson may perhaps be regarded as an *ur*-existentialist and early modern writer.

Stevenson's position in relation to the Victorian literary canon seems to be in rapid movement. The enquirer who consults *Victorian Fiction: A Guide to Research*[2] will find something odd. That is, he will find nothing. Disraeli's and Bulwer-Lytton's inclusion implies a widely flung net. It is fine enough for Moore. And yes, it has caught Wilkie Collins and Kingsley and Gissing and Reade. But not Stevenson. Worse, as if to justify the lapse of taste, a Preface explains that "Stevenson has been omitted, in spite of his influence on romantic fiction, because his adult novels are few and of debatable rank". I am not sure that I understand how "adult" is meant here. True, Stevenson spread his efforts among several popular kinds. But *Victorian Fiction*, influential as it is, exemplifies a common silliness about these. The error of demoting Stevenson's fiction to a 'debatable rank' arises from a confusion of evaluative and generic criteria. Generic hierarchies are still recognised in practice, however strenuously execrated in theory. And, because he wrote in kinds thought low, Stevenson has been fired from the canon.

But Constable's connoisseurs (who always think the art is already done) have blundered again. An increasingly educated liking for stories gathers strength with us. Jamesian critics may not all have quite learnt, yet, to rise to all of the Master's immense, really quite matchless admiration of the different art of Stevenson. But those who find high quality in Hawthorne and Melville should experience no difficulty in recognising the genius of Stevenson's romantic, un-novelistic stories. This is not an occasion to investigate differences between the novelistic genres and what James and Stevenson called the "romance". We need only recall that features admirable in the one group of kinds may be positively undesirable in the other. In speaking of romances and tales, questions of character development, or of authorial omniscience, will often be crassly impertinent. Who would be so generically idiotic as to question the probability of Poe's *MS. Found in a Bottle*? Yet to be less idiotic about stories that are not novels may call for critical methods of a new sort. We need a way, in short, of talking critically about effects of pure narrative. At present we only read and enjoy them, or read over and miss.

The need is nowhere greater than with Stevenson, who cultivated the forms of narration as an abstract art. What pleasures such an art can give seems to be little understood. E. M. Forster, who detested story as a tapeworm sapping a novel's life, expresses the common view of them, when he describes the storyteller keeping an audience of shock-heads (fatigued by contending against woolly rhinoceros) awake with suspense. "What would happen next?"[3] Suspense is certainly common in the adventure. Thus, even a reader tired by life's rhinoceros-race will want to know the result of the duel between St. Ives and the giant Goguelet in their pitch-dark prison-shed. But Stevenson's art has less to do with suspense than with surprise: with surprising turns of events: what Chesterton called "zigzag energy of action, as quick as the crooked lightning".[4] Not the least element of surprise is verisimilitude of detail. In the present instance, we have the invention of duelling weapons (not easy in a prisoner of war camp); the grim practicality of stripping to obviate bloodstains on clothes; and the unforeseen but appropriate staunchness of Goguelet, who saves St. Ives by his soldierly silence. A defeated duellist is generally seen to his carriage and out of the plot; we have to go to Tolstoi for the partial exception of Dólokhov.[5] But Goguelet—an authentic Stevensonian touch, this—lingers on with his castration-wound, leaching away our sympathy for St. Ives. The reader may feel suspense. (Will Goguelet talk?) But he may feel more strongly an unlooked-for respect for the hateful noble brute; together with a correspondent aesthetic surprise. In other words, suspenseful narrative serves as a medium of art, to be modulated, articulated, plastically formed. The narrative sequence, for example, may be ordered mimetically, even in so casual a work as *St. Ives*. Thus, the escape route from Edinburgh Castle is kept secret altogether, until the time comes to use it.[6] And the first mention that St. Ives started his climb without thought falls when he is already dangling by his hands: "I had never the wit to see it till that moment" (19.100). Again, St. Ives may be an unconvincing Frenchman. But would a truly French character quite have served Stevenson's purpose? He meant to lead us up the beaten path of patriotic British adventure, so as to trap us into a moralised adventure of psychology. The country of *St. Ives*, in fact, is on inward borders. It is a story taken up with the crossing and recrossing of lines of nationality, legality, and moral and sexual loyalty: a frequent theme is sympathy with the enemy, even such an enemy as the dark double Viscount de St. Yves. So fully moralised does the narrative become that the smallest practical detail may turn out to have a farther implication. St. Ives, about to descend by rope, offers himself with the gallows bravery "Here is the criminal". Boy's Own pluck? Not to the adult reader who thinks St. Ives guilty of a form of murder. He had better have hung in a noose, in more senses than one.

Most kinds of novel have a rule governing the selection of events, which might be called the constraint of the ordinary. It is often confused with the criterion of probability. But extraordinary events must occur sometimes; indeed, Aristotle even allows probable impossibilities. These would not do in novels. In romances, however, the unusual has its place and function: events, atmosphere, setting and other features compose a different world, as free as our own from the determinism of the ordinary. Yet Stevenson's romances also have their flavours of fact. He is indeed something of a specialist in unusual probabilities; a master at the admixture of likelihood beyond the ordinary. Only a Stevenson would make his duellists use authentic unscrewed scissor-halves lashed to wands with resined twine—"the twine coming I know not whence, but the resin from the green pillars of the shed, which still sweated from the axe" (19.47). Defoe (an early model of Stevenson's) might have managed the resin; hardly the scissors.[7] This is a classical art, delicately balancing and blending high tones of the unusual with a drab *repoussoir* of unmarvellous commonplaces. Only by working a long enough passage across mundane particulars—"the sun was setting with some wintry pomp" (19.201)—can Stevenson persuade us to accept St. Ives's precocious balloon escape courtesy Lunardi, or the encounter with Scott (that so bold superimposition of fictional worlds, which recalls the sighting of a huge eagle *en route* to still-suffering Prometheus, in the *Argonautica*). In fine, Stevenson's freedom from the constraint of the ordinary is far from unconditioned. Besides obeying formal patterns, as when St. Ives's last ascent answers his first descent, it also responds to introspective intimations. Indeed, the liberty seems to be taken in the interest of these. Stevenson's better stories often have the implication of an inner, secondary narrative. The common notion that his work grew away from childish romances towards "adult" novels (*Weir of Hermiston* is usually cited) oversimplifies the contrasted genres, and falsifies both the chronology and the direction of the actual development.

To the last, Stevenson's artistic development was less a progression of literary kinds than a search for fuller psychological mimesis. And from the first, he had used a wide range of forms as material for an art already idiosyncratic. There was never any such thing, for him, as "mere adventure". Even *Treasure Island* (to take an adverse example, serialised in a boy's magazine)[7] reaches out after very special narrative and descriptive effects. These Chesterton (pp. 42-3) has percipiently connected with Stevenson's fondness for the abrupt angularity and contrast of woodcuts. It is an eighteenth-century clarity: "just as all the form can best be described as clean-cut, so all the colour is conspicuously clear and bright". And besides this aesthetic shaping there are firm moral patterns; to which, however, the story answers with deeper questionings, less clear, less bright.

Not that it answers by offering much fine moral texture of characterisation. The narrator, Jim Hawkins, is of an age that easily excuses amoral externality: so easily that a reader may not notice when his inadequate moral standpoint is undermined. But to call *Treasure Island* a children's book without qualification, without acknowledging its deeper expressions, would be unthinkable. At least, it would be unthinkable if Robert Kiely had not done it. Professor Kiely accepts Jim's narrative on its own opaque terms, as a tale told by a child, signifying nothing, relating "an invigorating and harmless adventure".[8] Its whole pleasure is in the external conflict: "To try to speak seriously of good or evil in *Treasure Island* is almost as irrelevant as attempting to assign moral value in a baseball game, even though ... enjoying the contest involves a temporary if arbitrary preference for one side or the other" (p. 78). Morton Zabel, on the other hand, has Jim gaining stature as a mature character; risking his integrity to share in Silver's cunning; and learning the reality of manhood's battle.[9] There may be insufficient surface morality for this view, however, to carry much weight. Edwin Eigner, moreover, has questioned whether Stevenson (of all people) can have represented the goal of maturity in quite so favourable a light. May not the story's conclusion hint, chillingly, that to reject Silver is to exchange vitality for inglorious retirement? This note, of Jim's parting youth and separation from Silver, belongs not to the official theme but to a second subject, more intimate.

Every critic of *Treasure Island* has to begin by noticing the limitations of kind and Stevenson's zestful acceptance of them. But the disclaimers of "My First Book"—"a story for boys; no need for psychology or fine writing" (5.xxii)—need to be read together with the more considered account in "A Humble Remonstrance": "The author, for the sake of circumstantiation and because he was himself more or less grown up, admitted character, within certain limits, into his design; but only within certain limits" (12.216). A farther limitation (which Henry James remarked)[10] arises from our relative ignorance of the psychology of the Spanish Main. As Stevenson says in his defence, however, the boy is his own younger self, who searched for treasure, although not "in the fleshly sense". Within these limitations, the story deals with deep and night-marish experience—the emergence into the light of day, in fact, of Jim's fearful dreams. For "the seafaring man with one leg" turns out to be smiling Long John Silver. So far as this dream narrative is concerned, criticism may be said to begin with Wallace Robson's "The Sea Cook".[11] Professor Robson (p. 62) has given an admirable account of the increasingly unpleasant and progressively mutilated antifathers: Billy Bones, one sabre-cut; Black Dog, two fingers; Pew, blind. We can only be convinced by his tracing of "a line of candidate foster-fathers who constitute Jim's social relations in the story", beginning with Bones, whose death affects Jim more than that of his own father (p. 60). Our single hesitation concerns the status of the analysis: is it perhaps so penetrating as to go through the canvas of the picture Stevenson meant to paint? True, only the ignorant claim to know how far man's mysterious consciousness may extend. But is it conceivable that Stevenson should have been at all aware of the oedipal content of dreams and fantasies?

This question is very nearly answered by Stevenson's remarkable essay "A Chapter on Dreams" (written at Saranac and printed in *Scribner's Magazine*, Jan. 1888). Here he traces the genesis of his stories through dreams and half-waking fantasies. His unconscious faculties, which he calls "brownies" or lubber fiends, "do one-half my work for me while I am fast asleep, and in all human likelihood, do the rest for me as well, when I am wide awake and fondly suppose I do it for myself" (12.246). To illustrate he tells a dream of almost unbroken narrative coherence. (Its accessibility to interpretation, however, is equally notable.) He dreamed that he was the son of a bad-tempered father, and "had lived much abroad, on purpose to avoid his parent". Returning home, he found his father remarried to a young wife "supposed to suffer cruelly". Because of the marriage—"as the dreamer indistinctly understood"—father and son met on a desolate shore, and the son "struck down the father dead" (12.240-1). Most of the dream is taken up with the subsequent guilt, which works at cross purposes with the stepmother's misunderstood but at last openly declared passion for her son. Stevenson had realised, on waking, "that in this spirited tale there were unmarketable elements" (12.244). Unmarketable, that is, because of taboos that would lead to suppression—the actual fate of *The Travelling Companion* (an earlier attempt on the theme of *Dr. Jekyll and Mr. Hyde*), returned by an editor as 'indecent'. Stevenson himself, who was no Carus or Charcot, may have thought of his fantasies in moral terms. But—and this is my point—he allowed them within the pale of responsible consciousness. Instead of banishing them censoriously, he evaded his own censor to rehearse them carefully and explore their "crafty artifice" (12.245). Dreams had once taken him to "a certain doctor"; but now Stevenson could look at the 'spirited tales' of his unconscious with humorous detachment—perhaps even (who knows?) with a little understanding.

But we should distinguish between a psychoanalytic approach (tempting, but not my present idea) and a heuristic use of biographical information. The latter approaches the inner narrative of a meant fiction. For example, "A Chapter on Dreams", with its case history of childhood nighthags and adolescent repeated dreams, may encourage attention to the dreams in *Treasure Island*, not least in its fine closure: "Oxen and wain-ropes would not bring me back again to that accursed island; and the worst dreams that ever I have are when I hear the surf booming about its coasts, or start upright in bed, with the sharp voice of Captain Flint still ringing in my ears: 'Pieces of eight! Pieces of eight!' " Associated with his capture at the stockade, these are to Jim words of fear—"The name of Captain Flint ... carried a great weight of terror" (5.40-1). Of course, fear is a generic feature of the adventure; as Stevenson himself framed its rule, "danger is the matter with which this class of novel deals; fear, the passion with which it idly trifles" (12.216). But in this case the fear, which occasions a repeated dream, may be thought particularly deep and sustained. Fear of what, we may ask? Pirates, obviously; unpredictable killers; or, as Robson puts it in connection with the earlier dream of Silver, "the castrated father raging for revenge". Perhaps, with Stevenson's biography in mind, we might risk a more specific formulation: fear of an angry father and of forbidden aggression against him. Of striking the father dead, in fact, as Silver strikes Tom—aggression that Jim escapes consciousness of, by fainting (5.130). Stevenson confesses an auto-biographic relevance through the vestibular dream that ends the story. As Jim has told his dreams of a parrot with the voice of the murderer Flint, so the author has told the story of Jim, with a parrot voice very like his own, if not "in a fleshly sense". And as even Flint feared Long John Silver (5.101), so too Stevenson-Hawkins feared his loved father, his own aggression, and the maiming of challenged adulthood. Stevenson's "secret has been told to the parrot", Captain Smollett would say (5.84).

To open the open secret a little, one might first ask simply what *Treasure Island* is about. It would be too simple to answer, A quest for treasure. The "Treasure Hunt", after all, takes up only two chapters of thirty-four. And the comparative weakness of emotional charge in the treasure itself is quite problematic. Professor Robson asks (pp. 59, 67) whether Stevenson may not have avoided the theme because of inability to accommodate, at the time, representation of the possessed treasure (whose latent meaning is the mother's body). At all events, most of the story is not about a search. It recounts a series of contests for power. First comes the Admiral Benbow narrative, of struggle for a map; then the voyage under subverted authority; the mutiny and first struggle for the *Hispaniola*; the battle for the stockade; Jim's rebellious adventure and renewed struggle for the *Hispaniola*; and then (after his terrifying recapture) yet another power struggle, Silver's bid to retain the captaincy of the stockade. Throughout, the material consists of conflicts of authority, loyalty, obedience and duty. So far as these concern Jim, they could be shown to correspond to stages of growth in the scope of his volitions. To begin with, as critics have remarked, he displays little initiative, being caught up in events beyond his control. But later he achieves power of action, and becomes a sort of hero. We should not fail to notice (although children may) that this comes about through his flouting of Captain Smollett's authority: something that he is never quite forgiven for, even at the end—"You're a good boy in your line, Jim; but I don't think you and me'll go to sea again" (5.308).

Outwardly, Jim achieves this independence through his "Sea Adventure", which also forms a cardinal threshold for the action as a whole. He recaptures the *Hispaniola* single-handed. Or, almost single-handed. He receives one indispensable piece of assistance: the use of Ben Gunn's boat. Professor Robson regards the wild man as a mere *ficelle*, or piece of plot machinery. But Ben Gunn's function seems to me of a different order of significance. After all, who achieves the quest for Flint's treasure? Not the pirates; not Dr. Livesey; not even Captain Smollett; but Ben Gunn the maroon. The solitary, that is to say; one who has achieved independence and survived rejection by a society tired of the quest (5.140). We recall a possible meaning of what has been named the "treasure hard to attain" archetype: selfhood, independence, identity.[12] Treasure in this sense appears to constitute the story's goal. How significant, therefore, that Jim should achieve independence by entering Ben Gunn's dangerous coracle—by being, as it were, in the same boat with the solitary. This theme receives immediate development in Jim's brief, and very nearly disastrous, captaincy of the ship of life *Hispaniola*. Moreover, when he finally comes to possess the treasure, it takes the form of images of authority: his pleasure is to sort "the pictures of all the kings of Europe for the last hundred years" (5.311).

Stevenson's disclaimer of "psychology" (that is, detailed mimesis of emotions) should not be thought to imply disregard of motive or morality. *Treasure Island*, as Chesterton remarked, is almost too consistent in implementing moral patterns. These mostly concern Jim's shifting attitudes to various codes, such as ordinary decency (the Squire) and principled duty (Captain Smollett). In a limited sense, one might speak of development in the boy's character towards maturity or ambivalence. He learns, at least, that honest gentlemen in authority may not be fault-less, and that agreeable "gentlemen of fortune" may not be honest. It was in his first innocence that he "hated the captain deeply" for sternly eschewing favouritism (5.89); while finding Silver "unweariedly kind", ready always to favour Jim with a welcome to the clean, trim galley (5.93). However, the irony in Silver's characterisation—"he had a way of talking to each"—never quite becomes the narrator's. Even when villainy is unmasked at the apple barrel, Jim's artlessly remembered response is one of injured jealousy: he had felt like killing "this abominable old rogue addressing another in the very same words of flattery as he had used to myself" (5.99). Contrast the episode's original, a family anecdote of how Stevenson's father "with the devilish penetration of the boy" had seen through a sycophant called Soutar and deliberately eavesdropped from the *Regent's* apple barrel (12.458). Jim may hate Silver's disloyalty; but he never quite sees through him or ceases to take favouritism for granted. Even after witnessing murder, even in the enemy's camp, Silver is still, for Jim, "the best man here".

And one must admit some truth in this. Long John is a complex figure (although not a complex character), who has justly puzzled critics. One of them dallies with the idea that Silver and Jim really might have "done a power of good together" (5.261). The problem of Silver's attractive vitality is sometimes approached *via* "The Persons of the Tale", a fable in which Stevenson appears to offer a theological solution to it. This *parados* or interpolated frame or (if one may so describe it) *in persona personae* comment arises when Silver and Captain Smollett step outside *Treasure Island* after Chapter 32 into a limbo of indeterminate status. Silver (of course) exults in being the maker's favourite: "If there is sich a thing as a Author, I'm his favourite chara'ter. He does me fathoms better'n he does you—fathoms, he does. And he likes doing me" (25.184). Since the fable gives Smollett no effective answer, it is taken to imply the human liveli-ness of sin. But it may have more to do with the sinful creature's claim on God ("If there's an author ... he's on my side."), or with the paradox of the justified sinner. But Stevenson's fear of judgment could pierce deeper than this. The limbo has its own fictive deceptions; among which is its placement before Chapter 33. Silver's downfall and his worst hypocrisy lie ahead. "The Treasure Hunt" has just shown Silver turning his eyes on Jim "with a deadly look". Even Jim, then, realises something of Silver's evil—a realisation that the reader is to share: "Certainly he took no pains to hide his thoughts; and certainly I read them *like print"* (5.299): my italics). No longer neat but with "a hot and shiny countenance" (5.298). Silver has at last looked like his murderous self—the clean hands were those of hypocrisy. In fact, he is anything but a likeable rogue. What sort of author could love such a creature as this?

Yet Silver has a secure place in the narrator's feelings, at least. His domination of Jim is sharply set out in one of the book's strongest visual images. Fast as the action moves, it moves from one fully realised picture to another. We have only to think of the sabre-cut inn sign, or the attentive apple barrel, or the sloping mast of the beached schooner, to see why the tradition of *Treasure Island* illustrations should be so illuminating.) Often, the pictures take on an emblematic value (quite as much as any of Stevenson's so-called Emblems with their odd left-handed morals). The skeleton with hands "raised above his head like a diver's" (5.289) came, we know, from Poe; but it might have come from Quarles. Among all the pictures, none is more memorable than this: "We made a curious figure, had any one been there to see us. . . . I had a line about my waist, and followed obediently after the sea cook, who held the loose end of the rope, now in his free hand, now between his powerful teeth. For all the world, I was led like a dancing bear" (5.285). A dancing bear is made to perform, deprived of the power of independent action.

This is not to say that Silver merely symbolises what dominates Jim. He is too real, too much of a man, for that. To the end he retains convincing viability, if not as a leader then as a survivor. Think of his presence of mind, for example, when the treasure *cache* is found rifled:

> with Silver the blow passed almost instantly. Every thought of his soul had been set full-stretch, like a racer, on that money; well, he was brought up in a single second, dead; and he kept his head, found his temper, and changed his plan before the others had had time to realise the disappointment. . . . He passed me a double-barrelled pistol. (5.301)

Being a leader of pirates no doubt taught a man to respond rapidly to life's challenges; but by any standard Silver's is an outstanding human performance.

The ambivalence of Silver may have to do with his function in a symbolism of character formation. He is the worst of the story's evil fathers, a father of lies; but a father none the less. At his most threatening, in the enemy's camp, he voiced this paternity: " 'It's all that you're to hear, my son' . . . 'And now I am to choose?' " (5.255). If Jim had chosen as Silver wanted, he would indeed have become the son of a sea cook. On the other hand, Silver's kind treatment of his protegés as fellow-adults—"You're young, you are, but ... I'll talk to you like a man" (5.99)—seems to offer a genuine *entrée* to the insincere adult world. In a grown-up way he is tremendously knowing about his job, and full of unidealistic circumspection: "Now, the most goes for rum and a good fling, and to sea again in their shirts. But that's not the course I lay. I puts it all away, some here, some there, and none too much anywheres by reason of suspicion. I'm fifty, mark you; once back from this cruise, I set up gentleman in earnest" (5.100). Shrewd calculation of the odds, in fact, is what enables Silver to assert so frequently, and with such plausible confidence, "you may lay to that". How shockingly far-sighted his cool predictions sound, to the innocent ear: " 'It were fortunate for me that I had Hawkins here. You would have let old John be cut to bits, and never given it a thought, doctor.'—'Not a thought,' replied Dr. Livesey, cheerily" (5.306). Both have counted the cards; but Silver is the smoother at concealing this. He has more, so to say, maturity. If *Treasure Island* were a Renaissance work, one might speak of Long John as offering (like Autolycus) a mercurial component—a quicksilver facility in the change of roles, in persuasive eloquence, in lies.[13] At any rate, Silver helped Jim to form his adult identity. What moral identity, then, what character can that be? We cannot look to the narrator himself for much questioning of this. But a thoughtful reader may share Captain Smollett's view of Silver, and be disturbed to imagine how far the criminal may have influenced Jim for the worse: how far he too may have become, in the end, a "gentleman in earnest".

The autobiographical echoes from all this are too clear to need amplification. Stevenson himself lived through a passionate drama of adolescent rebellions, friendships with surrogate-parents and intense reconciliations with his father. But we should avoid the genetic cul-de-sac. No doubt intimate feelings were engaged. No doubt Louis would explore, as he was apt to do, intimations of unconscious passions. But subsequently he and his brownies formed these into a fuller communication than psychoanalysis, at its present stage at least, can hope to match. Certainly Stevenson, interested though he was in psychological research, would have preferred a moral statement of the main issue of *Treasure Island*. I mean the choice that Jim was faced with in the enemy's camp—"now I am to choose?" (5.255). It was a choice between hypocritical compromise, to save his skin, and loyal honesty. Jim chose to face the terrible father. In his finest hour, he even made an aggressive boast. And the reward for his boldness was not only that Silver kept him alive, but that the good father's party cut the tether of dependence and ratified the free selfhood that he had stolen.

So far, the story leads to individualism as much as individuation. But at last the achieved self is restored to society, and the individual to the fold. Outwardly, this comes about through reconciliation with Dr. Livesey and partial reconciliation with Captain Smollett. Indirectly, there are several statements of a similar idea. Perhaps the clearest is Ben Gunn's return to the human race. Another may be concealed in the treasure's final lodgement. We are are told that Jim was "kept busy all day . . . packing the minted money into breadbags" (5.310). The symbol of the achieved self is thus enclosed and fused with another symbol: containers of bread, the element of community.

The quest occasioned many deaths—fifteen, in fact, in the tradition of the island called The Dead Man's Chest. But the conclusion demands still more subtractions from the microcosmic community. Three mutineers were marooned to continue the harsh process of individuation. And Silver, helped by the anarchic Ben Gunn, subtracted himself, with a little Treasure-manna. His escape is variously interpreted. It may be merely to save him from the legal embarrassments of repatriation. Or it may imply doubt about civilised society's ability to arrest Silver's tendencies. Or perhaps Robson is right to see a connection with the abandonment of the bar silver (5.317). Stevenson may hint at deferred judgment and the silver of Jeremiah 6.30— "Reprobate silver shall men call them, because the Lord hath rejected them." If so, Ben Gunn was right to warn that the lives of the company "would certainly have been forfeit" had Silver remained aboard (5.316). It is sobering that Captain Smollett can think of a comparable exclusion of Jim, and proves to be right in his prediction: "I don't think you and me'll go to sea again. You're too much of the born favourite for me" (5.308). But to press the point farther might be "not to enrich but to stultify [the] tale" (12.216): to break a butterfly on the wheel, or make it walk the plank.

Similar existential questionings underlie the surface action of all Stevenson's better adventure novels, romances, and short stories. We have to think of a continuing inner search, passages of which might be traced throughout his writing: beneath the light improbabilities of *New Arabian Nights* and *The Wrong Box*; the doubles of *Dr. Jekyll and Mr. Hyde* and *The Master of Ballantrae*; the psycho-history of *David Balfour* and *Weir of Hermiston*; and the social questions of the underestimated late works, *The Wrecker* and *The Beach of Falesá*. In *The Ebb-Tide; A Trio and Quartette*, Stevenson's last completed work, the search reached a climacteric point. Partly for this reason and partly because it would be desirable, if possible, to bring more of the Stevensonian *oeuvre* into the critical canon, I should like now to draw attention to that "most grim and gloomy tale".[14]

To those who allow themselves the freedom of not condemning Story on principle, *The Ebb-Tide* offers a high pleasure. At the same time, it presents the problematic features of Stevenson's fiction in an acute form. (I am not thinking of its collaborative character, which is a problem only for the genetic critic.[15]) How does it relate to his other fiction? How seriously, in a literary way, is it meant? How are we to know, even, what it means? Or to take its unpalatable moral? It seems calculated, cynically, to disgust rather than convert. "That Grimy Work", as its author called it,[16] is at times very unpleasant; at times quite unsuccessful; at all times sharply interesting. Even its admirers must concede it to be uneven. Yet it remains a compelling work, and also one of some historical import. Within the narrow island limits of its derelict paradise, it holds, as who should say, *rationes seminales* of much of Conrad's fiction. Its weakness, but also in a way its strength, arises from excessive seriousness; which may explain why Stevenson found it so difficult to write. It was deeply involved in his quarrel with God.

The first part, "The Trio", follows the fortunes of three beachcombers on civilisation's Pacific margin. All lack the pliability, but also the firmness, to make a legal living: Davis is a former ship's captain, broken for drunkenness; Huish a hard, nasty, vulgar, indomitable Cockney clerk; and the quasi-authorial *persona*, Robert Herrick,[17] a timid failure and skulker from life's battles. (The Virgil that Herrick uses for *sortes* surely always opens at *facilis descensus Averni*: "each had made a long apprenticeship in going downward" (18.7).) We find the three starving in an old jail, which Stevenson based on the Papeete calaboose where Melville and his co-mutineers had been imprisoned.[18] Besides starving, Huish suffers from an influenza plague that has Tahiti in its grip—the same virus, we may suspect, as Camus's *peste*. The end seems close. But Davis's good fortune brings a reprieve. He is given charge of a schooner, whose drunken captain (an *alter ego*?) has died of a worse plague, small-pox. The three adventurers sail for Australia with a native crew and a cargo of champagne, having agreed—Herrick quite reluctantly—to steal the ship. Then Davis and Huish take to drinking the cargo, while Herrick is left to run the ship. And when the converted cannibals prove morally superior to their officers—"It was a cutting reproof to compare the islanders and the whites" (18.76)—the *Farallone* seems to be on a course well logged in *Typee* and *Omoo*.[19] As for the erring ship, surely it is a microcosm of civilisation, sailing the allegorical deep waters of *Moby Dick* or (rather) *Israel Potter*? But now the schooner comes about, for Stevenson's own form of fraud-within-fraud picaresque. The thirsty pirates discover that most of the wine is water—the *Farallone* voyage has been planned as an insurance swindle. This insight not only offers a fresh perspective on human society, but a new moral dilemma, another change of course, a deeper *bouge* of hell. The three will go along with the swindle so as to blackmail the dishonest owners. Immediately (presumably in consequence of their choice) they are lost and short of provisions; so that when they raise a mysterious island it is nothing at all short of providential.

The second part, "The Quartette", begins with arrival at the island.[20] As often with Stevenson, the shaping imagination plays over a setting, until full realisation of place gathers. In this, his art resembles Melville's, or Hugo's.[21] It patiently cultivates *mise-en-scène*, so discreetly that one only realises later how deeply the meditation has gone. In *The Wrecker* it dwells on the bird-obliterated *Flying Scud*; in *Weir of Hermiston* on the Covenanter-haunted moors; and in *The Ebb-Tide* on a bare atoll. When the island is first sighted, by one of the Kanakas, it appears as "a greenish, filmy iridescence . . . floating like smoke on the pale heavens" (18.102). Farther in,

> The isle was like the rim of a great vessel sunken in the waters; it was like the embankment of an annular railway grown upon with wood: so slender it seemed amidst the outrageous breakers, so frail and pretty, he would scarce have wondered to see it sink and disappear without a sound, and the waves close smoothly over its descent. . . . A spur of coral sand stood forth on the one hand; on the other, a high and thick tuft of trees cut off the view; between was the mouth of the huge laver. . . . The sea turned (as with the instinct of the homing pigeon) for the vast receptacle, swept eddying through the gates, was transmuted, as it did so, into a wonder of watery and silken hues, and brimmed into the inland sea beyond. The schooner worked up, close-hauled, and was caught and carried away by the influx like a toy. She skimmed; she flew; a momentary shadow touched her decks from the shoreside trees; the bottom of the channel showed up for a moment, and was in a moment gone; the next, she floated on the bosom of the lagoon; and below, in the transparent chamber of waters, a myriad of many-coloured fishes were sporting, a myriad pale flowers of coral diversified the floor. (18.108-10)

Simply as description, this would be well enough. But consider that it is only a correlate, or outward husk, and its achievement may seem of a high order indeed. Jacques Rivière has noted the "free, radiant curiosity" of this landfall, "the delightful unfurling of our spirit before the future, very near but still silent", with congenial sensitivity:

> During those moments when nothing is yet happening, when events are still in preparation—not a breath of wind on the deck of the ship—I feel myself quietly growing equal to everything prodigious in the universe. And my ecstasy resembles that of Herrick who, leaning over the diaphanous scarce-moving water of the lagoon, saw "a trail of rainbow fish with parrot beaks" swim by.[22]

It is the characteristic moment, for him, of the *roman d'aventure*.

After the suspense, surprise. The island, itself not quite ordinary in its presentation, is inhabited by a distinctly extraordinary white aristocrat, Attwater, able to offer Herrick "a dry sherry that I would like your opinion of" (18.144). Yet the uncertainly-charted Zacynthos is no ideal Shangri-La. It has been so ravaged by smallpox that only four inhabitants survive. True, it is wealthy. But its wealth has a mundane basis in pearl-fishing. The pearls come as welcome news to the adventurers, who scent plunder more valuable than anything from the *Farallone*. Plainly

Zacynthos is another microcosm of the undeveloped native society to which Europeans "carry activity and disseminate disease" (18.5). The urban similes in its description may thus be more apt than Kiely (p. 181) allows. Now, however, a counter-action develops: Attwater's attempt to divide the adventurers. At first he treats Herrick as a favoured elect, Davis and especially Huish as reprobate. But when the complex *entrainement* of conversion engages with the machinery of the pirates' intrigues, the plot turns and alignments change. Now Davis is with Herrick, now with Huish. And the self-righteous Attwater: is he always on the side of Stevenson's angels? We wait in suspense to know who will control the island when the pearl-fisher's private schooner, *Trinity Hall*, returns. In the end it is Attwater who wins, but with Davis as repentant sinner instead of Herrick. This edifying turn may provoke the same response that Huish made to Herrick's story: "It's like the rot there is in tracts".[23] But cooler reflection will find that Stevenson means the *dénouement* (which went through much revision) to stimulate analytic appraisal. The four characters make up a quartette indeed, of psychological forces contending for a single mind: Herrick and Huish even share the same *nom de guerre*. All along the story has been a psychological investigation. The conclusion, therefore, should be seen as raising a question whether there may be other, deeper, religious strata underlying the psychomachic material. It remains a question that gives *The Ebb-Tide* enduring interest.

Doubt particularly attaches to the character of the failed missionary, who is central enough for the story to have been called, at one stage, *The Pearlfisher*.[24] Attwater belongs with Stevenson's most powerful father-surrogate characters: he is in the same class, as a moral invention, with Long John Silver and Weir of Hermiston. He is clearer than the first, more felt than the second, subtler than either. As a character, however, he may be too uncertainly realised—by turns flattering and insolent; brutal and pious; evangelically sincere and unscrupulously machiavellian; the object of satire and subject of enigma. Some will find him implausible as soon as he leans (swiftly) to Herrick and says "University man?" (18.116). Too abrupt, surely, even allowing for *temps* and *moeurs*? Perhaps. But the point is a nice one: Herrick has shown himself pained by Huish's vulgarity, and Attwater may be seizing his chance. Besides, the enquiry implies—though not in terms of character—judgment of the snobbery. A similar jolt may be felt when Attwater later appeals to Herrick, with evangelical fervour, to "come to the mercy seat". The atheistical Herrick will not surely be alone in calling this "beyond bearing" in its presumptuous directness. He cannot, cannot believe. But notice the ex-missionary's response: "The rapture was all gone from Attwater's countenance; the dark apostle had disappeared, and in his place there stood an easy, sneering gentleman, who took off his hat and bowed. It was pertly done, and the blood burned in Herrick's face" (18.138). This *volte face* momentarily recalls *Confessions of a Justified Sinner*; but the effect seems here more tactical. Stevenson makes Attwater so often surprising that he seems to challenge the reader to come to terms with him. Sometimes the surprises suggest Providence. Attwater is ready for the adventurers when they first arrive; sees through them immediately (18.161); acts with the inevitability of foreknowledge; and is a fatalist. Yet he also prevents the thought of a "God figure": "I have nothing to do with the *Sea Ranger* and the people you drowned. ... That is your account with God. ... I do not kill on suspicion" (18.166). Is he, then, a religious fanatic, for whom the chief end justifies any means however grimy? But his ruthlessness is too casually cruel for that, his foresight too readily that of a Winchester. It is a Braxfieldian anecdote of his, about inflicting summary justice with his two-handed engine, that precipitates Herrick's breakdown, attempted suicide and final submission. (He runs off, tries to drown himself, but elects instead to swim to the island and give himself up to Attwater and salvation). Some have seen in Attwater the Accuser himself—"dark apostle" indeed. But if that naïve machinery is present, it can only form a part of the author's own advanced conversion machine. To Herrick-Stevenson, the cruelty of the universe seemed quite evil enough to be hated—or to warrant "an insultin' letter to Gawd" (18.99).

But Stevenson as Tusitala, as story-teller, presents a larger parable. And perhaps it is one with political or anthropological edge. In the end, Herrick and Davis are to leave on the *Trinity Hall*, the *Farallone* having been destroyed as incriminating evidence. (It is none of Attwater's affair.) Religion's main effect on them, Herrick seems to imply, has been to make a "sure thing" (18.208) surer, more respectable. It has certainly been hardest on the proletarian reprobate Huish ("Whish", Attwater class-consciously calls him): he is not spared, like the others, to embark in the security of the Trinity, or the more secular *Trinity Hall*. Zacynthos, in short, could be represented as the image of a society quite as unacceptable, politically, as the Tahiti of the opening chapters. Only, Davis has achieved now the respectability of the Scotch Captain who earlier humiliated him; and he belongs to a community too lost in self-delusion to recognise itself as satirised. It is more than a community of colonialists, for Attwater embodies every respectable believer. He locks up the pearls of his faith in a safe, hoping to make a good thing out of them. He builds his life around an efficient monopolistic business enterprise. And he is quick to defend in-groups: believers, whites, Cantabrigians, *bourgeois*. Herrick's submission to him, therefore, is cynical despair, Herrick's final cynicism enlightenment. The sequel will be to move away from the island's old, doomed, religious state.

This view might explain much. It would help, for example, with the Melvillean icon of the buried ship's figurehead, a "woman of

exorbitant stature and as white as snow ... beckoning with uplifted arm",
set into the beach, "the ensign and presiding genius of that empty town"
(18.112). Once, the figurehead was on a ship of state moving on some
great historical course.[25] Now, it is grounded among the bones of a dead
atoll. But it has enough force still for Herrick to regret that he cannot
commit himself to it in the simple old way:

> From the crown of the beach, the figure-head confronted him with
> what seemed irony, her helmeted head tossed back, her formidable
> arm apparently hurling something, whether shell or missile, in the
> direction of the anchored schooner. She seemed a defiant deity from
> the island, coming forth to its threshold with a rush as of one about to
> fly, and perpetuated in that dashing attitude. Herrick looked up at her,
> where she towered above him head and shoulders, with singular
> feelings of curiosity and romance, and suffered his mind to travel to
> and fro in her life-history. So long she had been the blind conductress
> of a ship among the waves; so long she had stood here idle in the violent
> sun that yet did not avail to blister her; and was even this the end of so
> many adventures, he wondered, or was more behind? And he could
> have found it in his heart to regret that she was not a goddess, nor yet
> he a pagan, that he might have bowed down before her in that hour of
> difficulty. (18.127-8)

As it is, the image seems too ambivalent: "shell or missile" punningly
directs aggression that takes simultaneous forms of trade and war. Here
the thrust of European civilisation is hard to miss. We cannot be so sure,
however, as to whether the figure-head's gesture of hurling meets a
response in Huish's attempt to throw acid. (Had he succeeded, Attwater
too might have been a "blind conductor".) At least Huish is the
adventurer who seems closest to honouring the figure-head (18.198). And
it would be in character for Stevenson to prefer the outcast: in the fable
"Faith, Half-Faith, and No Faith At All" it is the rover with his axe who
goes "to die with Odin" (25.228). Huish is defiant enough; although if the
figure-head figures "high adventure" (Kiely p. 191), it is hard to see him
as a worshipper, exactly. He seems to have a more social import—to
embody, perhaps, the coarse yet vital energy of the European colonial
volition. In any event, white civilisation's dynamic marine emblem is now
run aground, bogged down, stuck. That does little to reduce the level of
its aggression, however. Huish has to be violently repressed by the super-
egotistical Attwater (himself a hurler of shells). Indeed, "The Quartette"
brings a marked accentuation of the aggression earlier displayed towards
the cockney only in threats. Obviously Stevenson does not mean us to
wish that the acid-thrower had lived to inflict a power-emasculating
injury on Attwater. But maybe there is relief in the final prospect of
embarkation: of moving on after the episode (to put it a little crudely) of
Christian Capitalism.

The various ships and *mises-en-scène* thus symbolise forms of social organisation progressively, in order of chronology. (Or of viability: The island itself, we recall, was first described as a "fragile vessel".) Turns of plot that Kiely dismisses as mechanical stimuli really function organically to exfoliate more and more radical ideas of human society. For Stevenson, indeed (as for Kipling), the whole adventure form served a revelatory or exploratory purpose, ever disclosing deeper, less suspected and more surprising insights. Its type is the gradual uncovering of the *Farallone's* fraudulent cargo: "Deeper yet, and they came upon a layer where there was scarcely so much as the intention to deceive" (18.91). In some ways the form anticipated post-modernist fabulation. But Stevenson continued to use conventional generic terms, such as *romance* and *parable*—even if he applied the latter with a new-old Aesopian ambivalent emphasis. We can almost see a self-referring sequence of kinds, in *The Ebb-Tide*, from the epic of the 'tattered Virgil'; through the letters home (Huish's being pure romance); Herrick's "tract" and *graffiti;* and the "sea-romances" (18.55) that provide nautical words of authenticity; to the parables of Attwater and of Stevenson.

"Fond of parables?" asked Attwater abruptly when he came upon Herrick in the diving shed. And he told him the parable of the diving suits:

'I saw these machines ... come up dripping and go down again, and all the while the fellow inside as dry as toast ... and I thought we all wanted a dress to go down into the world in, and come up scatheless. What do you think the name was?' he enquired.

'Self-conceit,' said Herrick. ...

'And why not Grace? Why not God's Grace, Hay?' asked Attwater. Why not the grace of your Maker and Redeemer, He who died for you, He who upholds you, He whom you daily crucify afresh? There is nothing here'—striking on his bosom—'nothing there'—smiting the wall—'and nothing there'—stamping—'nothing but God's Grace! We walk upon it, we breathe it; we live and die by it; it makes the nails and axles of the universe; and a puppy in pyjamas prefers self-conceit!' (18.131-2)

This comes dangerously near to giving God the best tunes. Can such words have come from the same pen as "The Yellow Paint", that anti-parable of religion's worthlessness as a life-preserver? Understandably, Herrick was baffled. He still saw Attwater's iron cruelty and insensibility. But now there was something else—"to find the whole machine thus glow with the reverberation of religious zeal, surprised him beyond words"; so that he laboured (in vain) to piece together Attwater's character. Perhaps the reverberation was deeper than he recognised, deeper than even the author could quite have sounded. The episode suggests genuine puzzlement and introspective ("psychological") search; not least in its description of the diving shed. This fascinated Herrick with a "disorder of romantic things", profuse debris from "two wrecks at least", and "commonplace ghosts". Doubtless, the wonderfully inventorised detritus is emblematic (a compass, for example, "idly pointing, in the confusion and dusk of that shed, to a forgotten pole"). It was a voyage of empire that had failed: the *Asia* from whose wreck Attwater preserved relics. But there may also be less conscious tones. The episode uses the sort of material that furnishes dreams—material that may well have had a source in experiences far anterior to the Anstruther period, when Stevenson himself learnt to wear an unfigurative diving suit and come up scatheless.[26] Similar depths seem to yield up religious images and symbolic actions throughout; in which even the unbelieving Herrick participates unawares. Even when he attempts suicide by drowning, it constitutes the "immersion" of a baptism of repentance.[27] He is conscious, however, only that his cowardice is ignoble; and "with the authority of a revelation" that "another girds him and carries him whither he would not" (18.172). Similarly, Attwater's killing of the *alter ago* Hay-Huish enacts the mortification of the body of sin. And, more obviously still, the island itself is a vessel of the Grace of repentance. ("We walk upon it, we breathe it.") It is called a "huge laver": the water that Attwater lives "at" represents the cleansing water of life. For this reason, too, Stevenson makes each description of water vibrantly alive; as when "the silence of death was only broken by the throbbing of the sea" (18.109). In the most pervasive way imaginable, the story's myth is implicitly Christian. In other words, Attwater's religion makes a real challenge, however much we may dislike the man. His fatalism (to mention only one trait) has a character hard to distinguish from Stevenson's own.[28] Both believed in a distinctly savage deity. But then, it is the coward who "loathes the iron face of God" (25.213).

Attwater epitomised not so much Stevenson's missionary enemies, in fact, as his missionary heroes. The ex-missionary was even a part of himself. This he thinly disguised by chronological reversal. Attwater's romantic interest in missions declined (18.133); whereas Stevenson, at first temperamentally antipathetic to the missionaries, later revised his view. After visiting a Molokai leper colony, he defended Father Damien, and in Samoa he became very friendly with James Chalmers the New Guinea missionary. It would be presumptuous (in several ways) to assert that between *The Beach of Falesá* and *The Ebb-Tide* Stevenson experienced religious conversion. In time of composition, indeed, they overlap. In spite of the latter's epigraph from *Julius Caesar*, the eponymous tide is beyond doubt that of Arnold's sea of faith (which must ebb, for a ship to leave Zacynthos's lagoon). But at least Stevenson was swimming with Herrick, "without illusion", for Canaan's side. The Christian atheism of "If this were faith"[29] accorded well enough with

Sunday-school teaching and pious addresses. Perhaps, to use the terms of *The Ebb-Tide*'s fable, we may say that in it Stevenson perceived civilisation as a fragile vessel, more dependent than he had thought on the faith and duty and discipline that keeps ships of various kinds from being put on the rocks. Certainly his own sense of duty became quite intense. It is not impossible, after all, to see *The Ebb-Tide* as something of a tract, in its fashion: quite in line, say, with "The House of Eld".[30]

Or does this view miss the best of the story, its finer psychological intimations? Attwater, besides being a fatalist, is also an experimentalist. And I have hardly touched on the psychology of true and false belief; of the relation of ageing to believing; and of moral reformation. The exploration is conducted allegorically, through the interactions of four personifications of internal faculties. Sometimes they compose a moral spectrum, or form a psychodynamic series—as when Huish threatens Davis in such a way as to remind him of "something he had once said to Herrick, years ago, it seemed" (18.192). Herrick acts as Davis's better self, Davis as a better self to Huish. Considering, too, that Davis often initiated action—at least until Huish "carried him on to reprobation" (18.194)—one thinks of psychological schemes such as the Platonic souls (with Huish as the concupiscible), or the various Renaissance triads (*mens-ratio-passio; intellectus-anima-voluntas*).

These adumbrations, however, are strongly over-printed by others. Stevenson, like many nineteenth-century writers, was fond of the motif of doubles. He used paired characters not only in *Dr. Jekyll and Mr. Hyde*, *Kidnapped* and *The Master of Ballantrae* but also in minor works such as *The Owl*. This interest in divided or multiple personality, which he pursued in correspondence with F. W. H. Myers the psychical researcher,[31] found some of its farthest reaches in the intricacies of *The Ebb-Tide*. The story so coruscates with doubled pairs as to dazzle with their excess. As Stevenson told an interviewer in February 1893 (the same month when he returned to revising *The Ebb-Tide*): "My profound conviction is that there are many consciousnesses in a man ... I can feel them working in many directions". The doubling of Hays is an explicit instance of something pervasive: there are doubled ships, wrecks, islands, and incidents—Attwater's laving Davis's face as Davis laved Herrick's (18.159 and 204); Davis's and Attwater's calling Herrick to Jesus; and many others. But it is no static array of diptychs. The quartette continually rearranges itself (like the Pythagorean elements) to form new pairs of pairs. Thus, the fatalistic Attwater and superstitious Davis are believers, the others sceptics. This pairing seems to be confirmed by the authoritarian roles of the first pair—the ex-missionary's stern paternalism and Davis's captaincy, natural fatherhood and respect for forceful command (18.152-3). Davis is fond of the expression "my son" (18.14 etc.), and it is his prayer for his children that saves his life, to put him at last on

Attwater's side. However, a different grouping altogether brings
Attwater and Herrick together. It makes them gentlemen, university
men, 'respectable', but puts Davis and Huish in the same boat as grosser
natures (18.193). At times this class structure can seem fundamental:
Davis says to Herrick, "He's your kind, he's not ours. . . . Save him if you
can!" Yet another grouping is generated by the axis of moderation and
extremity. Attwater and Huish are both, in their different ways,
"sinister": given, that is, to non-natural behaviour (e.g. 18.187). But
Davis and Herrick normally inhabit a more average middle ground of
ordinary experience and half-faith. It is they who are liberals perplexed
about whom to betray. So Herrick resists an "immense temptation" to
warn Attwater, while agonising over the three lives that "went up and
down before him like buckets in a well" (18.139); just as Davis later
agonises over the ethics of vitriol. The dilemmas are not so much moral as
existential—which part of experience should be eliminated: the supernatural, or the natural body of sin? Even Herrick can see that to eliminate
Attwater might be to lose a living energy and purpose vital to human
existence. And yet. . . .

The reader may never resolve the quartette into a settled scheme of
relations. Perhaps because he is reading about change, his feelings are
perpetually disturbed by some unanticipated turn, or some new
valuation, which forestalls the equilibrium of mere understanding. Each
characteristic he counted best turns out to have its repellent aspect; each
truth to be a form of "romance". The monstrous Attwater, explicitly,
makes Herrick say "I am attracted and repelled" (18.123). A reader may
agree that "circumstance was like a consecration of the man" (18.140);
but then the dominating personality will be given unpleasantly hard, or
else homosexual, overtones ("You are attractive" 18.135; cf. 141).
Similarly with honest Captain Davis. Nothing could be more sincere than
the father's love for Ada—until we learn that he has no daughter. But
after we learn about the glass menagerie? False or doubtful emotions of
this sort abound. Indeed, familial sanctities seem in this story to operate
more often as means of justifying crime than as ameliorating influences.
The paternal Davis could even be construed as a tempter. But how could
Herrick be expected to cut the human bond he embodies? It is the
dilemma of "The House of Eld" again. Davis's ambivalence culminates
in the last invitation to Jesus. If a reader is capable of compassion, it may
trouble him to think that Davis's weakness caused, among other things,
Huish's death. Moral readers will have no time for vitriol throwers. Yet
Stevenson more than once writes of the "innocence" of Huish, whose
courage commands Davis's respect, and who can fairly be called "the
least deserving, but surely the most pitiable" (18.169, 192, 187, 13).
Attwater, we recall, threatened Davis: "Whatever you do to others, God
shall visit it again a thousandfold upon your innocents" (18.203). In this

way, every value has its opposite; every absolute becomes relatively fictional. But the effect is not, in the end, quite like that of Poe's nihilistic *exposé*. With Stevenson, demystification goes farther; demythologising itself is shown to be a form of fiction. The outcome reminds one of the practicalities of Tolstoi (another harsh fabulist).[33] For all its scepticism, *The Ebb-Tide* offers a sort of bleak faith, in a savagely rational religion that never forgets its origin in folklore. Stevenson could call the concluding chapters "the most ugly and cynical of all" (Letter to Colvin, 23 Aug. 1893: 23.312). But "was even this the end of so many adventures ... or was more behind?" (18.127) Ulysses' course, after all, led on past Zacynthos to Apollo's shrine *formidatus nautis*. We can take the parable, like Attwater's, in different ways; but each leads to our own next change of heart.

The tract-like seriousness of such a parable carries fiction to a limit. And surprisingly the limit lies on the instrumental, not the formal, border of literature. Some have regarded the fineness of Stevenson's style as an obstacle to modern readers (presumably they prefer literature to be written badly). But Stevenson's own search during his last years, an opposite endeavour to Henry James's, was always for simplicity. In particular he had come to dislike the forced "alembicated" or high-pitched style, to which the earlier beginning of *The Ebb-Tide* partly committed him. In a letter to Colvin of 23 May 1893 he writes: "I am dis-contented with *The Ebb-Tide*, naturally; there seems such a veil of words over it; and I like more and more naked writing; and yet sometimes one has a longing for full colour and there comes the veil again" (23.239). But the veil was drawn only comparatively; *The Ebb-Tide* depended most on its "intrinsic horror and pathos"—and on its "fierce glow of colour" in another, far from rhetorical, sense (23.238). Stevenson meant it, even, anti-mechanistic as it was, to appeal to admirers of Zola's "pertinent ugliness and pessimism" (Letter to James, 17 June 1893: 23.261).

Rivière wished to promote kinds of fiction that might provide models for an emergent French form of the 1920s. But in the event, ironically, it was Conrad, that drawer of many veils of words, who most immediately found inspiration in Stevenson's South Sea fiction. Critics trace the connection through narrative motifs. Thus *The Ebb-Tide* anticipates *Victory*, in its plot of three adventurers bent on another man's wealth; *Lord Jim*, in its failure recouped. Or, Donkin is modelled on Huish.[34] And many passages give atmospheric hints of Conrad's doomed, rotting, "tenebrous land", where only stars and heroes stand out from the vile darkness: "On shore, through the colonnade of palm stems, Attwater's house was to be seen shining steadily with many lamps. And there was nothing else visible, whether in the heaven above or in the lagoon below, but the stars and their reflections."[35] A more significant resemblance between the two *romanciers*, however, may reside in the tentative forms of meaning towards which they liked to grope. Each develops a firm setting of "formidable immobility", splendidly described and deeply considered, with its roots in memories of experience; and each recounts, within this eloquent symbolic world, a story with numerous moral facets. But neither the facets nor their sum exhaust the story's meaning. In a famous passage, Conrad says that to Marlow "the meaning of an episode was not inside like a kernel but outside, enveloping the tale which brought it out only as a glow brings out a haze, in the likeness of one of these misty halos that sometimes are made visible by the spectral illumination of moonshine".[36] Stevenson, although he considered himself "preoccupied with moral and abstract ideas",[37] seems to have illuminated *The Ebb-Tide*, at least, according to a poetic that Marlow would have found congenial. An encompassing yet elusive phosphorescence of moral meaning was a quality of several nineteenth-century writers—one thinks of Melville, Hawthorne, Dickens. Not the least valuable legacy to the literature of our own century, however, has been variously inherited by Conrad and Greene and Borges, and such postmodernists as Donald Barthelme, from Stevenson. For the special obliquity of moral that he taught is remarkably close to the way in which serious dreams often convey their sense; as Stevenson himself realised:

> Sometimes a parabolic sense is still more undeniably present in a dream; sometimes I cannot but suppose my Brownies have been aping Bunyan, and yet in no case with what would possibly be called a moral in a tract; never with the ethical narrowness; conveying hints instead of life's larger limitations and that sort of sense which we seem to perceive in the arabesque of time and space. (12.249).

Among all Stevenson's late works, *The Ebb-Tide* is not only the most interesting as a work of narrative art, but also one of the most commanding as a work of intellect. It may not stand out as *Weir of Hermiston* a massive crag from the moorland. But like its own atoll it is founded deep.

NOTES:

1. For many suggestions, corrections and references throughout this paper, I am indebted to Roger Swearingen.
2. Ed. L. Stevenson (Cambridge, Mass., 1966). The forthcoming new edn. has a Stevenson section.
3. *Aspects of the Novel* (London, 1927), 41.
4. G. K. Chesterton, *Robert Louis Stevenson* (London, 1927), 51.
5. Stevenson was an admirer of Tolstoi's later work but there is no evidence that he knew the novels. See n. 33 below.
6. Works, 19.90. Throughout the present chapter, references in this form are to the Vailima edition, ed. L. Osbourne and F. Van de G. Stevenson, 26 vols. (London, 1922-23).
7. They came from the *Annual Register* for 1813; see correspondence in *TLS*, 3,

10, and 17 February 1940.

7a, *Young Folks,* 1 October 1881-28 January 1882.

8. R. Kiely, *Robert Louis Stevenson and the Fiction of Adventure* (Cambridge, Mass., 1965), 55.

9. Introduction to *Robert Louis Stevenson: The Two Major Novels* (New York, 1960), xvii-xviii.

10. "The Art of Fiction", rept. in *Henry James and Robert Louis Stevenson: A Record of Friendship and Criticism* ed. J. A. Smith (London, 1948), 80.

11. *On the Novel* ed. B. S. Benedikz (London, 1971), 57-74. *The Sea Cook* was the primal title of the book now called *Treasure Island.* See also, however, some very perceptive remarks in David Daiches, *Stevenson and the Art of Fiction* (New York, 1951). Stevenson intensified this element in revising for book publication.

12. See, for instance, C. G. Jung, *Psychology and Alchemy* tr. R. F. C. Hull (London, 1953), 113-4.

13. Stevenson's interest in Autolycus goes back to 1879, when he was planning *Autolycus at Court.* From 1878-83 he worked on the play *An April Day; or Autolycus in Service.*

14. RLS-Baxter, 1 March 1893, from *R.L.S.: Stevenson's Letters to Charles Baxter* ed. D. Ferguson and M. Waingrow (London and New Haven, 1956), 324.

15. According to Osbourne himself, most of Part 1 was planned jointly, drafted by him, but revised and finally written by Stevenson (who left the first four chapters, however, much as they were drafted). The rest was entirely rewritten by Stevenson: Osbourne "never even touched" the end, and there was discussion as to whether his name should go on the title page at all. See RLS-Colvin, 23 August-12 September, 1893: 23.314; Graham Balfour, *The life of Robert Louis Stevenson* II, 33-4, 133 (1901)

16. RLS-Baxter, 19 July 1893; *Letters to Baxter,* 335.

17. Stevenson referred to himself as "a kind of prose Herrick" (RLS-Henley, cit. Furnas, 71). Herrick was one of the three poets most often quoted in Stevenson's letters: see *Collected Poems,* ed. J. A. Smith (rev. edn, London, 1971), 25ff. Stevenson's annotated copy of *Hesperides* is in the Beineke Collection (2536).

18. And near to where Stevenson himself once lay desperately ill: see Furnas, 279, 315.

19. On Stevenson's taste for Melville see Furnas, 274. He thought Typee "a howling cheese"—i.e. a dandy.

20. Even the division makes a sour ominous point. As 18.38 makes clear, there is an allusion to *Aen.* I, 94-6 "O three and four times blest, whose lot it was to die before their fathers' eyes". The island is obviously based on Penrhyn, with which it shares many features, including a perilous entry to a brilliant lagoon; a white trader's house with salvage from a wreck; a figurehead (feared by the natives, in the case of Penrhyn); ravages of plague; and a strict disciplinarian. Stevenson visited Penrhyn on 9 May 1890: See the accounts in "A Pearl Island: Penrhyn" (*Letters from the South Seas,* Vailima edn. 26:427-35) and *The Cruise of the "Janet Nichol" Among the South Sea Islands: A Diary by Mrs. Robert Louis Stevenson* (New York, 1914), 53-65. A photograph of the figurehead is reproduced opposite p. 56. On the same cruise Stevenson met three beachcombers (p. 40).

21. Whom Stevenson admired: see "Victor Hugo's Romances" (1874) in *Familar Studies of Men and Books.*

22. Jacques Rivière, *The Ideal Reader* ed. and tr. B. A. Price (London, 1960), 80.

23. 18.16. Cf. Stevenson's joky description of *The Ebb-Tide* to Baxter: "It would make a boss tract: the three main characters—and there are only four—are barrats, insurance frauds, thieves, and would-be murderers ..." (*Letters to Charles Baxter*, 325).

24. *Op. cit.* 246.

25. For the ship's company as a microcosmic community in Romantic literature see W. H. Auden, *The Enchafèd Flood or The Romantic Iconography of the Sea* (London, 1951). For a real-life original of the figurehead, see n. 20 above.

26. Furnas, 48. The immediate original, of course, was probably the white settler's house on Penrhyn: see n. 20 above.

27. Cf. Kiely, 190.

28. See, for instance, 141-2 and cf. "The Poor Thing". The antinomian dangers of the position are guarded against in "The Sinking Ship", another fable where Stevenson grapples with fatalism.

29. *Collected Poems* ed. J. A. Smith (London, 1950), 261-2.

30. The above paragraph owes much to Furnas, especially to pp. 288, 303, 325, 337.

31. F. W. H. Myers, *Human Personality and its Survival of Bodily Death* (London, 1903). On the motif and its psychological background, see R. Tymms, *Doubles in Literary Psychology* (Cambridge, 1949); also Mark Kanzer, "The Self-Analytic Literature of Robert Louis Stevenson", *Psychoanalysis and Cultre: Essays in Honour of Géza Róheim* ed. G. B. Wilbur and W. Muensterberger (New York, 1951), 425-35.

32. Interview with W. H. Triggs, Christchurch, N.Z. *Press.*

33. For the influence of Tolstoi's religious teaching on Stevenson, see Furnas, 229. Stevenson discusses Tolstoi's *Powers of Darkness* in "The Lantern-Bearers" (1888).

34. See Furnas, 358-9; Kiely, 185. An anonymous reviewer of *The Nigger of the Narcissus* in *The Saturday Review* (12 February 1898) explains that Donkin is not plagiarised but "only reminds us of somebody else": see *Joseph Conrad's Letters to R. B. Cunninghame Graham* ed. C. T. Watts (Cambridge, 1969), 80.

35. 18.169; cf., for example, *Almayer's Folly* Collected Edn. (London, 1947), 182.

36. *Heart of Darkness* Collected Edn. (London, 1946), 48.

37. Gosse, cit. Furnas, 217.

FURTHER READING:

The standard bibliography is by W. F. Prideaux (1903), revised edition 1917), but important supplementary material is to be found in the catalogue of the Beinecke Robert Louis Stevenson Collection at Yale (6 vols, New Haven, 1951-64) and in R. L. Swearingen's "Stevenson's Prose Writings 1850-1881: An Index and Finding-List", *Studies in Scottish Literature* XI, (January, 1974), 178-96. The revised edition of Janet Adam Smith's collection of Stevenson's poems appeared in 1971. From the many biographies, one may select Graham Balfour, *The Life of Robert Louis Stevenson* (London, 1901); J. C. Furnas, *Voyage to Windward: The Life of Robert Louis Stevenson* 2 vols. (London, 1952); and the illustrated short biography by David Daiches, *Robert Louis Stevenson and his World* (London,

1973). Chesterton's *Robert Louis Stevenson* (London, 1927) remains interesting; and there are two useful modern studies, R. Kiely, *Robert Louis Stevenson and the Fiction of Adventure* (Cambridge, Mass., 1965) and E. M. Eigner, *Robert Louis Stevenson and Romantic Tradition* (Princeton, 1966). Recent publication indicates that interest in Stevenson's life and works remains high.

THE KAILYARD REVISITED

by Eric Anderson

"There grows a bonnie brier bush in our kail-yard,
And white are the blossoms on't in our kail-yard."

THESE LINES from Johnson's *Musical Museum*, printed by way of motto at the beginning of *Beside the Bonnie Brier Bush*, suggested to W. H. Millar the title for his article on "The Literature of the Kailyard" in *The New Review* of 1895[1] and gave the Kailyard School its name. The three authors brought together in the article as they never were in real life were James Matthew Barrie (1860-1937), Samuel Rutherford Crockett (1859-1914) and John Watson (1850-1907). Most of Barrie's contribution to the Kailyard was made before he become a successful West End playwright. It consists of *Auld Licht Idylls* (1888), *When a Man's Single* (1888), *A Window in Thrums* (1889), *The Little Minister* (1891), *Sentimental Tommy* (1896) and *Margaret Ogilvy* (1896), a biography of his mother. S. R. Crockett, a Free Church minister who resigned his charge to become a full-time novelist, wrote thirty-seven volumes of prose fiction, of which the best-known are *The Stickit Minister* (1893), *The Raiders* (1894), *The Lilac Sunbonnet* (1894), *The Grey Man* (1896) and *Kit Kennedy* (1899). Dr. John Watson, also a Free Church minister, published his fiction under the name of "Ian Maclaren". He is remembered as a writer of short stories rather than novels—in particular for *Beside the Bonnie Brier Bush* (1894) and *The Days of Auld Langsyne* (1895). His other works include *Kate Carnegie* (1896), *Afterwards and Other Stories* (1899) and *St. Jude's* (1907).

FOR ITS time, the unfriendly article in *The New Review* which gave the Kailyard its name struck a dissonant note. The author's principal target was S. R. Crockett's *The Lilac Sunbonnet*, but he had harsh things to say about Ian Maclaren's "diseased craving for the pathetic",[2] and allowed only Barrie ("*pars magna*, if not *pars maxima*, of the Great Kailyard Movement"[3]), to emerge with some of his reputation still intact. Yet *Beside the Bonnie Brier Bush*, first published the year before, was already in its ninth edition and had sold nearly sixty thousand copies, twelve years later its popularity would be unabated and its sales in Britain and America would be close to three-quarters of a million. Maclaren's biographer declares that the author received no unfavourable review,[4] and if we exclude Millar's article that seems indeed to be the truth. Barrie's kailyard work also was enthusiastically received by reviewers and reading public alike. Crockett was not always quite so lucky, but the truth remains that the Kailyard, in its time, had an immense popular and critical success.

It is also true that its reputation has not endured. The movement has been derided for its sentimentalism, attacked as a partial and inaccurate picture of Scottish life, or ignored as more or less beneath notice. Cunninghame Graham thought that no one "who thinks in 'guid braid Scots' would recognize himself dressed in the motley which it has been the pride of kailyard writers to bestow".[5] George Blake in *Barrie and the Kailyard School* echoes this "purely Scottish complaint against the betrayal of national dignity"[6] and regrets that they wrote "sweet, amusing little stories of bucolic intrigue as seen through the windows of the Presbyterian manse" (*B&KS*, 13) while the "mainly ugly sort of life" (*B&KS*, 9) of nineteenth-century industrial Scotland remained unrecorded. Kurt Wittig finds Barrie's earliest work "not bad", but criticises the "sickening sentimentality and quaintness" of his imitators: Maclaren and Crockett, "Whatever their merit . . . have nothing to add to the Scottish literary tradition".[7] David Daiches sums it all up admirably in his wry suggestion that the Kailyard "is generally agreed to be something that one shakes one's head over".[8]

If we do not expect any writer of fiction (let alone one whose concern is rural life) to give a total picture of his country or his time, and if we do not entirely exclude sentimentality from the range of emotions acceptable to reader or writer, we may find the Kailyard worth revisiting. It is unlikely that the blooms on the brier bush will have retained the fragrance enjoyed by Victorian readers, but equally they may now seem less sickly-sweet than the school's detractors maintain. In any case the Kailyard is on the native soil. We cannot pretend that it is not a part of the Scottish literary tradition simply by ignoring it.

Barrie's *Auld Licht Idylls* (most of which originally appeared in the *St. James's* and *The British Weekly*) is the *fons et origo* of the "Great Kailyard Movement". The irony of the title is almost immediately apparent, although it has escaped those who insist that the Kailyard is merely sentimental or bucolic. The Auld Lichts are narrow-minded, poverty-stricken weavers, living for the most part "in retiring little houses the builder of which does not seem to have remembered that it is a good plan to have a road leading to houses until after they were finished".[9] At harvest time as many as fifty men and women are herded together to sleep in the straw of a farm garret, "Up as early as five in the morning . . . generally dead tired by night" (*ALI*, 49). The post-mistress steams open all letters. Salmon-poaching at times turns to violence, and the visit of the neighbouring townsfolk on their Fast Day leads to bloodshed in the streets. As the strictest of the four denominations in Thrums the Auld Lichts watch their minister for unsound doctrine and their members for Sabbath-breaking. The narrator's landlady (for Barrie distances himself from his subjects by using the old dominie as his narrator) laments the "want of Christ" in the minister's discourses: "Her case against the minister was that he did not call to denounce her sufficiently often for her sins" (*ALI*, 11). There is nothing idyllic about Thrums.

It is important to notice that neither Thrums nor the Auld Lichts are contemporary pictures. Barrie goes out of his way to remind the reader that "There are few Auld Licht communities in Scotland nowadays" (*ALI*, 11), that "For forty years they have been dying out" (*ALI*, 61), that the election described in one chapter is that of 1832 (*ALI*, 196). *Auld Licht Idylls* is a series of vignettes, illustrative of social change, and Barrie's source was his mother's memory of what she had seen and heard tell of as a girl. Maclaren and Crockett are less evidently antiquarians in their early works. Maclaren drew from experiences on his uncles' farms as well as from his mother's stories, and Crockett took as much from his Galloway childhood as from the tales of the grandparents who brought him up; but like Barrie neither pretended to offer a contemporary picture of Scotland. They assume, as Scott assumed, that their readership is interested in the manners of the age that has just passed.

The instant success of *Auld Licht Idylls* is not far to seek. It is well-written and extremely funny. Barrie's humour characteristically catches the reader by surprise, the sentences finishing in other manner than he has been led to expect. "The only pleasant story Thrums could tell of the [English] chapel", he tells us for instance, "was that its steeple once fell". (*ALI*, 20) In the Auld Licht kirk, "The plate for collections is inside the church, so that the whole congregation can have a guess at what you give" (*ALI*, 64). Absurdity, especially when the subjects seem unaware of it, is his delight. There is nothing better of this kind than the description of the "very old family" at the beginning of Chapter X:

> They were a very old family with whom Snecky Hobart, the bellman, lodged. Their favourite dissipation, when their looms had come to rest, was a dander through the kirkyard. They dressed for it: the three young ones in their rusty blacks; the patriarch in his old blue coat, velvet kneebreeches, and broad blue bonnet; and often of an evening I have met them moving from grave to grave. By this time the old man was nearly ninety, and the young ones averaged sixty. They read out the inscriptions on the tombstones in a solemn drone, and their father added his reminiscences. He never failed them. Since the beginning of the century he had not missed a funeral, and his children felt that he was a great example. (*ALI*, 206-7.)

The most important of the *Idylls* is the single short story included in what is otherwise a collection of essays. Apart from being one of the best of Scottish short stories, "The Courting of T'nowhead's Bell" points the way forward which both Barrie and his immediate successors in the

Kailyard were to take. The plot is simple and close to farce: the wooing of Bell by two inarticulate suitors who finally race each other from church to be the first to propose. The excellence lies in the unexpected conclusion when the winner is manoeuvred into giving his prize to the loser, and in the brilliance of the dialogue:

'Sam'l,' said Sanders.
'Ay.'
'I'm hearin' yer to be mairit.'
'Ay.'
'Weel, Sam'l, she's a snod bit lassie.'
'Thank ye,' said Sam'l.
'I had ance a kin' o' notion o' Bell mysel,' continued Sanders.
'Ye had?'
'Yes, Sam'l; but I thocht better o't.'
'Hoo d'ye mean?' asked Sam'l, a little anxiously.
'Weel, Sam'l, mairitch is a terrible responsibeelity.'
'It is so,' said Sam'l, wincing.
'An' no the thing to tak up withoot conseederation.'
'But it's a blessed and honourable state, Sanders; ye've heard the minister on't.'
'They say,' continued the relentless Sanders, ' 'at the minister doesna get on sair wi' the wife himsel.'
'So they do,' cried Sam'l, with a sinking at the heart.
'I've been telt,' Sanders went on, ' 'at gin ye can get the upper han' o' the wife for a while at first, there's the mair chance o' a harmonious exeestence.'
'Bell's no the lassie,' said Sam'l, appealingly, 'to thwart her man.'
Sanders smiled.
'D'y ye think she is, Sanders?'
'Weel, Sam'l, I d'na want to fluster ye, but she's been ower lang wi' Lisbeth Fargus no to hae learnt her ways. An a'body kins what a life T'nowhead has wi' her.'
'Guid sake, Sanders, hoo did ye no speak o' this afore?'
'I thocht ye kent o't, Sam'l.'
They had now reached the square, and the U.P. kirk was coming out. The Auld Licht kirk would be half an hour yet.
'But, Sanders,' said Sam'l, brightening up, 'ye was on yer wy to speir her yersel.'
'I was, Sam'l,' said Sanders, 'and I canna but be thankfu ye was ower quick for's.' (*ALI*, 185-6.)

"T'nowhead's Bell" is Barrie's first extended excursion into the dramatic. It looks forward to his novels, and, beyond them, to his plays. Before both, came *A Window in Thrums*. It is not quite a novel, but a series of sketches of family life assembled into a loose narrative. Its appeal lies in its characters—first among them Jess, the crippled mother who dominates the household—and its evocation of the little world in which Barrie grew up. What action there is passes almost entirely inside the house on the brae or within sight of Jess's window. The humour, less biting than in *Auld Licht Idylls*, is the humour of character revealed in ordinary situations. The seemingly insignificant comings and goings in the village, for instance, as observed by Jess and Leeby from their window, can lead them to elaborate deductions about Sunday's preacher and every detail of the meals he will eat and with whom.[10] In another chapter the fun lies in Hendry's total incomprehension of the effect of his casual remark "that he had seen Tibbie Mealmaker in the town with her man" (*AWT*, 20), the womenfolk's total certainty that she will call—as of course she does—and the upheaval as the entire house is transformed in readiness to receive her:

> Fresh muslin curtains had been put up in the room. The grand foot-stool, worked by Leeby, was so placed that Tibbie could not help seeing it; and a fine cambric handkerchief, of which Jess was very proud, was hanging out of a drawer as if by accident. An antimacassar lying carelessly on the seat of a chair concealed a rent in the horse-hair, and the china ornaments on the mantelpiece were so placed that they looked whole. Leeby's black merino was hanging near the window in a good light, and Jess's Sabbath bonnet, which was never worn, occupied a nail beside it (*AWT*, 25).

The new element in *A Window in Thrums* is its pathos. The main incident in the book is the visit of Jess's favourite son from London and the struggle between them for the lady's glove he carried in his pocket. His mother's power over him at length persuades him to burn it. There is pathos both in the young man's submission and in the inevitability of Jess's eventual defeat, a pathos enhanced by the admission of failure implicit in the final words of the chapter: "But she saw 'at he laid it on the fire fell fond-like" (*AWT*, 192).

A Window in Thrums is a sad book. The life it describes has its pleasures, just as in "a garden of kail and potatoes . . . there may be a line of daisies, white and red, on each side of the narrow footpath, and honeysuckle over the door" (*AWT*, 5), but the ever-present thought is "that all braes lead only to the grave" (*AWT*, 5). Thrums is both a kindlier and a more realistic place than in *Auld Licht Idylls*, but it remains far from idyllic, and the narrator (who is again the dominie) hints ever and again at the sadness which lies ahead. The greatness of this minor masterpiece lies not in its humour and pathos, nor even in the brilliance of the dialogue and the spare prose of the descriptive passages, but in the sense of significance with which Barrie invests the humble lives which he describes. The short and simple annals of the poor are annals, not of the parish, but—he convinces us—of all humanity.

With *Sentimental Tommy*, which was published seven years later, Barrie reaches the peak of his achievement as a novelist, and the Kailyard its top-most point. It can stand comparison with the best novels of childhood. Tommy—a precocious, affectionate and maddening youngster, full of imaginings and self-deception, and convincing even in the unexpected-ness of his actions—is Barrie himself and a writer in the making. (The novel's title is clearly intended to be ambiguous: *Sentimental Tommy: The Story of His Boyhood*, by J. M. Barrie). There is humour in plenty—especially when the two children set out to view Thrums and find the promised land small, dirty and without magic—but also a pervasive sadness. Barrie concludes the novel, as Crockett could not have brought himself to do, with the failure of the young hero to win his bursary to Aberdeen University and an agonising farewell from his sister.

At times there is the sound of a new note, alien to the Kailyard. When little Grizel becomes "mother" to the family (*ST*, 188), or Tommy's shadow "strained a muscle in turning with him" (*ST*, 203) or the make-believe Jacobites' enemies are made to walk the plank (*ST*, 261) the pan-pipes are distinctly heard. For Barrie the Kailyard was too restricted a field. Within it he wrote better than anyone else, but his Kailyard period was a prologue only. It helped him to develop an astringent style and a more and more effective mastery over character and dialogue, but in due course he turned, as he was bound to do, to the place where these qualities could find their fullest expression.

The short story of Scottish rural life was the form initially adopted by both Barrie's principal followers—by S. R. Crockett in *The Stickit Minister*, and by Ian Maclaren in *Beside the Bonnie Brier Bush* and *The Days of Auld Langsyne*. His two strands of humour and pathos—the humour often enhancing the pathos by its unexpectedness—became the characteristics of the school. It is probably true to say that the taste for Scottish stories exploited by Crockett and Maclaren was not created by Barrie so much as discovered by him, for a glance at the weekly newspaper in which some of Barrie's and Maclaren's sketches first appeared strongly suggests that the audience was already assembled and waiting. The first number of *The British Weekly* (a church newspaper with liberal and non-conformist leanings edited in London by Robertson Nicoll, a former Free Church minister from Aberdeenshire) has a page and a half of politics; the rest of the issue is concerned almost exclusively with church affairs and literature with a religious slant. Most space is given to "Our Religious Census of London", the first of a series of articles on morning and evening attendances at each church and chapel in London on Sunday, October 24th. The "Sermon Column" carries summaries of addresses by the Rev. C. H. Spurgeon and the Rev. Marcus Dods. Three pages are devoted to "News of the Churches" and "Table Talk" about church affairs, and the literary section includes reviews of five religious books and periodicals. The advertisements, which are numerous, give a further indication of the kind of people who might be expected to take the paper. The Edinburgh Life Assurance Company takes half a page; the Scottish Union and the Scottish Provident a quarter-page each. Oliphant, Anderson and Ferrier of Edinburgh advertise nine novels by Annie S. Swan, lighter reading perhaps than Dr. Talmage's *Marriage and Home Life*, or the fourth edition, revised, of *The Practice of the Free Church of Scotland in her Several Courts*. Among the smaller advertisements one for "McVitie's Genuine Scotch Oatcakes" is prominent.

In such a periodical Scottish readers would be tempted by more than oatcakes, and it is not surprising that Ian Maclaren's stories of small Perthshire farmers and their conversation in the kirkyard on Sundays should receive a ready welcome. With the single exception of Barrie's sketches, they were easily the best things that had appeared in *The British Weekly*. Published in book form they quickly proved that their appeal was not limited to the audience which Robertson Nicoll had assembled. Despite characters remote in place and experience, and speaking a dialect not all of whose *nuances* were immediately obvious, Maclaren's two volumes became best sellers on both sides of the Atlantic. That does not, of course, prove that they were, or are, works of art. In point of fact the Drumtochty stories are not all excellent, but the best of them are, and in their small way they deserve to endure.

The Rev. John Watson's metamorphosis into Ian Maclaren was an accident. He had published nothing, apart from a brief sketch of a friend, when Robertson Nicoll asked him for a series of articles on the leading ideas of Jesus for another of his ventures, *The Expositor*. When Watson visited him, Nicoll was so impressed by the racy stories and character-sketches with which he enlivened his conversation that he asked him to make articles of them. The first four chapters of *Beside the Bonnie Brier Bush* were the result, and the first article appeared in *The British Weekly* for 2 November 1893.[11]

Watson was as far from the conventional stereotype of a Free Church minister as can be imagined. Physically he was a big man; he had inherited from his Highland mother (a Maclaren) her gifts of repartee and mimicry, and in his social circle he was a notable raconteur and humorist. By choice he would have been a farmer or a land agent, but to please his father, a devout Free Kirk elder, he finally agreed to the ministry. On the surface, the life chosen thus was surprisingly successful. Three happy years at Logiealmond in Perthshire were succeeded by a less agreeable spell in Glasgow and then by a ministry of twenty-five years at Sefton Park Church, Liverpool. He wrote twelve religious works as well as eleven works of fiction; he was a popular guest preacher, Moderator for a year of the Presbyterian Synod in England, and a lecturer in demand both in Britain and America. But beneath the surface, he yearned for country life.

"If sometimes I have been almost choked in the atmosphere of ecclesiastical courts", he said when resigning his charge, "it was because my lungs were accustomed to the wind blowing over the moors or across a field of ripe, golden wheat; and if I have not understood the subtleties or the phraseology of esoteric piety, it was because I had been so much at home with open-air folk".[12]

For him his fiction was an escape back to the company of the open-air folk he had left for Glasgow and Liverpool. His best works, *Beside the Bonnie Brier Bush* and *The Days of Auld Langsyne* ("The two books are in reality one", said Nicoll, "and should go together"),[13] are written with the passionate intensity of the exile whose vision of people and places has been focussed by absence. It is on these two books that his reputation must rest.

Drumtochty, the glen about which he writes, is Glen Almond, where he had his first charge. The name may perhaps have been suggested by his aunt's farm at Drumlochy, some of the characters by people he had met on his uncles' farms near Blairgowrie. Certainly Burnbrae and Drumsheugh share some of his uncles' characteristics; Dr. Davidson was modelled on Dr. Barty of Bendochy, and George Howe was William Durham, Watson's school-fellow at Sirling who was always in his form "*facile princeps*"[14] and denied a brilliant career by his death at the age of twenty-one in much the manner described in "Domsie".

For modern readers these tales present the two almost insuperable barriers of being both churchy and sentimental. The church is of real importance to his characters. They are small tenant-farmers, and for all of them, Free Kirk or Established Kirk, "intellectual life centred on the weekly sermon".[15] Apart from the train journeys to and from market, they meet only at church on Sundays. The great events of the glen, its deaths, illnesses, sales, the triumphs and disasters of sons and daughters who have gone south or gone abroad, are the weekly topics of discussion in the kirkyard and the occasional subject of prayers from the pulpit. Rightly, Maclaren brings the reader into the church itself at times, for the prayers of thanksgiving for the recovery of Professor Ross or for Burnbrae's return to his farm are a proper part of the world he is describing, a world in which the minister is expected to give expression to deep feelings which otherwise remain unarticulated. But the men and women of Drumtochty are far from ideal Christians: Milton and Lachlan Campbell are pharisees, Dr. Maclure and the dominie scarcely believers. There is nothing of the tract-writer about Maclaren. For his characters, however, religion matters (the Bible, as Crockett reminds us, was "in some wise also the key to Scotland and to its history for three hundred years"),[16] and Maclaren gives it its due place, treating it, without comment, as a normal and important aspect of human life. In this respect the contrast with Barrie is revealing and much in Maclaren's favour. Barrie treats religion as a joke. The reader is invited to watch the antics of his Auld Lichts—their absurdly narrow views and humbugging self-righteousness—and to laugh. Maclaren records the piety of his characters as a simple fact and assumes that we shall find it natural. There is little doubt that his is the more faithful picture of religious life in rural Scotland at the time of which he writes.

Maclaren's sentimentality we may find less easy to accept. His deathbed scenes do not share the reticence which he commends in so many of his characters. Like Drumtochty, which "never acquitted itself with credit at a marriage", he "had a genius for funerals" (*BBB*, 40). The death and funeral of George Howe, the death of Dr. Maclure and the death of Lily Robertson spare the reader very little. The dying words of the doctor, as he remembers learning the twenty-third psalm as a boy and asks his long-dead mother for a kiss ("for a've been waiting for ye, an' a'll sune be asleep" (*BBB*, 304)), cross the border for most readers between sentimentality and sickliness, but Maclaren's touch is surer with the prayer of George Howe the scholar, dying of consumption. The old schoolmaster who first noticed his talent ("The first year o' Latin was enough for me. He juist nippet up his verbs" (*BBB*, 25)) is making his farewell visit to the divinity student and, unbeliever as he is, is impressed by the boy's steadfastness and asks him to pray for him. Howe extemporises as follows:

"Lord Jesus, remember my dear maister, for he's been a kind freend to me and mony a puir laddie in Drumtochty. Bind up his sair heart and give him licht at eventide, and may the maister and his scholars meet some mornin' where the schule never skails, in the kingdom o' oor Father" (*BBB*, 39).

An age like ours which approves frank description of the sexual act but finds the act of dying embarrassing in reality and in fiction cannot quite respond as did Maclaren's original readers, whose taboos we have neatly reversed. If the only response we can make to sentimentality is embarrassment then great areas of Maclaren's achievement—as well as his intentions—lie beyond our comprehension. It is perhaps a sobering reflection that such a response would also limit our reading of many of the greatest Victorian novelists including Dickens and George Eliot, who are not shy of sentimentality themselves.

Sentimentality is one of Maclaren's weapons. He uses it deliberately to play on his readers' feelings and, having made use of it, he puts it away again. He is sentimental in moments of pathos, but far from sentimental about the world he has created. Drumtochty is not as brutal as Thrums, but life there is also far from idyllic. Death and sadness are frequent visitors. The love of mother for son, father for daughter and old couples for each other is usually love in adversity. Maclaren's world has its kindly side to the fore, but the background to the neighbourly charity which is the theme of many of his tales is a hard world in which a farmer will be ruined if illness keeps him from ploughing his fields, in which sons who go abroad or daughters who go into service in the city may never return or may come home in disgrace. There is drunkenness in the glen, and meanness, and not all those who leave to seek a fortune are paragons of virtue and learning. Jamie Soutar's summary is fair: "There's a puckle gude fouk in the pairish, and ane or twa' o' the ither kind, and the maist o' us are half and between" (BBB, 194). The final impression is of optimism, for adversity brings out the best in Maclaren's characters rather than the worst, but it is of an optimism based on a realistic view of how people can and will behave, not on the wishful thinking of a sentimental clergyman.

Maclaren's attempts at a full-length novel expose his limitations. He can follow the implications of one incident over several chapters in "Domsie" or "For Conscience Sake", but the demands of an extended and more complex plot are beyond him. Kate Carnegie, which is set in the glen, begins with a vivid lively scene on Perth station on the busiest day of the year and quickly establishes the characters of Kate and her military father, returning from long service abroad, and of Carmichael, the young Free Kirk minister. It is clear that Carmichael and Kate will marry each other, but it soon becomes equally clear that Maclaren does not know how to prevent that conclusion from arriving too soon. The hint of a theme of social change, connected with the Carnegies' poverty, is not developed, and the second half of the book is filled out with an improbable accusation of heresy made by a neighbouring minister. With sketches of this eccentric cleric at home and the deliberations of the presbytery, we find ourselves back beside the brier bush. Maclaren was a raconteur, rather than a novelist. His range was confined to dialogue, to a group of characters carefully and sparingly etched, to the humour and pathos of their lives at a particular time and a particular place.

His Drumtochty is an island-world. The railway (for Hardy the sinister symbol of the town's influence on the country) is used by Maclaren to emphasise Drumtochty's isolation and immunity to change. It ran, he tells us, from Muirtown to the Junction and thence to the neighbouring village of Kildrummie, but "did not think it worth while to come to Drumtochty" (BBB, 133). The final journey home, therefore, is on foot through the woods, and the farmers, who have kept off local affairs until then, hold their confidential parley at walking pace on the road. No stranger can arrive unseen, for Peter Bruce, "the factotum of the little Kildrummie branch" (BBB, 140), is at once gate-keeper to the glen and commentator upon its affairs. His exclamation as the train brings home the coffin of Lily Robertson sums up Drumtochty with admirable economy: " 'Kildrummie platform's black', cried Peter from the foot-board; 'the'll be twal gin there be a man. Ye stick by ane anither weel up the wy' ".[17]

This clannish community of "sound education, unflagging industry, absolute integrity, and an undying attachment to Drumtochty" (*ALS*, 209) has all the fascination of a closed society to which the reader slowly earns admission. As character is revealed almost entirely in speech the reader gets to know the glen, as in real life, little by little, and there is always the possibility of surprise, as when Jamie Soutar the cynic takes on an errand of mercy in London or Dr. Maclure's need for affection is suddenly betrayed when he drops Drumsheugh's territorial name and calls him Paitrick (*BBB*, 293). The reader is invited to identify with Drumtochty as he is not expected to do with Thrums. He is to share Drumtochty's disapproval of servant-girls with fur on their jackets and "Miss" on their envelopes, and applaud Lily's attitude to organ-music in church: "As for the organ, it juist boomilled awa', an' she never lat on she heard it" (*ALS*, 285). When the famous surgeon protests that he will be damned if he crosses a river in spate and is silenced by Dr. Maclure's, "Sit doon ... condemned ye will be suner or later gin ye shirk yir duty, but through the water ye gang the day" (*BBB*, 261), the reader delights in the local man's victory. This is the secret of Maclaren's success with the reading public of his day. He offers an escape into the kind of world which everyone believes they would prefer to their own, yet conceals that it is an escape by the realism of the dialogue and the humour with which his characters reveal themselves.

Is Maclaren any more than a clever writer of popular fiction? I think he is. His range is narrow but the two Drumtochty books are enough to establish a continuing reputation. His ear for speech and his disciplined determination to reveal character "in dialogue exclusively"[18] allowed him to create characters which have survived beyond their time and locality. In their reticence and their self-righteousness, their lapses into sentimentality and their steadfastness in adversity, they are recognisably Scottish, of their own and other ages; but, beyond that, their little world whose loves and deaths, triumphs and disasters, are rooted in the particular and local is recognisably a part of universal human experience.

S. R. Crockett's first published prose was *The Stickit Minister*, a collection of short stories set in a particular region and concerned with a small circle of characters. Although modelled on Barrie, it introduces an element of melodrama, a striving for a startling or shocking conclusion, which is new. The stickit minister of the title, for instance, has sacrificed his career and his health for an ungrateful brother who is about to stand by and watch as the dying man is turned out of his farm before the year's end. "I thank you kindly," he concludes, in reply to an offer of help, "but *I'll be flitted before that*".[19]

The other stories in the collection are of a piece. "Accepted of the Beasts" is a melodramatic sketch of a minister who loses his congregation little by little, is suspended from his charge and turns to singing Handel to

the cattle before dying in the field. "The Heather Lintie"—melodrama
with a dash of pathos—describes a lonely spinster poetess waiting for a
review of her poems and dying in the night, clutching, as yet unread, the
paper which contains a slashing review by a clever young satirist. There is
further melodrama in "The Split in the Marrow Kirk" when the boy
Jaikie is injured near to death by the action of his own father, and the
sentimental ending to which the other stories have accustomed the
reader: "When it was time for Jiminy to go to college he had for companion, at Maister Adam's expense, a lame lad with a beautiful countenance. His name was Jaikie" (*SM*, 65).

Each of these tales has one point, usually a slight one. There is no twist or
turn to the plot, which reaches its expected end in a moment of melodrama or mild pathos. The characters scarcely have time to develop; they
are merely vehicles for the story which Crockett takes from his own
experience or from a traditional local tale. *The Stickit Minister* is
journalism of quite a high order, far superior to the usual standard of *The
Christian Leader* in which, as a series of articles, it first appeared, but in
two respects it also makes a claim to be considered as literature.

The first is Crockett's easy mastery of his native Galloway dialect, used
to reveal character through speech. "Trials for Licence" is worth reading
because Saunders McQuirr tells his story in his own pithy words. Mrs.
McQuirr, one of those decided, managing wives who people Crockett's
novels, is deftly etched in a few words of her own and a few from her
husband, who is, he confesses, "ower slow for the wife; she kind o' likes a'
things to gang forrit gye-an sherp, an' wad gar a' the hens hae their layin'
dune i' the mornin' an' their nests made afore they gaed oot to pick a
single corn" (*SM*, 30). The second is the excellence of the best story in the
collection, "The Tragedy of Duncan Duncanson, Schoolmaster". Like
the others this short story deals with one simple incident, but on this
occasion the present is set between a past and a future. The central
character, the deposed minister of the Parish of Shaws, is a solid creation,
sad rather than pathetic, and dangerous in his drunkenness. The post-
script verges on the over-sentimental, but the inscription on the schoolmaster's tombstone sets the incident in the longer perspective which gives
the story its power. There is a fine picture of the village school at work, a
splendid description of the dog inserted into the class, and a carefully
built-up moment of tension, even of horror, as the fuddled dominie turns
from the dog to attack the boy.

The Stickit Minister, which appeared a year before *Beside The Bonnie
Brier Bush*, places Crockett in the Kailyard, but unlike Maclaren he soon
stepped outside it into the larger field of full-length historical and
domestic romance. Crockett had enormous creative energy. He published, on average, two novels a year, besides other works. He had an eye
which noticed things, a pen which could describe them and a burning

urge to tell a story. Above all he knew his Gallovidians and their speech. "At home", he once said, "we all spoke Scots. My old grandmother, I remember, spoke the beautiful Scots which now, except in Carrick and the rural districts of North Galloway, is almost a dead tongue. We spoke exactly the words of Burns . . . and in our daily speech his most recondite words were used".[20] As a result his slow countrymen and quicker-tongued countrywomen are as genuine as any in Scottish literature. Yet Crockett does not get near to attaining the utmost round. *The Lilac Sunbonnet*, his first domestic romance, shows us why. Its plot, a number of its incidents, and occasional verbal reminiscences suggest that as he wrote it Crockett had in mind *Tess of the d'Urbervilles*, published not long before. No serious comparison, however, is possible. For all the small similarities the tone and the intention are quite different. There is none of the social and moral comment implicit in the sub-title of *Tess: "A Pure Woman"*. Crockett's world is an altogether undisturbing place. The tone of the novel is obstinately cheerful and the love-talk sickeningly coy. References here to the Garden of Eden are not balanced by the crushing drudgery of Flintcombe Ash; his characters are not living on a blighted star. For Hardy there is the threat of social change which may corrode the lives of his characters, and the dark perversity of a hostile or uncaring universe which may destroy them. For Crockett it is enough to create a world in which real-seeming people act out a drama with a happy ending.

Kit Kennedy, the autobiographical novel which is most nearly Crockett's masterpiece, is flawed by the same fudging of life's darker side. The cruelty of Mrs. MacWalter to young Kit is tempered by the reader's knowledge that the boy's father is close enough to prevent real harm, and the melodramatic conclusion to the novel is robbed of its proper excitement by the presence of too many would-be rescuers. It is clear that the ending will not be allowed to be unhappy. Crockett's determination to spare his reader is a pity, for there is real merit in the account of Kit's struggle for an education and in the descriptions of a Galloway childhood and student life in Edinburgh. This is Crockett's best novel.

The historical novels are recognisably in the same mould as the domestic romances. In effect Crockett merely shifted his scene through time rather than place. He took care, but not too much care, over historical accuracy. He liked to read every book published during the period he was describing, but that was more to immerse himself in the spirit of the times than to search out the details of clothing and equipment, life and manners, which clog some of the lesser Waverley Novels.

The Raiders, with which Crockett sprang into prominence as a writer, is a good example of his practice. The date (the first quarter of the eighteenth century) is never expressly mentioned. It hardly matters. The tale is one of adventure and love—of Patrick Heron's search for the raiders who have burnt the farm of Craigdarroch and his wooing of May Maxwell, one of Crockett's tomboy heroines. He makes use of Galloway legend in a powerful scene by the Murder Hole, but little of history. The period is established, adequately enough for his purposes, by the archaic rhythms of the first-person narrative. We can be pedantic, as an early reviewer was,[21] and object that Patrick Heron uses occasional anachronisms, but by and large Crockett's method works and *The Raiders* is gloriously free of being too consciously historical. On the level of a thorough-going adventure story *The Raiders* is a success. It has not held favour as well as *Kidnapped* or *Treasure Island*, but it is very much in that class. It is, as Andrew Lang said, "such a book as boys delight in, and wise men do not despise".[22]

In *The Grey Man* Crockett comes closer to historical events. Set in the reign of James VI, it finishes with the trial and execution of John Mure of Auchendrayne. The hero and narrator, is, however, a squire to Sir Thomas Kennedy of Culzean, and the winning of his spurs and his lady are his principal concern; only gradually does he realise the significance of the feuding in which the two families of Kennedies are caught up and the way in which John Mure, the grey man, manipulates events for his own advantage. Launcelot Kennedy establishes himself as a solid personality in whose affairs we can be sufficiently interested, but the merit of the novel lies in some stirring scenes of action: the battle in the snowstorm, the murder of Sir Thomas Kennedy among the sand-dunes and the execution of John and James Mure in Edinburgh. If it is enough that the age should be suggested and that the interaction of historical and fictional characters should be skilfully managed, *The Grey Man* passes muster pretty well. But there are grave weaknesses. Particularly towards the end Crockett fails to resist the urge to pile incident upon incident and improbability upon improbability. Above all, there is no wider perspective or theme, no longer view of history—merely a story of more or less historical events, for the most part rather well told.

We have come some way from the Kailyard. It is important to make the point, however, that Crockett is at his least effective precisely when he is furthest from it. The enduring passages in his novels are the moments of homely life and the conversations of homely characters, Scottish scenery described with passionate affection and an unerring eye for detail, and Scottish talk recorded in richly expressive words. When the Kailyard reappears, as in this brief incursion of Gordon the natural into a breathless love-scene between the hero and heroine, Crockett is playing from strength:

'Now go on; tell me what else you see,' said Winsome.

'Your lips—' began Ralph, and paused.

'No, six is quite enough,' said Winsome, after a little while, mysteriously. Now she had only two, and Ralph only two; yet with little grammar and no sense at all she said, 'Six is enough.'

But a voice from quite other lips came over the rising background of scrub and tangled thicket.

'Gang on coortin',' it said; 'I'm no lookin', an' I canna see onything onyway.'

It was Jock Gordon. He continued still more delicately:

'Jock Scott's gane hame till his breakfast. He'll no bother ye this mornin', sae coort awa'.[23]

Crockett's fatal flaw is that he settled too early and too easily for romance. His first novels were successful, but as time goes on we get the uneasy feeling that he is writing the same novel over and over again. For all his creative energy, his range was narrow. He understood young love, but seldom attempted a serious description of other human relationships. Every hero resembles the "dreamy long-legged callant who, with a staff in his hand and a whang of soda scone in his pocket" (*R*, viii) so marvellously turned into Crockett, the best-selling novelist. Every heroine (and they are convincing heroines) is a tomboy of considerable accomplishments who can whistle, ride, climb rope-ladders and handle dogs, horses and young men. The setting is probably Galloway, and the plot suggested, as often as not, by Galloway legend. None of this is quite enough to make an agreeable story-teller into a serious novelist. Crockett's domestic romances lack shade, his historical romances that sense of time passing, of the old order giving place to new, which makes *Rob Roy* and *Redgauntlet*, for instance, into historical novels rather than mere tales of a vanished age. When all that has been said, Crockett's achievement remains far from negligible. His best work is intensely alive. You may not like it all, but it is immensely readable.

The Kailyard writers were not innovators. For everything they wrote, their reading of Scottish literature provided them with ample precedent. They responded in particular to two characteristic features of Scottish life and letters: the cult of homeliness and nostalgia for the past.

The cult of homeliness is best summed up by Burns in his poem "To Dr. Blacklock"—

> To make a happy fireside clime
> To weans and wife,
> That's the true pathos and sublime
> Of human life

but those lines proved so powerful an echo of Scottish feeling that they are repeated over and over again, less and less well, throughout the nineteenth century. The words are different in *Whistle-Binkie*, but the sentiment is the same:

> "How gladsome pass my hours wi' my bonnie Meg sae leal!
> An', to see our tender pledges rompin' roun' our cozie biel;
> Where, i' their gleesome faces, ilka mither-feature's seen,
> For we live an' love thegither at our ain hame at e'en.

> My ain hame at e'en,

Tho' o' this warld's gear we can boast but little share,
We're contented aye, an' happy, sae we wish for naething mair;
I wadna change for kingley ha', or pearl-muntit Queen!
Sae dear to me is Maggie, an' my ain hame at e'en."[24]

The cult of home and the homespun virtues is central, too, to the Scottish novel. "To every Scot," wrote Crockett,

his own house, his own gate-end, his own ingle-nook is always the best, the most interesting, the only thing domestic worth singing about and talking about.

'So, deep in the lowland nature, began the Humour of About-the-Doors. It is little wonder, then, that the Scottish romancers have generally begun with descriptions of their own kail-yairds—which are the best kail-yairds—the only true kail-yairds . . .' (R, 96).

Crockett named Galt as "the most excellent, as he was the first of all those students of 'my ain hoose', and my ain folk' " (R, 97),[25] but Scott, "the great Wizard of all time, and the master of all who weave the Golden Lie" (R, 94) was an even more powerful example. The way in which the Waverley Novels dominated the nineteenth century should not be forgotten. They were Maclaren's favourite reading, and Robertson Nicoll's. Their influence on the Kailyard Movement is predictably considerable. Although Scott has his big bow-wow delight in rumbustious scenes and an exciting story, he is often at his most memorable in the kailyard. It is his humble characters that have endured best, and it is to them (to Mucklebackit, Ochiltree, Fairservice and Jeanie Deans, not to his heroes) that he gives the best words to speak. Scott shares with Burns the Scottish belief that, since rank is but the guinea-stamp, wisdom is often to be found in the common sense of common-life characters. In prose and in poetry the kailyard was flourishing long before Barrie began to cultivate it.

Nostalgia for the past is a strongly-developed strain in Scottish fiction, as it is in the Scottish character. The past is important to small nations living close to powerful neighbours, for they must take a pride in their history if they are to keep their identity. Scotland's past, thanks above all to Scott, is habitually viewed romantically or sentimentally, so that Mary Queen of Scots and Charles Edward Stuart are accorded the same veneration as Bruce and Wallace by people who in real life would certainly have fought against all they stood for.

Crockett was predisposed towards the historical novel by his early reading of Scott and Dumas, but also by his upbringing. He worshipped at the Cameronian kirk and visited the graves of the martyrs with the grandfather who brought him up, and he adopted "Rutherford" as his middle name in honour of the famous Covenanter. Past and present merged easily into one in the Galloway of his youth; to set his romances in the Scotland of previous ages was to write on subjects still alive in the minds and talk of people he knew.

Barrie and Maclaren, not historical writers in the same sense, nonetheless shared the national veneration for what is unchanging in a shifting world. The Scots are antiquaries at heart. Sir Walter Scott was pleased that *Waverley* might "really boast to be a tolerably faithful portrait of Scottish manners"[26] and saw his first three novels as an attempt to "illustrate the manners of Scotland at three different periods".[27] The Kailyarders followed in this tradition. Barrie's Thrums would have delighted Scott. Crockett did for Galloway what the Waverley Novels had done for the Borders and Edinburgh. Maclaren preserved, in his sketches of Drumtochty where "manners retained the fashion of the former age" (*BBB*, 133), not only the memory of a Perthshire glen earlier in the century but by implication a record of those moral qualities on which Scotsmen used to pride themselves.

None of these writers, nor all three taken together, give a complete picture of Scotland in their own time or in the past. They wrote about three different, distinctive, remote and self-contained country areas. They were not critics of their times, nor social reformers. The sadness of change and the collision of cultures, the sort of themes explored by novelists as diverse as Tolstoy and E. M. Forster, they ignored. They remained determinedly parochial. Literature is concerned with great issues and great movements, with the tide of times and what it sweeps away—but also with the small, the eccentric and the individual. The Kailyard's importance is that in writing (and generally writing well) of parochial matters, its authors conjured up at the same time much of the essential Scottishness of the Scot, those qualities which in modern times may in large measure have been eroded by city life and the influence of easy travel. Eroded, but not yet destroyed. The Kailyard identified the courage in adversity, the general approval of "getting on" (and the particular jealousy felt for some who get on), the kindliness, opinionatedness, undemonstrativeness, sentimentality, provincialism and stubborn insistence on what is thought to be right, which are not untypical eighty years on.

NOTES

1. *The New Review*, XII, 384-94.
2. *op. cit.*, 385.
3. *op. cit.*, 384.
4. W. R. Nicoll, *Ian Maclaren: Life of the Rev. John Watson, D.D.* (London, 1908), 168.
5. T. W. H. Crosland, *The Unspeakable Scot* (London, 1902), 152.

6. G. Blake, *Barrie and the Kailyard School* (London, 1951), 75. (hereafter referred to as *B&KS*).

7. K. Wittig, *The Scottish Tradition in Literature* (Edinburgh and London, 1958), 254.

8. David Daiches, *Literary Essays* (London, 1956), 132.

9. J. M. Barrie *Auld Licht Idylls* (London, 1888), 12. (hereafter *ALI*).

10. J. M. Barrie, *A Window in Thrums* (London, 1889), chap. 2. (hereafter *AWT*).

11. Nicoll, *Maclaren*, 166.

12. *op. cit.*, 46.

13. *op. cit.*, 183.

14. *op. cit.*, 30.

15. Ian Maclaren, *Beside the Bonnie Brier Bush* (London, 1894), 200. (hereafter *BBB*).

16. S. R. Crockett, *Raiderland* (London, 1904), 32. (hereafter *R*).

17. Ian Maclaren, *The Days of Auld Lang Syne* (London, 1895), 307. (hereafter *ALS*).

18. Nicoll, *Maclaren*, 167.

19. S. R. Crockett, *The Stickit Minister* (London, 1893), 14. (hereafter *SM*).

20. R. H. Sherard, "Crockett at Home", *The Idler* (1894), 804.

21. In *The Athenaeum*, 7 April 1894, 441.

22. M. M. Harper, *Crockett and Grey Galloway* (London, 1907), 103.

23. S. R. Crockett, *The Lilac Sunbonnet* (London, 1894), 291.

24. "My Ain Hame at E'en", *Whistle-Binkie*, 4th series, (Glasgow, 1832-47).

25. See also Crockett's introduction to D. S. Meldrum's edition of *Annals of the Parish* (Edinburgh, 1895).

26. H. J. C. Grierson *et al.*, *Letters of Sir Walter Scott* (London, 1932), III, 478.

27. W. Scott, *The Antiquary* (1816), Introduction.

FURTHER READING:

An early study, brief and often oversimplified, but valuable, is George Blake's *Barrie and the Kailyard School* (London, 1951). Barrie himself is the subject of a good introductory survey by Allen Wright (Edinburgh, 1976), and there has been considerable recent discussion of his fiction suggesting that a wider revaluation is in progress. MacLaren's most successful stories were re-issued in hardback and paperback (Edinburgh, 1977) indicating their continuing popularity. Crosland's *The Unspeakable Scot* (London, 1902), often unfairly but often wittily ridicules the kailyarders; they get rougher treatment from Lewis Grassic Gibbon and Hugh MacDiarmid in their joint *Scottish Scene* (London, 1934).

GEORGE DOUGLAS BROWN: A STUDY IN OBJECTIVITY

by Ian Campbell

GEORGE DOUGLAS BROWN was born illegitimate to a farm labourer in Ochiltree, Ayrshire in 1869. Poor, morbidly conscious of his unhappy parentage, sensitive and very gifted, he struggled through village schools, Glasgow University, Oxford, and settled in 1895 in London. He died in 1902, with only *The House with the Green Shutters* (1901) to make his name famous. His academic career had promised well, but eventually fizzled out. He produced a few odd commissioned publishers' jobs and some powerful literary essays, and was at work on interesting projects when he died, suddenly, of a mysterious illness in London. His first, early success gives some indication of his mordant gift for observation of his native country; the twentieth century lost a penetrating and perhaps brilliant commentator on the Scottish scene.

SHORTLY before his tragically early death in 1902, George Douglas Brown wrote from London to an old acquaintance in Ochiltree.

Dear Mrs. Watson,

I thank you very much for the kindly letter you sent me, and am glad to have your father's verses. I am afraid, however, you will be sadly disappointed by "The House with the Green Shutters". It is anything but a kindly book. Yet it was written with a kind enough intention. I hate scandal, malevolence, and all manner of cruelty; and in this book I tried to hold them up to scorn and loathing. Hence the unpleasantness of the characters. But, believe me, not one of the characters was drawn from Ochiltree. Ochiltree has always treated me well, and never better than on my last visit.

I am yours very truly

G. Douglas Brown.[1]

Mrs. Watson might have been a little surprised by this innocent claim; since his searing picture of realistic Scottish country life in *The House with the Green Shutters* Brown had been identified in Ayrshire circles as the man who incorporated Ochiltree into the unflattering picture of Scottish "reality", peopled by the "Scot malignant" whom he believed to be more realistic, more honest to the facts, than the sugary sentimentalities of the "kailyard" popular at the turn of the century, the often able but hopelessly over-romanticised pictures of Barrie, Crockett and MacLaren. Like Lewis Grassic Gibbon two generations later, he seemed to have saved up his unhappiest childhood observation to flesh out the skeleton of his novel, incorporating barbed pictures of people and places which were all the more realistic for being (or so it seemed) not altogether fiction.

There was a lot for him to remember with malice; the discomfort of subsistence-level crofting life outside Ochiltree; the stigma of his illegitimate birth in 1869; the slighting of his mother, Sarah Gemmel, who loyally worked to support him through his school years and University career, in Glasgow and Oxford, where a minimum budget and prickly sensitive character made him slow to appreciate the dreaming spires; the mixed reception, in Scotland as in England, of a sardonic and often wounding novel which, in his own words, had "too much black for the white in it". He withdrew from the uncomfortable memories of his youth, and in his isolation achieved an ability to incorporate them in his fiction. He worked fiercely to control his ideas and his memories, and to climb out of the Ochiltree social class, and background, and take advantage of his education.

Education was an important thing for Brown: it released him from the countryside of his youth, from his upbringing, from the stigma of his illegitimacy sardonically or unfeelingly observed by the community, and from the prospect of living out an existence of drabness, monotony and intellectual dullness intolerable to his morbidly sensitive mind. Clearly he enjoyed life in Scotland, clearly he also hated some aspects of it. "Our insight is often deepest into those we hate" (115),[2] he was to write in *The House with the Green Shutters,* and by the time of his solitary mature novel[3] his insight was sharpened into an acid, sardonic view of country life which while doubtless it had "too much black for the white in it", was even so

> more complimentary to Scotland, I think, than the sentimental slop of Barrie, and Crockett, and Maclaren. It was antagonism to their method that made me embitter the blackness ... Which was a gross blunder, of course. A novelist should never have an axe of his own to grind. If he allows a personal animus to obtrude ever so slightly it knocks his work out of balance. He should be an aloof individual, if possible, stating all sides and taking none.[4]

To some extent Brown achieved this lonely view of the world: although he craved the society of literary London he recorded in the same letter that "I wrote the greater part of *The House with the Green Shutters* when I was living all alone in a little cottage in Haslemere". He was a lonely individual at Glasgow University, and later at Oxford: his few friends found him intensely loyal, occasionally intensely unsociable. They faced long silences from him by letter, yet they recognised that the painful solitary character was accompanied by genius. He took offence easily, and dreaded the falsetto social encounter, though he could blend easily when he tried to revisit his native Scotland (*V*, 66). Writing of Burns he clearly saw analogies in their situations. "It is a great thing to have the detachment, the self-mastery, that ignores insult":[5] that Brown had *not* achieved this detachment is clear from such incidents as his angry outburst in the trap when he overheard himself casually referred to as his father's "bastard". The incident appears transformed in *The House with the Green Shutters* as the baiting of Gourlay in the Skeighan trap (159-60). Gourlay's threat to Brodie is real enough, but it merely mirrors the intensity of Brown's anger, recorded by John Veitch. " 'I'd rather be auld Broon's bastard than the son o' any man in this brake!' he ground out between his teeth" (*V*, 67) Even in repose he found it difficult enough to readjust: again writing to Barker he unbosomed himself freely.

> I was in Scotland for about five weeks at the New Year (in a very irresponsive circle, I admit), and I was sadly gravelled for topics of conversation. If you flung out an idea above the level of food, liquor, and local politics, you were met by a blank stare of unintelligence. It is difficult to knock sparks out of mud (*V*, 164).

Never a man at his ease, he found it easy to be outside his community. An educated man, he was set apart in any case, both by his own attitude to life and by the attitude of others to his privileged position. One thinks of Thomas Carlyle's father being advised by an acquaintance not to give his son "education": "James Bell (one of our wise men) had told him: 'Educate a boy, and he grows up to despise his ignorant parents.' My Father once told me this; and added: 'Thou hast not done so. God be thanked for it!' "[6] A nice story, but one notices the parenthesis; Carlyle's education allows him the ironic reference to "our"—Ecclefechan's—wise men. He was glad to go back to revisit Ecclefechan for holidays, but notably not to settle again in the village from which education had alienated him. Perhaps he was lucky he was not a woman, for then his chances of emancipation would have been even slimmer. Lewis Grassic Gibbon's Chris Guthrie experiences amply the alienation from her community which "education" brings, but there is no immediate escape. Her mother freshly dead, Chris sits in the family kitchen and sees the ruin of her education.

> *You'll be leaving the College now, I'll warrant, education's dirt and you're better clear of it. You'll find little time for dreaming and dirt when you're keeping the house at Blawearie.*

And Chris in her pit, dazed and dull-eyed, said nothing ...[7]

The alienation, interestingly, is a compound of thoughtlessness and cruelty. The remark is monstrously tactless, but it also comes from a social tradition which quite omits subtleties of verbal interchange on this level. Brown underlines this tactlessness, quite brilliantly, in the handling of Gourlay's inarticulacy in *The House with the Green Shutters*. Perhaps this point would bear some closer inspection.

Gourlay (senior) is far from inarticulate. His gifts of character come from enormous self-possession, brute masculine courage, a bigness of presence which earns him the bodies' grudging respect as a "gentleman" in a book where such are woefully few (226). On his own ground, he can dominate (or domineer) verbally without question: witness his dismissal of Gilmour (15-32), and his handling (105) of Templandmuir. That his powers of verbalisation, particularly under stress, have their limitations is painfully obvious at the public meeting which precedes his break with Templandmuir (113-19). In a village where modern manners, improving contact with the outside world and a gloss of civilisation mean more and more, his brute strength of character counts for less and less. He is never beaten down, but all too easily outmanoeuvred. Brown makes the point, but is not content to leave it at that—he turns it splendidly to advantage in one of the most subtle points of characterisation.

It is necessary for us to some extent to identify with Gourlay before his tragic downfall: Brown was too well versed in his Greek dramatic studies (both his University degrees were in Greek) not to know the Aristotelian injunction that the tragic character must have elements of good and bad together, not merely bad. There is small tragic pleasure to be had out of watching a purely bad character fall to a deserved punishment. Rather the ambiguous response must be cultivated by showing a potentially good, but flawed, character. Such a man is Gourlay—how are we to bypass Brown's heavy-handed insistence on his limitations, and achieve a genuine rapport with him?

The answer lies in part in his limited powers of verbalisation. " 'I was always gude to the beasts at any rate,' Gourlay muttered, as if pleading in his own defence". He didn't have to talk to them, nor could they answer back. Yet the power of the writing Brown brings to bear on this description is undeniable. "For a long time he stared down at the sprawling carcass, musing. 'Tam the powney,' he said twice, nodding his head each time he said it; 'Tam the powney'; and he turned away" (154). The control of emotion is hinted at purely suggestively; the restraint of the writing is its strongest point. There is nothing to say, after all, just a hint of the emotional attachment to a horse which had been, we know, his favourite. Nature's gentleman does not need to make speeches: his silence is more eloquent.

Occasionally he does make speeches, and their effect is closely related to that of the foregoing passage. Particularly is this so when, near to financial ruin, he has to dismiss the last of his servants, the half-wit Peter Riney. Communication between master and man is not difficult between these two, for Gourlay has nothing to fear from willing old Peter (71). All the more painful when Gourlay parts with this last vestige of his empire; significantly, the day before he had sold "Black Sally, the mare, to get a little money to go on with" (232).

The scene of Riney's dismissal is handled with total economy of dialogue. Gourlay watches him at work on the potatoes, and uncharacteristically hesitates.

. . . The old man, encased in senility, was ill to disturb . . . Gourlay, so often the trampling brute without knowing it, felt it brutal to wound the faithful old creature dreaming at his toil. He would have found it much easier to discharge a younger and a keener man.

'Stop, Peter,' he said at last; 'I don't need you ainy more.'

Peter rose stiffly from his knees and shook the mould with a pitiful gesture from his hands. His mouth was fallen slack, and showed a few yellow tusks.

'Eh?' he asked vaguely. The thought that he must leave the Gourlays could not penetrate his mind. (233)

The response is exactly and beautifully caught: again the comparison comes to mind with Lewis Grassic Gibbon, recalling his own pride at winning the bursary which would emancipate him from a hated life at subsistence level on the croft. " 'I've won a bursary', he said. 'What?' said Chapel o' Seddel."

His father cannot take in the idea; nor will be budge. 'Na, na', he says, 'we canna spare ye. Ye'll hae to tak Peter's place when he leaves hame and gangs to Redleafe. We canna spare ye. Na.'[8] So Gibbon catches the blank incomprehension in *The Thirteenth Disciple*, as Brown does in the earlier novel. There is no patronising in the episode, rather an observation from life. Riney cannot understand for a long time, and he drives Gourlay further and further onto the insecure ground of explaining himself. Peter unwittingly twists a knife in Gourlay's wounds by rambling on. "Man, have ye noathing for us to do?", he asks.

Gourlay's jaw clamped. 'Noathing, Peter,' he said sullenly, 'noathing': and slipped some money into Peter's heedless palm.

Peter stared stupidly down at the coins. He seemed dazed. 'Aye, weel,' he said; 'I'll feenish the tatties at ony rate.'

'No, no, Peter,' and Gourlay gripped him by the shoulder as he turned back to his work, 'no, no; I have no right to keep you. Never mind about the money—you deserve something, going so suddenly after sic a long service. It's just a bit present to mind you o'—to mind you o'—' and he broke off suddenly and scowled across the garden. (234)

The breakdown of the cash nexus indicates keenly how this hurts Gourlay. With other men he dominates by personality or money: with Peter he can do neither. He is vulnerable. Peter is insensitive to both. Yet he shows his feelings in the unthinkable gesture, presumptuous and touching—he shakes Gourlay's hand.

Without a word of thanks for the money, Peter knocked the mould off his heavy boots, striking one against the other clumsily, and shuffled away across the bare soil. But when he had gone twenty yards, he stopped, and came back slowly. 'Good-bye, sir' he said with a rueful smile, and held out his hand.

Gourlay gripped it. "Good-bye, Peter! good-bye; damn ye, man, good-bye!'

Peter wondered vaguely why he was sworn at. But he felt that it was not in anger. He still clung to his master's hand. 'I've been fifty year wi' the Gourlays,' said he. 'Aye, aye; and this, it seems, is the end o't.'

'Oh, gang away!' cried Gourlay, 'gang away, man!' And Peter went away. (235)

This is Gourlay at the end of his tether; unable to verbalise his intense feeling, he resorts to swearing (in a quite unmalicious way, but it is the only weapon in his armoury), then to dismissiveness. As in the case of Gourlay with the dead pony, Brown ends with the skilful, brief anti-climactic sentence. Peter went away, and with him the last trace of the Gourlay empire.

The breakdown of communication is one of the most effective ways in which Brown evokes the breakdown of the social contract in Barbie, and by extension in the "real" Scotland which he, partly from memory, tries so hard to recreate in opposition to the sugar-candy picture of the kailyard. That the same attempt was in progress in the Victorian social novel in England needs little underlining here: the gulf is not only between the Deadlocks and the lower ranks, but between the Gradgrinds and Veneerings and those relatively little removed from their social position. *Mary Barton* and *North and South* both show how difficult it is even for communication—charity—to take place between members of a hard-pressed working class where *sauve qui peut* is a necessary slogan for all but the exceptional. But then *The House with the Green Shutters* is not quite on that level; like the kailyard novels whose form it cleverly imitates, it selects its social *milieu* from well above the ranks of destitution and starvation; apart from Peter Riney and (when it suits the author) Jock Gilmour, the narrator's eye is fixed at the level of the comfortable, the independent, the body who has time to gossip at the Cross, the middle-class family who can send their sons to University, the genial (if not actually comfortable) student world, the busy market-place of those who trade on their own behalf, not of those who work for others. John Gourlay does not descend to the indignity of Michael Henchard, ruined Mayor of Casterbridge, whom Hardy sends out to resume a life of manual toil. Rather the Gourlay fortunes are played out against a consistent social background, and the total ruin which Postie so gleefully announces at the end (325) is forestalled by the mass suicide of the surviving family.

Brown the outsider was ideally suited to observe life from either social level. He felt at home in neither. James Veitch prints a most interesting excerpt from the plot-outline for Brown's unfinished novel *The Incompatibles*, in which Brown apostrophises himself to "forget, to let the past slide, [express a] dislike to open communication with it when once you have entered on a new world. Get this very vividly from your own relation to Ayr in particular and Scotland in general since you have been up here in London." (*V*, 172). He chooses the rootlessness of the socially mobile as one major theme of *The House with the Green Shutters*, but treats this difficult, because very personal, subject with startling flexibility. By contrast Gissing's treatment of Reardon's flawed marriage in *New Grub Street* seems curiously static in the unwillingness of either party to give way or adjust, and Hardy's sympathetic treatment of Tess, caught between two social pressures in her marriage, much too gentle. Brown focuses grimly on the inarticulacy of the trapped individual, locked in an uncaring, inflexible, frequently needlessly abusive and hostile society which has the outside trappings of kailyard pleasantness, and is widely held by millions of readers to be an archetype of country calm and virtue. The irony of the situation lends savagery to his treatment of it.

So far this paper has dealt with the generation in power, the businessmen like the Provost, Gourlay, Wilson, Gibson. Yet their power is a transitory one, and even in the brief span of *The House with the Green Shutters* the balance of power in Barbie shifts quite startlingly from Gourlay's hands. At the outset of the novel his house is new, his grip of the carting trade in Barbie iron; he ruthlessly tramples his rivals (10), he externalises his pride in achievement by the excellence of the house (17), right down to the fender and poker specially imported from Glasgow, the poker with heavy tragic irony introduced as the murder-weapon which is to strike down its owner (70, 294). A smaller but a more flexible man, Wilson can undo him when a bigger and more direct man could not; one bigger and more flexible—but not more admirable—like Gibson can out-manoeuvre both of them. Change is the great factor operating against Gourlay, the change which brings such transformation to Glenburnie and Dalmailing, yet is largely excluded from Brown's hated kailyard. Change brings the advent of the railway and the coal mines, the factories and the immigrant workers, the Wilson Emporium and its associated business empire, the redistribution of power which ousts Provost Connell by Provost Wilson (yet fails to unseat the malignant Bodies, the real Town Council). In fiction, change prepares a new generation to succeed the previous one; in *this* fiction, there is no such exception to the general attack on Scottish life. The younger generation will *not*, on the evidence of *The House with the Green Shutters*, be better able to cope with change, and bring about the improvement their elders failed to achieve. Unlike *Grey Granite*, Brown's novel fails to offer this consolation to Scotland: rather, in George Blake's phrase, it "forced a neglected truth upon the Scot".[19] The younger generation share their fathers' faults, the constrictions of

their environment and the mean-ness of their lives, without the
redeeming feature of learning from their experiences.

A superficial examination of the medium in which young John Gourlay
and his contemporaries grow up shows an alarming lack of sustaining or
morally improving forces. Each force incorporated in Barbie is the
deliberate antithesis of his kailyard prototype. The Established Kirk
minister is a pompous and disgusting ass (209), the Free Kirk
Minister—for Gourlay persists in the kailyard habit of playing up to the
post-Disruption divided Scotland)—a botanising weakling (36); provost
and Doctor are nonentities (112, 53); perhaps most serious (as Brown
would know), the schoolmasters are failures as moral influences. He
himself owed his start in life to early good teaching, and *The House with
the Green Shutters* is dedicated to William Maybin, the excellent schoolmaster of Ayr who encouraged his *protégé* Brown to University, and
disciplined his early writing.[10] Young John Gourlay and his associates
have no such strong early guides. Gemmell, the Barbie schoolmaster, a
stern disciplinarian, has little idealism for his task and contents himself
with keeping order (58). McCandlish, a weaker but a more humane man,
fails to brace young Gourlay's character and weakly tolerates his truancy
from a hated environment (149). Perhaps most serious of all, though the
Barbie schoolmaster follows young John Gourlay's progress and under-
stands him, he fails to intervene when his intervention could have saved
not only suffering, but four lives.

Young John Gourlay is in many ways the antithesis of his father; where
the older man is straight, bluff, masculine, animal, superb, coarse, the
younger is weak, effeminate, unphysical, yet noticing, clever, articulate in
an undisciplined way. Brutally domineered by his father, he shelters in
his mother's uncritical adoration. Gourlay likes his daughter, the
unlovely and neglected Janet; Mrs. Gourlay loves her effeminate and
clever, but weak son. So it goes.

Sneered at, repressed, bullied and shouted at, John can hardly express
himself freely at home. In his father's presence he is cowed (67), or easily
shouted down (160). His terror of lightning (shared by his creator), and
his pathetic gratitude for the baker's unthinking protective sympathy in
the Skeighan station yard during the thunderstorm, show how little
affection he has known in the house with the green shutters (146-7). Yet
he has talent; he *is*, in his mother's fond words, a "noticing boy" for little
trifles (64), though significantly he cannot share his mother's taste for
trashy "novelles" since he cannot handle even the limited externalisation
of his imaginative world necessary to relive the experiences of any
coherent plot. He can handle only flashes, and the immediately
memorable is all he can grasp. "His mind was full of perceptions of which
he was unconscious, till he found one of them recorded in a book, and that
was the book for him. The curious physical always drew his mind to hate

it or to love". (66) Human inter-relations hold no interest for him; brutally callous to his mother's sufferings, and apparently unconscious of his own sister's steady decline into tuberculosis, he is as bored by his home life as by the love-interest of fiction. "An Arctic Night" catches his fancy for the Raeburn prize essay title just for the cold purity of its matter, experienced, vivid, uncluttered by messy human beings. To let such a boy loose in the city, to give him an unwanted University education for purely social reasons, to keep up with neighbours, is tantamount to a crime against his developing personality, and the Barbie schoolmaster, in choosing not to become involved, could be thought guilty of a grave dereliction of duty.

A brooding and taciturn man, he said nothing till others had their say. Then he shook his head.

'They're making a great mistake,' he said gravely, 'they're making a great mistake! Yon boy's the last youngster on earth who should go to College.'

'Aye man, dominie, he's an infernal ass, is he noat?' they cried, and pressed for his judgement.

At last, partly in real pedantry, partly, with humourous intent to puzzle them, he delivered his astounding mind.

'The fault of young Gourlay,' quoth he, 'is a sensory perceptiveness in gross excess of his intellectuality.'

They blinked and tried to understand.

'Aye man, dominie!' said Sandy Toddle. 'That means he's an infernal cuddy, dominie! Does it na, dominie?'

But Bleach-the-boys had said enough. 'Aye', he said drily, 'there's a wheen gey cuddies in Barbie!'—and he went back to his stuffy little room to study *The Wealth of Nations*. (163-64)

This is a crucial moment in the book. The bodies would not have lifted a finger to save young Gourlay, indeed they would have refrained from doing so if it could have injured old Gourlay, but the public figure of the schoolmaster should perhaps have had higher ideals. Yet the scene here, in addition to reinforcing the degenerate nature of Barbie's public institutions, is quite in keeping with what has been argued to be the main intention of this novel, to parody the kailyard by incorporating its familiar characteristics, applied in an inverted way. In Maclaren and Barrie the dominie moves heaven and earth for the good of his poor pupils, and to get them to College is the limit of his ambitions; not so Bleach-the-boys. For the sake of a thin joke he breaks off the subject; for a cheap point against the Bodies (hardly worth engaging in verbal battle) he hides his analysis of young Gourlay's trouble in verbiage and walks off, unwilling to become engaged. The system has failed; neither Gemmell nor McCandlish try to talk Gourlay out of sending his son to Edinburgh University, and of course the inarticulacy of young John makes his feeble protests easy to overcome.

'But I don't want to gang!' John whimpered as before.

'Want! What does it matter what *you* want? You should be damned glad of the chance! I mean to make ye a minister—they have plenty of money and little to do—a grand easy life o't. MacCandlish tells me you're a stupid ass, but have some little gift of words. You have every qualification!'

'It's against *my* will,' John bawled angrily.

'*Your* will!' sneered his father. (160)

Again, as with Peter Riney, Gourlay resorts in bafflement to the putting-down, the abrupt dismissal. There is nothing to say, because neither party is equipped to say it. Riney may shake his employer's hand at the crucial moment of inarticulate communication, but young John has to resort to the cruder, if more effective, instrument of the poker.

If the school system of John's youth fails to diagnose and cure this weakness, so does the University system, with a vengeance. Though set in Edinburgh, these scenes can with little difficulty be attributed to the memories of the lonely years Brown spent as a poor, undistinguished undergraduate in Glasgow, living in cheap digs and working spasmodically between bouts of depression and apparent inertia. Apart from Gilbert Murray, the gifted and youthful Greek professor, the staff seem to have paid little attention to him, and in particular it is interesting to note Brown's biographer singling out James Veitch as a subject of young Brown's dislike. Veitch was a gifted philosopher but not a beguiling teacher like Murray; small wonder that Auld Tam, the clever but uncaring pedagogue who does much to destroy young Gourlay in the University passages of *The House with the Green Shutters*, should be a professor of philosophy. It is not too much to ascribe this to Tam; he *is* careless of his audience with the same superb contempt as Bleach-the-boys in Barbie, but with a wider audience and a greater potential power to damage. The University cared little for young Gourlay, as it cared little for his creator. Enormous classes seem to have been enlivened by no individualised tutorial discussion. Junior staff barely met the students, except to impose discipline (251). Outside lectures, the students merely walked to and from lonely digs, or gathered in public houses for discussions which seemed more an escape from, than an extension of, their learning experience. This is not quite fair, for the view of Edinburgh University is as viciously limited by the author's intention (and by his chosen social sample) as is his view of rustic Scotland. Yet when Allan and his cronies attempt the philosophical discussion at the Howff, the sort of scene Brown must have grown accustomed to in Oxford and missed sadly when revisiting his native village, the attempt does not come off given the background of the Scottish cubs, their limited powers of conceptualisation, and above all their halting verbalisation of the unfamiliar. They descend easily to the anecdotal, Jock Allen "opening his usual wallet of stories when the dinner was in full swing" (180), and seek to "cap" each other's stories rather than analyse the reasons behind the subject under discussion—the extraordinary vividness of the Scottish peasant's speech.

'To hear Englishmen talk, you would think Carlyle was unique for the word that sends the picture home—they give the man the credit of his race. But I've heard fifty things better than 'willowy man,' in the stable a-hame on a wat day in hairst—fifty things better!—from men just sitting on the corn-kists and chowing beans.' (180-81)

Oddly enough, Carlyle would probably have been among the first to agree—witness his eloquent testimonial to his own father's uneducated power of speech,

... that bold glowing style of his, flowing free from the untutored Soul; full of metaphors (though he knew not what a metaphor was), with all manner of potent words (which he appropriated and applied with a *surprising* accuracy, you often could not guess whence) ...[11]

"It comes from a power of seeing things vividly inside your mind", is young Gourlay's explanation, piping up from a corner of the dinner table where he has been sitting unperceived (182). The author's ironic distance is exactly Carlyle's, as the parenthesis will show.

'Metaphor comes from the power of seeing things in the inside of your head,' said the unconscious disciple of Aristotle,—'seeing them so vivid that you see the likeness between them ... A man'll never make phrases unless he can see things in the middle of his brain. *I* can see things in the middle of my brain ...' (183)

So could he; so could his creator. "He was unusually susceptible to the season", wrote one of Brown's student contemporaries ". . . ordinary things which leave no impression on the ordinary mind were to him full of a definite relish" (*V*, 47). He was, after all, a Scottish peasant, and to this class he attributed a share of "Burns's terrible vividness". Everywhere among them he expected to ". . . find men who can plant a picture in the mind for every single terrible phrase" (*V*, 94). To add to this the ambition of being a novelist was to put a terrible strain on the writer, the strain of having to live with the gift of the vivid imagination. His imaginary writer in the notes he made called "The Novelist" ". . . ran from note-book to note-book—he left notes half finished in the hurry of inserting others. His mind seemed to tower, to achieve; he was abundantly content" (*V*, 130). When all was not well, the strain was extreme, as he rushed to put down ideas, then strained to give them shape. The sparking of congruous ideas did not take place; Brown's notebooks are full of half-finished, desperately unfinished work. He honestly admitted to Ernest Barker that his style was "too tense" (*V*, 164), and young Gourlay "subjected to too much analysis" (*V*, 165). Wryly he agreed with Balzac's sister, when she diagnosed her brother's problem as "congestion of ideas": ". . . straining on one phase of thought spoils the general satisfying effect of the whole concatenation of thought" (*V*, 169).

Lucid order, clarity, control lead to relaxation of tension; it was rarely that Brown knew this relaxation, and more rarely still that he permitted it to young John Gourlay, the product of all the stresses and injustices in the Scottish educational system which had plagued his creator, and which are largely responsible for the downfall of *The House with the Green Shutters*, after the more obvious reasons of pride, character defect and personal animus are accounted for. The Scottish system made John Gourlay the man he was, and his interaction with it made Barbie the twisted place it was; his son was educated to that system, and in its highest development the Scottish educational system could not rescue him, nor release him from the inner tensions which, sternly repressed in the father (who only rarely gave way, as when his pony died, or he had to part with Peter Riney) break out and demoralise the son.

Far from helping, the system by uncaring actually hastens the harm to young Gourlay, by the heedless judging and awarding of the Raeburn prize. A minor essay prize (a scathingly reduced version of the prestigious Snell Bursary which Brown won, its money and its scholarship to Balliol College in Oxford being the escape from all he had found restricting in his early manhood), it had been won several times by Barbie men, and by winning it young Gourlay seemed deceptively set on a career of academic success for which he was plainly unfitted. Auld Tam the professor who liked the essay (it is shrewdly hinted) as much for its brevity as for any other quality, should have hesitated before inflating the ego of a weakling like its author by the public award of the prize at the final lecture. Yet, like the dominie in Barbie, he cannot resist making a *bon mot* of the occasion, and his prosy words of advice flow unheeded by young Gourlay, whereas a private admonition would perhaps have changed his whole lifestyle.

'You know, Jack,' said Gillespie, mimicking the sage, 'what you have got to do next summer is to set yourself down for a spell of real, hard, solid and deliberate thought. That was Tam's advice, you know.'

'Him and his advice!' said Gourlay. (196)

Tam plainly did not even know who the author was; carelessly he awarded the prize, and set young Gourlay off on a hard-drinking course of several months which culminated in his expulsion, return to Barbie in disgrace, murder of his father, and eventual suicide. Could Tam have prevented it? In no very obvious way. Yet what he *said* from the rostrum was exactly what Gourlay needed to hear.

Tam, in returning the essays, distinguished between the lowest kind of imagination, which "merely recalls something which the eyes have already seen, and brings it vividly before the mind", and a higher kind which "pictures something which you never saw, but only conceived as a possible existence". Beyond this is a kind which can both see and hear another man's experiences "entering into his blood", and the finest, highest imaginative act is both "creative" and "consecrative", and "irradiates the world" (194-5). It is just this which is lacking in Gourlay's writing, though there is much evidence of nervous perception. "It displays, indeed, too nervous a sense of the external world".

There are very ironic levels of writing here, for Brown clearly saw in this analysis some of the weaknesses of his own hypersensitive character. He wrote, with feeling, the final admonition of the professor. "That almost morbid perception, with philosophy to back it, might create an opulent and vivid mind. Without philosophy, it would simply be a curse ... Without philosophy, it would simply distract and irritate the mind" (195-96). That philosophy is something Gourlay does not attain; his creator is out to make sure we do not sympathise too much with Gourlay as a fallen sage. He cannot, as can Tam, see the value of a "wise indifference". With it, a man is "undaunted by the outer world. 'That, gentlemen, is what thought can do for a man.' 'By Jove,' thought Gourlay, 'that's what whiskey does for me!' " (188-89). The bathos is calculated; Gourlay is a fool and soak as well as a victim of his upbringing. Yet the uncaring professor who swells his head by the award of the Raeburn delivers him into the environment from which he has failed to escape; the bodies love to play on his new arrogance, to inflate his absurd self-importance, and they accelerate his tragedy.

Education in itself, the ultimate goal of the kailyard dominie, is exposed as a chimaera by this novel. The untutored soul in James Carlyle may have been vividly metaphorical, in John Gourlay it was (just as credibly) trapped in inarticulacy, though still possessed of boundless brute courage. After all not all Scots are phrasemakers, even in the kailyard, and most of the Scots in *The House with the Green Shutters* are very poor verbalisers indeed. What little *tendresse* there is in the novel—between the baker and his wife, in their memorable encounter during one of the bodies' gossips (226)—is unspoken and suggested, as is the bond between the baker and young Gourlay. In Barbie public speech-making is cruelly parodied, public exchanges reduced to the spiteful buzzing of the bodies, or the crude raillery of the bar-room or the Skeighan brake. At University the flow of reason is sadly interrupted, and public discourse from the professoriat self-indulgent and unfocussed. Young Aird and Gourlay may come back to Barbie in the vacations to show off, with new clothes and newly Englished vocabularies to match—but they have not learned to communicate, any more than have those who stayed behind in country obscurity. The climactic scenes at the end are all on a level of failed communication. Gourlay tries to inflict mental torture on his son more by calculated silence and half-speech than by command of words; John's attempts to explain his near-insanity after his father's death are whimperingly inarticulate. His mother's magnificent speech on charity (322-24) is little more than unvarnished Biblical quotation, and only poor, colourless Janet is allowed one splendid speech, in Scots, (321) before she, too, dies. Her achievement is a very partial success; her mother was not even listening. Even outside, when the murder is discovered, the postie surprises Sandy Toddle struggling to tell the bodies (as he had solemnly promised not to do) the Gourlays were "sequestered", instead of "sequestrated" (328).

There are many levels of irony in *The House with the Green Shutters*, all of them worthy of the ironic man who could write as his own epitaph, "Here lies a man whose ideals were so high that he never tried to realise them" (*V*, 154). If the book is an "honest brute" then it achieves its effect partly through its form (its satire of a dishonestly sentimentalised Scotland), partly through its characters (inversions of a dishonest parody), partly through the life-philosophy it projected *in its characters*, unrelieved by any objective standard which suggests the validity of higher ideals. Moving as Mrs. Gourlay's reading on charity from Corinthians is, on the verge of her suicide, it does not really give the reader much hope that it will be put into effect in Barbie, even that it will be heard by any of the natives who cluster round to witness the House's fall the following morning. There is no honest dominie, no worthy professor, no struggling reforming minister, no ideal parent trying to bring up his children despite the influences of environment. Perhaps Brown's dissatisfactions were so high that he did not try to picture his ideals in this first, angry novel, but this is not to say that the novel is not without ideals implicit in the novel which is there. The book is, it has been suggested, a sustained critique of a Scotland which can subsist without real communication, which can stumble on uncaringly and uncomprehendingly ignoring suffering or actually rejoicing in it, and rejoicing in causing it. It is a plot which touches on tender areas of Brown's own childhood experiences, on the injustices of fathers to sons, the difficulties of working-class schoolchildren trying to get on in a world seemingly quite alien to all they know, the uncaring or hostile reception that success—the outside world's success—meets with in the home town. Wilson's first return to Barbie, and his putting-down by Gourlay, is so bitterly written that it must be intended to relive some experience Brown knew. The University fails to diagnose and cure the weakness in Gourlay, as presumably it fails through indifference to see similar weaknesses in scores of boys from similar, if less restricted, backgrounds. The town fails to diagnose the trouble with the Gourlays, or if it does it opts out of involvement.

Change sweeps through this novel, and the social and economic upheaval of the closing decades of the nineteenth century is vividly recalled by its rapid evolution. George Douglas Brown's concern is not to

trace the true social effects of population change, to analyse the breakdown in communication between master and servant, urbanite and
countryman; he is not concerned with the work ethic, nor with the
aesthetic problems forced on an industrial society by a machine age.
George Douglas Brown is an observer, keen, too keen for his own
comfort; if *The House with the Green Shutters* is an angry book it is in part
because it *does* have ideals, but the anger comes in the way of the ideals.
Instead the reader is offered the embittered irony of the outsider, the man
alienated from his early Scotland yet fascinated by the very features
which embitter. Above all, he is fascinated by the character of the "Scot
Malignant", and allows the ironies of his society to speak for themselves,
however ambiguously.

'Tyuts,' said the baker, 'folk should be kind to folk. There may be a
possibeelity for the Gourlays in the youngster yet!'

He would have said more, but at that moment his sonsy big wife
came out, with oh! such a roguish and kindly smile, and, 'Tom, Tom,'
said she, 'what are ye havering here for? C'way in, man, and have a dish
o' tea wi' me!'

He glanced up at her with comic shrewdness from where he sat on
his hunkers—for fine he saw through her—and 'Ou aye,' said he, 'ye
great muckle fat hotch o' a dacent bodie, ye—I'll gang in and have a
dish o' tea wi' ye.' And away went the fine fuddled fellow... (226).

If that is the only unquestioned moment of fine interpersonal affection in
the book, it is as ambiguous as the only unquestionably "moral" moment:

Wylie looked at him for awhile with a white scunner in his face. He
wore the musing and disgusted look of a man whose wounded mind
retires within itself, to brood over a sight of unnatural cruelty. The
Deacon grew uncomfortable beneath his sideward, estimating eye.

'Deacon Allardyce, your heart's black-rotten,' he said at last.

The Deacon blinked and was silent. Tam had summed him up.
There was no appeal (305-306).

Of course, Brown's untimely death meant there was no appeal from the
picture of Scotland he painted in *The House with the Green Shutters*. Yet
with all its errors of overstatement and personal animus, the power of this
novel suggests the power of feeling which lay behind Brown's self-
picture, and his picture of the Scotland of his youth. To label it "anti-
kailyard" is as dangerous as to label all kailyard "sentimental slop": *The
House with the Green Shutters* was a timely warning against false self-
analysis, and a timely and welcome reflection of a rapidly-changing
Scotland as the country left the nineteenth century behind.

NOTES:

1. Brown—"Mrs. Watson", 18 January 1902. MS: Carnegie Library, Ayr. Cf. J. Veitch, *George Douglas Brown* (hereafter *V*) (London, [1952]), 163.
2. Page numbers in parentheses refer to the first edition, published in London by John Macqueen in 1901.
3.. *Love and a Sword* was published, judiciously, under the pseudonym "Kennedy King". For some discussion of this early work see I. Campbell, "George Douglas Brown's Kailyard Novel", *Studies in Scottish Literature* XII, 1 (July, 1974), 62-73.
4. Brown-Ernest Barker, 24 October 1901, quoted from *V*, 153.
5. Quoted from *V*, 92. The main article by Brown on Burns was published in *Blackwood's Magazine* in August, 1896: Veitch seems to have access to further unpublished material.
6. Carlyle records this in his "reminiscences" of his father. See T. Carlyle, *Reminiscences* (London, 1972), 12.
7. "Lewis Grassic Gibbon" [J. L. Mitchell], *Sunset Song* (London, [1932]), 84.
8. J. L. Mitchell, *The Thirteenth Disciple* (London, [1931]), 40.
9. Quoted from the preface to his Modern Library edition of *The House with the Green Shutters* (New York, 1927), xi.
10. Of Ayr Academy, Brown wrote: "To it I owe everything that I am." Quoted from C. Lennox, *George Douglas Brown* (London, 1903), 51.
11. Carlyle, *Reminiscences*, 3.

FURTHER READING:

There is little discussion of Brown, beyond a scathing attack in T. W. H. Crosland, *The Unspeakable Scot* (London, 1902), and the sympathetic treatment by George Blake in *Barrie and The Kailyard School* (London, 1951), and by James Veitch (London 1952) in his biography. The reader can find more discussion in the recent re-issue of the novel by Holmes MacDougall ed. J. T. Low (Edinburgh, 1974), and in Ian Campbell, "George Douglas Brown's Kailyard Novel", *Studies in Scottish Literature* XII, 1 (July, 1974), 62-73, and "D. E. Edward, George Douglas Brown, 'The Poor of Coylton' ", *Library Review* 1977/3, 197-201.

For wider further reading, the editor recommends in conclusion three very different books. Maurice Lindsay's *History of Scottish Literature* (London, 1977) gives a wide-ranging if occasionally narrow view of the authors treated in these essays; David Craig's trenchant *Scottish Literature and the Scottish People, 1680-1830* (London, 1961) was a pioneer work of criticism and still has much to offer in the way of stimulating, if occasionally infuriating, criticism; finally George Elder Davie's *The Democratic Intellect* (Edinburgh, 1964, second edition) is an invaluable introduction to some of the changes in ideas and attitude which were taking place at this time in Scotland.

As the book goes to press, further critical work is appearing, and is announced. Exploration continues.

Spring, 1978

Moir, D. M., 3, 91
Moncrief, H., 53
Moore, G., 105
Murray, G., 157
Myers, F., 123

New Review, 130
Nichol, W. R., 135, 136, 145
"North, C." SEE Wilson, J.

Oliphant, M., 4, 89-103

Poe, E. A., 106, 113, 125

Quarterly Review, 66
Quarles, F., 113

Ramsay, E., 90, 93, 94
Reade, C., 105

Saintsbury, G., 66
Scott, Sir W., 3, 6-17, 39, 42, 48,
  49, 52, 53, 57, 58, 89, 90, 91,
  94, 142, 145, 146

Shakespeare, W., 10, 12, 122
Smith, A., 52
Southey, R., 12
Spenser, E., 11
Stevenson, R. L., 4, 91, 93, 105-
  29, 143
Stewart, D., 19
Story, R., 90, 101
Swan, A. S., 136

Tasso, T., 11
Thackeray, W., 9
Tolstoy, N., 125, 146
Trollope, A., 92
Tulloch, J., 90

Veitch, J., 157
Walton, I., 8
Watson, J., 130-47, 149, 156
Wilson, J., 91
Wood, Mrs. H., 92
Wordsworth, W., 57, 66

Zola, E., 125